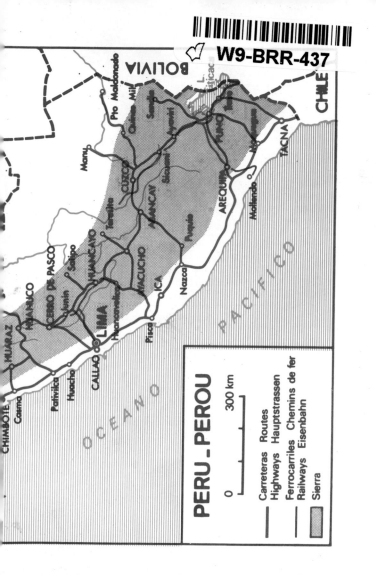

PERU - PEROU

0   300 km

Carreteras   Routes
Highways   Hauptstrassen

Ferrocarriles   Chemins de fer
Railways   Eisenbahn

Sierra

PERU

NAGEL'S

ENCYCLOPEDIA - GUIDE

GOLD MEDAL OF THE CITY OF ROME
GREAT SILVER MEDAL, PARIS
INTERNATIONAL MEDALS, VIENNA, 1968, 1972

PERU

320 pages

3 maps and plans in colour

17 pages of maps and plans in black and white

NAGEL PUBLISHERS

GENEVA · PARIS · MUNICH

This Guide was prepared by Mme **J. Brisseau-Loaiza,** D. ès L.;
M. **H. Favre** and Mlle **D. Lavallée,** of the Centre National de la
Recherche Scientifique; and Sr **H. Loaiza,** the Peruvian writer.

ISBN 2–8263- 0712–6

PUBLISHER'S NOTE

Although a latecomer in the field of international tourism, Peru has now established itself firmly as a tourist country. Air travel has opened up the land of El Dorado to thousands of visitors from Europe and North America, attracted in increasing numbers every year by the beauty of its scenery and the grandeur of the Andean peaks, its archaeological and artistic wealth, its lively and colourful folk traditions. For those reluctant to explore the country on their own the travel agencies offer a range of package holidays at very reasonable prices. Only yesterday a remote country almost inaccessible to the ordinary traveller, Peru is now in the world tourist league, vying with India, Ceylon and Bangkok in its appeal to visitors.

Like other volumes in the series, this Encyclopedia-Guide is in three parts: a General Introduction devoted to the natural setting and the history, art, literature and economy of Peru; a descriptive part, with precise and detailed itineraries; and a section of Practical Information concerned with all the practical details of a visit to Peru. The Guide also includes a series of maps and plans, some of them in colour. Our aim has been to make it as complete and up-to-date as possible, while at the same time remaining compact and convenient for the traveller.

Our thanks are due to those responsible for the preparation of the Guide, all of whom have lived and worked in Peru and know the country well. Mlle Danielle Lavallée, a research assistant with the Centre National de la Recherche Scientifique and a member of the Institute of Andean Studies in Lima, wrote the sections on pre-Columbian Peru and on folk arts and traditions. M. Henri Favre, also of the C.N.R.S. and the Institute of Andean Studies, was responsible for the account of colonial and Republican Peru and of public life in present-day Peru. Sr Hector Loaiza, the Peruvian writer, prepared the sections on art, language and literature. The brunt of the work, however, fell on Mme Janine Brisseau-Loaiza, who not only prepared the itineraries but wrote the introductory chapters on the natural setting, the population and the economy of Peru.

We should also like to express our gratitude to all those who have helped so generously in the preparation of this Guide, in particular to Sr Arq. Ferrari of the Peruvian Ministry of Tourism; Sr Abelardo Indacochea, General Manager of the Organización

Sudamericana de Promoción Turística; Sr P. Usselmann, Director of the Institute of Andean Studies in Lima; and M. J. Fabre,
Director General of Air France in Peru.

A work of this kind must be constantly improved and updated
if it is to remain helpful to its readers. We shall therefore welcome
comments and suggestions which will enable us still further to
improve the next edition of this Encyclopedia-Guide.

Like all the other Nagel Guides, this volume contains no
advertising matter. The information it contains can therefore be
relied on as being absolutely objective and unbiassed.

CONTENTS

8. Peruvian Amazonia 249

MAPS AND PLANS

The table shows the distance by road (kilometres). After

	Abancay	Arequipa	Ayacucho	Cajamarca	Cerro de Pasco	Cuzco	Chachapoyas	Chiclayo	Chimbote
Abancay, *2398*		820	396	1766	907	197	2132	1675	1334
Arequipa, *2378*	820		1217	1868	1335	623	2235	1777	1437
Ayacucho, *2857*	396	1217		1417	511	594	1783	1326	986
Cajamarca, *2860*	1766	1868	1417		1164	1963	333	265	431
Cerro de Pasco, *4338*	907	1335	511	1164		1104	1530	1073	732
Cuzco, *3399*	197	623	594	1963	1104		2329	1872	1532
Chachapoyas, *2334*	2132	2235	1783	333	1530	2329		457	798
Chiclayo, *29*	1675	1777	1326	265	1073	1872	457		340
Chimbote, *6*	1334	1437	986	431	732	1532	798	340	
Huancavelica, *3900*	665	1055	269	1305	399	862	1672	1214	874
Huancayo, *3260*	655	1330	258	1159	252	852	1525	1068	727
Huánuco, *1915*	1012	1440	615	1268	105	1209	1634	1177	837
Huaraz, *3127*	1317	1420	969	637	715	1514	1003	546	205
Ica, *402*	609	711	612	1157	619	806	1523	1066	725
La Oroya, *3412*	778	1207	382	1035	129	976	1401	944	604
LIMA, *203*	917	1020	569	848	315	1115	1215	757	417
Piura, *29*	1947	2049	1598	536	1344	2144	529	272	612
Pucallpa, *205*	1432	1860	1035	1688	525	1629	2055	1597	1257
Pto. Maldonado, *256*	729	1061	1125	2495	1636	532	2861	2404	2063
Puno, *3870*	584	296	980	2164	1491	387	2531	2073	1733
Tacna, *568*	962	400	1358	2184	1646	764	2550	2093	1752
Trujillo, *61*	1465	1568	1117	300	863	1663	667	209	131
Tumbes, *33*	223	2326	1874	813	1621	2420	805	548	889

DISTANCES

the name of each town is shown the altitude in metres.

Huancavelica	Huancayo	Huánuco	Huaraz	Ica	La Oroya	LIMA	Piura	Pucallpa	Pto. Maldonado	Puno	Tacna	Trujillo	Tumbes
665	655	1012	1317	609	778	917	1947	1432	729	584	962	1465	2223
1055	1330	1440	1420	711	1207	1020	2049	1860	1061	296	400	1568	2326
269	258	615	969	612	382	569	1598	1035	1125	980	1358	1117	1874
1305	1159	1268	637	1157	1035	848	536	1688	2495	2164	2184	300	813
399	252	105	715	619	129	315	1344	525	1636	1491	1646	863	1621
862	852	1209	1514	806	976	1115	2144	1629	532	387	764	1663	2420
1672	1525	1634	1003	1253	1401	1215	529	2055	2861	2531	2550	667	805
1214	1068	1177	546	1066	944	757	272	1597	2404	2073	2093	209	548
874	727	837	205	725	604	417	612	1257	2063	1733	1752	131	889
	147	503	857	344	270	457	1486	923	1394	1249	1371	1005	1762
147		356	710	490	124	310	1340	777	1384	1239	1641	858	1616
503	356		819	723	233	420	1449	415	1740	1595	1750	968	1725
857	710	819		708	586	400	818	1240	2046	1716	1735	336	1094
344	490	723	708		490	308	1338	1143	1338	1005	1027	856	1614
270	124	233	586	490		187	1216	653	1507	1362	1517	735	1492
457	310	420	400	308	187		1029	840	1646	1316	1335	548	1306
1486	1340	1449	818	1338	1216	1029		1869	2676	2345	2364	481	276
923	777	415	1240	1143	653	840	1869		2161	2016	2170	1388	2145
1394	1384	1740	2046	1338	1507	1646	2676	2151		824	1202	2194	2952
1249	1239	1595	1716	1005	1362	1316	2345	2016	824		378	1864	2621
1371	1641	1750	1735	1027	1517	1335	2364	2170	1202	378		1883	2641
1005	858	968	336	856	735	548	481	1388	2194	1864	1883		758
1762	1616	1725	1094	1614	1492	1306	276	2145	2952	2621	2641	758	

NATURAL REGIONS OF PERU

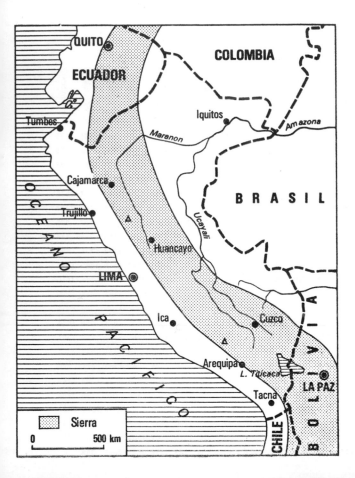

General Introduction

THE NATURAL SETTING

Few countries have such a varied natural setting as Peru; and indeed this is one of its chief tourist attractions. Its latitude makes it a tropical country, extending from 3º S. on the frontier with Ecuador, and indeed from the Equator on the Colombian frontier, to 18º S. — giving it an area of 1,285,215 sq. km; but the presence of a cold coastal current and the mountain mass of the Andes radically modify the climatic conditions normally found in these latitudes. Three main natural regions are distinguished, varying in altitude, climate, vegetation and development: the *Coast* (Costa); the *Sierra*, i.e. the Andes above an altitude of 1500 m; and the *Montaña* or *Selva*, i.e. the Amazonian forest. See the map on p. 15.

The Coast

This region consists of the western slopes of the Andes and, to the south, the discontinuous ridges of the coastal cordillera. There is no coastal plain except in the extreme north, in the Piura-Tumbes area. The Peruvian coast surprises the visitor by its desertic character. From Lima to Talara in the north and to Tacna in the south extends a region of bare rocky spurs, expanses of ochre, greyish or tawny sand (often blown into dunes), weathered banks of hard rock, tumbles of boulders and scree. The Peruvian desert has the advantage, however, of lying at the foot of the Andes, from which flows down an abundance of water. Some twenty rivers, fed by glaciers and the perpetual snow as well as by the hot-season rains of the Sierra, have created a series of oases along the coast, densely populated swathes of fertile soil in striking contrast with the almost inhabited deserts which surround them.

The desert owes its existence to the anticyclones of the South Pacific and the influence of a cold marine current, the *Humboldt Current*. This current of cold water from the South Pole is driven along the Peruvian coast by the very strong and regular southeast trade winds. During the southern hemisphere's winter (June to December) it reaches the latitude of Cabo Blanco, north of Piura. The whole coast then has a long "dry season" notable for a very low rainfall but also for a very high level of atmospheric humidity, with low clouds and often with fog (*neblina*) or even sometimes fine drizzle (*garúa*). Temperatures remain moderate and sometimes cool; the mean annual temperature at Lima is 18° C, with little variation over the year. One need only climb the lowest slopes of the cordillera, however, to find a dry climate and clean air. The Trujillo area in the north and the Moquegua-Tacna area in the south also also have a sunnier and drier climate which contrasts with that of the cloudy central region.

During the southern hemisphere's summer an equatorial counter-current—known as "El Niño" or "the Infant (Jesus)" because it makes its influence felt around Christmas—flows past Cabo Blanco, bringing warmth and heavy humidity. In some years it drives back the Humboldt Current, leading to heavy rain and flooding along the coast north of Trujillo. In others, however, it affects only the Tumbes area, leaving the drought to continue in the oases farther down the coast. It only very rarely makes its influence felt in the central region, producing torrential rain which has catastrophic effects in a city not designed to cope with wet weather. During the summer the temperature rises rapidly, and from the end of November to the end of March there is beautiful weather, with abundant sunshine and a mean monthly temperature of 22° C.

The Sierra

Between the Pacific and the Amazon basin lie the Andes, a range of mountains which reaches its highest point in Mt Huascarán (6768 m). The chain widens out from north to south, reaching a width of 400 km on the Bolivian frontier. Except in the north the passes are all above 4000 m, and there are some 20 peaks over 6000 m. The Andes are the result of an upthrust beginning at the end of the Tertiary period which involved a very varied range of geological structures—a granitic batholith along the coast, huge expanses of sandstones, limestones and secondary conglomerates in the centre, folded primary series with granite intrusions in the east, and everywhere traces of volcanic activity in many different periods. That the Andes are relatively young mountains is shown by the frequent occurrence of thermal activity and, even more markedly, by the seismic and volcanic activity still present in the south.

For the most part the Andes consist of two cordilleras roughly parallel to the coast running from north-west to south-east, separated by collapse basins and slashed by deep valleys. In the

north are the small Jaén and Cajamarca basins; then comes the
deep and sharply hewn valley through which flows the river
Santa, the Callejón de Huaylas, caught between the Black
Cordillera on the Pacific side and the White Cordillera (in which
is Mt Huascarán) to the east. The two cordilleras join in the
centre at the "Pasco Knot", where the Marañón (the Upper
Amazon) rises; then they diverge again, separated by the wide
Mantaro depression, in which the town of Huancay is situated.
The western cordillera widens out into a high rolling plateau,
slashed by valleys which frequently take on the character of
canyons (the Mantaro valley below Huancayo and the Urubamba
and Apurímac valleys in the province of Cuzco). In the Arequipa
area this cordillera contains a number of magnificent snow-
capped volcanoes, some of them still active (see the Lima-
Arequipa route, chapter 3). The eastern cordillera, which is
lower in the central stretch, rises again towards the south to
form a chain of high snow-covered mountains with peaks of over
6000 m (Salkantay, 6271 m, and Ausangate, 6384 m, in the Cuzco
area). To the east the two cordilleras are separated by the depression containing Lake Titicaca, on the Bolivian frontier. Titicaca is
one of the largest high-altitude lakes in the world (area 8100 sq.
km, altitude 3812 m), the residue of an immense inland lagoon
which in the Quaternary period occupied the Peruvo-Bolivian
altiplano, now a large grass-covered sedimentary plateau.

The Sierra has the climatic pattern of the tropics, with a fairly
warm rainy season from November to April and a colder dry
season. There is little temperature variation over the year, but
there are sharp daily fluctuations, particularly during the dry
season, when it frequently freezes at night at altitudes over
3000 m. The following climate and vegetation types are found at
different altitudes:

—the *yunga type* (above the coastal desert at altitudes of
around 600 m in the north, 1200 m in the centre and 1800–
2000 m in the south), with a semi-desertic vegetation of organ-
pipe cactuses, prickly pears and *molle*, a small red-berried acacia.
This ecological pattern extends into the bottoms of the inter-
Andean valleys below 2500–2800 m, in some of which the
Spaniards introduced sugar-cane growing with the help of
irrigation.

—the *Quechua type* (around 2000 m in the north, between
3000 and 3400 m in the south). The temperature range in this
zone produces a temperate climate. Cuzco has a mean annual
temperature of 12° C, with fairly wide daily variations and

nights which are often cold. The rainfall ranges between 500 and 700 mm, with heavy showers in the early afternoon or during the night from November to March. In recent years the dry season has been less marked, and Cuzco sometimes has snow and rain in July and August. The original vegetation consisted of shrubs with gnarled trunks, including many evergreen coniferous species like *chachacomo* and *queshuar*, but the Spaniards introduced willows, poplars, mulberries, broom (*retama*) and various European fruit-trees. The tree which is now most characteristic of the Quechua zone, the eucalyptus, is a very recent introduction (late 19th century, during the development of the railways). The resultant general pattern is of mixed woodland and grassland, a green and fertile landscape in which the agaves and cactuses along the roads and round the edges of fields are a reminder of the underlying dryness of the climate. This is also a cereal-growing area. Maize — an indigenous species — is grown on well irrigated terraces in the valleys, while European cereals (mainly wheat and barley) grow on the poorer soils of the hillsides, in fields extending to heights of over 3500 m in the Suni zone. In this zone grow tuber-bearing plants like the potato (*papa*), *olluco* and *oka*.

— the *puna type* (above 3900 m). This is a treeless steppe, made up of various grasses, in particular the coarse grass known as *icchu*. This zone is known in the north as the *jalca*, a greener version of the *paramo;* in the south the *jalca* is the glacier zone. The climate is cold (mean annual temperatures 4–6° C), with precipitations of around 600–800 mm, and allows no plants of any size to grow apart from a few clumps of *quinoas* (*Polylepis*) in sheltered areas. Crops can be grown only round the numerous lagoons and on certain slopes with an eastern exposure (potatoes, barley and *cañihua*). It is a vast stock-rearing region, with large numbers of llamas, alpacas, etc., as well as the cattle, sheep and horses introduced by the Spaniards. With its vast empty expanses, its deep blue lagoons, its herdsmen with their primitive way of life and its mineral wealth, this is a kind of Peruvian Far West, full of fascination for the tourist, even though most visitors tend to pass it by in favour of the temperate valleys.

— the *rock and glacier zone* (above 4800 m in the south, 4200 m in the north), in which even the grass disappears. This is a region of valleys formed by ice action, with floors consisting of tundra and peat-bogs in which rivers flow in wide bends. The level of perpetual snow ranges round 4800 m in the north and 5300 m in the south, varying according to exposure.

This series of vegetation zones is not found on the Amazonian slopes of the Andes on account of the high humidity. The humid-

ity is produced by the condensation of the mass of warm air in
the Amazonian basin when it comes in contact with the mountains, and is accentuated by altitude. Rainfall is everywhere
higher than 1000 mm annually and frequently exceeds 6000 mm.
There is a zone of permanent fog at an altitude of about 4000–
3500 m, and this gives its name to the whole of the climatic zone,
the *ceja de montaña* or "eyebrow of the mountain". At 1800 m
(Huánuco) the mean annual temperature has risen to 18° C; at
700 m (Tingo María) it is 23°. The relief is rugged and much
indented, carved into a multitude of ravines by the rivers of the
Amazonian system. The tropical forest which covers the mountain
slopes has been cleared for cultivation in the principal valleys
below 3000 m, and here various hot-country crops like sugar-
cane, cacao, coffee, tea, rice, manioc, sweet potato and oil palm
are grown. This zone, extending from the glaciers of the Eastern
Cordillera at an altitude of 5600 m to the tropical forest of the
Amazon basin, has one of the most impressive and rapidly
changing ranges of climate to be found anywhere in the world.
Visitors travelling to Machu Picchu by train get some impression
of these swift changes, but for those who can spare the time it is
well worth while continuing to Quillabamba or taking one of
the roads which run down to the tropical zone.

The Selva or Montaña

The south-western part of the huge Amazon basin lies within
Peru, occupying more than half its total area (600,000 sq. km).
This is a large area of subsidence which has been filled up with
sedimentary deposits since the Secondary era. Quaternary
alluvium has been laid down in terraces by the mighty rivers
which form the upper part of the Amazonian system — the
Marañón, the Huallaga and the Ucayali flowing north and the
Madre de Dios and its tributaries flowing from west to east. The
climate is equatorial, with high temperatures (an annual mean of
25–26°C), very little variation in temperature and heavy rainfall
throughout the year (an annual 2500–3000 mm at Iquitos). It
is a region of dense forest, with very tall trees and an impenetrable undergrowth of bamboos, ferns, lianas and parasitic
plants. With its rivers of slow and regular flow the Amazonian
forest is more accessible to human penetration than the forests of
Central Africa. It is also healthier, having no malaria and no
tsetse flies. It remains, however, very thinly populated.

PRE-COLUMBIAN PERU

The Origins

As early as the 16th century Peru's past was the subject of curiosity, interest and even of serious study. The fabulous descriptions of the Conquistadors, embellished and often grossly inflated in successive re-tellings, the huge quantities of gold — and this at any rate was real and genuine — brought back by the galleons to the Iberian peninsula, and the detailed accounts of the chroniclers, the monks or officials who tried to set down systematically what they had seen and heard — all this soon created the picture of a fabulous kingdom ruled by a mighty prince, the *Inca*.

No one at that time knew anything of a period before the Inca dynasty. The chroniclers had gleaned from the mouths of ordinary Indians, or from the "wise men" whose task it was to preserve and transmit the country's traditions, a medley of information about great military exploits or about social life and religion. But pre-Hispanic Peru was a country without an alphabet and without any written texts[1], and its earlier traditions had either been forgotten or had been relegated to the status of legend and adapted to their own ends by the ruling Inca caste, concerned to create an official "history" which should attribute to them all the glory of building up the splendid civilisation which was then in full flower.

It is only within the last sixty years that archaeology has gradually revealed the long history of Peru, in which the Incas now figure as relatively late arrivals. In the light of the most recent discoveries the peoples of the Andes have a past going back some 20,000 years, and the story may yet be carried back to even remoter periods.

It is true that the arrival of man on the American continent is still very recent in comparison with the antiquity, reckoned in millions of years, of the earliest traces of human life in East Africa. The theory now accepted, confirmed by scientific evidence, is that the population of America mostly came from northern

---

[1] *It has recently been suggested, however, that the Incas did in fact possess a system of "writing" in the form of the ideograms which appear on textiles and on ceremonial wooden vessels.*

Asia. Small nomadic groups had made their way across the Bering Strait at a time when the sea level was lower than it is today (more water being then locked up in glaciers and pack ice) and there was a land bridge across the strait. This first arrival of man in America is thought to date back over 50,000 years.

Evidence of the presence of man in South America some 20,000 years ago has been found in Peru, in the *Ayacucho* basin, situated in the heart of the Cordillera at an altitude of 3000 m. Here small human groups lived in caves and rock shelters, maintaining themselves by hunting the last large mammals of the Pleistocene, like the now extinct American horse and the Andean camelidae (ancestors of the llamas, alpacas, vicuñas and guanacos of the present day). The type site for this period is the *Pikimachay* cave, discovered by an American archaeologist, MacNeish, in 1966. At that time the highest parts of the Andes, above 4000 m, were still occupied by huge glaciers, which did not retreat until about 12,000–10,000 B.C. As the last offshoots of the glaciers retreated small groups of nomadic hunters set up their encampments in rock shelters on the *puna*, the high plateau of the Andes (*Lauricocha* and *Toquepala* caves, c. 8000 B.C.). On these sites men have left traces of their presence in the form of remains of hearths, broken or carbonised animal bones, and weapons and implements of flaked flint. Sometimes, too, they decorated the walls of the caves with hunting scenes painted in red ochre.

On the coast, which was already desertic but had a rather wetter climate than today, leading to a seasonal growth of vegetation on the *lomas*, the hunters (perhaps the same men who hunted on the high plateau during the dry season) also set up their encampments, remains of which have been found at several points, particularly near *Ancón*, in the central area. Here they found herds of guanacos and deer which were drawn, like them, to these miraculous oases in the middle of the desert. Their main subsistence came, however, from gathering wild grains and tubers — the first systematic use of natural vegetation by man.

At this early period man still depended on non-cultivated species of plants, wandering perpetually about in quest of his daily food. The next step took place about 5500 B.C., when the first signs of the domestication of plants appear, both in the Sierra and on the coast. This was followed a little later by the first settled human establishments: all along the Pacific coast huge masses of shells and small groups of huts half buried in the ground bear witness to the existence of the first villages at the mouths of rivers and close to the coastal beaches (*Cabezas Largas* and *Chilca*, in the south). Their occupants lived by fishing, gathering shellfish and hunting the marine mammals which were abundant along the coast, but they also cultivated a few plants — gourds, beans, tomatoes and, rather later (about 3000 B.C.), cotton, from which they wove clothes and made fishing nets. This period, extending from 5500 to 3000–2500 B.C., which succeeded the long Lithic (Stone Age) or Pre-Agricultural period, is known as the Pre-Ceramic period; for although a radical change had taken place in man's way of life the art of making pottery was still unknown.

It was probably in the favoured regions of the large inter-Andean basins that, some time between 4000 and 3000 B.C. (dates obtained in the Ayacucho basin), man first began to grow maize: a step forward which was to have a profound influence on the whole technological and cultural development of Peru. The appearance of this new resource — at a rather later date (c. 2000 B.C.) on the coast — coincides approximately with the first appearance of pottery and the weaving loom; we do not know, however, whether this is a mere coincidence, or whether these were associated cultural elements brought by new human groups from the northern part of the South American continent. At any rate the domestication of maize marked a decisive stage in the progress of Andean civilisation. Men no longer needed to live precariously from hand to mouth: they could lay down reserve stores and produce a surplus which enabled them to maintain non-productive members of society like warriors, priests or craftsmen. We can now observe the emergence of a social stratification, the development of military and religious ruling castes, the appearance of more and larger villages centred on larger buildings with a ceremonial function. The *Temple of the Crossed Hands* at *Kotosh* (1500 B.C.) in the northern Andes is the counterpart of the adobe "temples" on the coast, at *La Florida* and *Río Seco* (1800 B.C.) in the central coastal area, and the large ceremonial complex at *Las Aldas* in the Huarmey valley, to mention only the most important.

Chavín and the Cult of the Feline God
(c. 1000–800 to 300 B.C.)

Although preceded, as we have seen, by many millennia of prehistory during which man gradually moved towards civilisation, the name of *Chavín* symbolises the ancestral culture of

Peru, and Dr J. C. Tello, the Peruvian archaeologist who discovered it around the year 1920, saw it as the cradle of all the great cultures which later succeeded one another in Peru. For Chavín represented the appearance for the first time, quite suddenly, of an extraordinarily elaborate and refined culture, apparently the result of a movement of religious fervour unparalleled in the country's subsequent history.

The large architectural complex of *Chavín de Huantar* is situated at an altitude of some 3200 m in the northern Andes, on the eastern slopes of the White Cordillera. It consists of a series of truncated pyramids separated by esplanades or plazas, terraces, sunken courts and staircases, the construction of which extended over several centuries. The best-known and most prominent building, known as the *Castillo*, is probably fairly late; it contains an extraordinary maze of dark narrow passages, in which was found a monolith carved with a grimacing figure, half human and half feline. This may have been the principal idol of the Chavín temple.

The stone carving of Chavín is undoubtedly the finest in South America. On all the carved or engraved stelae, columns and slabs found on the site is a representation, in varying degrees of stylisation, of the god with feline fangs, sometimes with attributes belonging to other animal species like snakes or birds of prey. We do not yet know what is the origin of these terrifying images, or which people erected this huge structure in honour of its gods. Although some scholars believe that this culture evolved gradually in the area, others are convinced that it reflects an outside influence, that of the brilliant Mesoamerican culture of the Olmecs in southern Mexico.

The influence of Chavín extended for several centuries over much of the country. The figure of the feline god is found on the pottery of the northern coastal area (the *Cupisnique* style, in the Chicama valley) and the central coastal area (*Ancón-Supe*). At *Kuntur Wasi* and *Pacopampa*, near Cajamarca in the northern Andes, and at *Kotosh* near Huánuco the same stylistic features are found in the pottery, and at *Cerro Blanco* and *Punkuri* in the Nepeña valley and *Moxeque* and *Pallka* in the Casma valley the worshippers of the feline god built adobe temples for their idol. In the southern coastal area, too, the earliest pottery of the *Paracas* culture (*Ocucaje* and *Cavernas* styles) shows markedly Chavinoid features.

The Emergence of Regional Cultures
(300 B.C. to 100 A.D.)

The Chavinoid expansion which characterised the period known as the "Middle Formative" appears to have begun to to decline, quite suddenly, about the end of the 1st millennium B.C. During the following two or three centuries a trend towards regional differentiation begins to appear; and this "Late Formative" saw the progressive diversification of cultures and the emergence of distinctive artistic styles, sometimes still showing features inherited from Chavín.

It was also during this short phase of experimentation that man finally mastered the techniques of agriculture, the domestication of plant and animal species and a variety of crafts. The areas of settlement were mainly round the mouths of rivers, where artificial irrigation was already practised. Villages sprang up in large numbers—small groups of adobe huts contrasting in their simplicity with the magnificence of the buildings erected to honour the gods.

In the northern coastal area cultures of this type have been identified at *Salinar*, *Puerto Moorín* and *Vicus*, characterised (particularly the first two) by red pottery in simple shapes with decoration in white ("Red-on-White"). In the southern coastal area the culture of *Paracas* is noted for its extraordinary mastery of weaving and needlework. Around 1929 Tello discovered almost 500 "mummy bundles", laid out in rows or piled on top of one another, buried in the remains of a village at the foot of a hill on the Paracas peninsula. Each bundle contained a human mummy huddled in a wicker basket and wrapped in several metres of cotton fabrics—the famous *mantos*, masterpieces of the textile art unequalled anywhere else in the world, the finest examples of which are to be seen in the Museo Nacional in Lima. Associated with the bundles were a few pieces of cream or orange pottery decorated with representations of fruit. The name of *Paracas Necropolis* was given to this new style. In the Highland areas the Late Formative period is represented by the cultures, still very imperfectly known, of *Chiripa* and *Pucará* (the latter similar in many respects to the Paracas culture), round Lake Titicaca.

All these developing regional cultures reached their peak about the end of the 1st century A.D.

The Classic Cultures (100–800 A.D.)

In every coastal valley and every basin within the Andes there now flowered an independent and original culture. Not all of them, of course, attained the same degree of artistic development — the Highland cultures in particular being considerably behind the others — but some of the coastal centres achieved such a high standard of refinement in art and technology that this has been called the period of the Master Craftsmen. In this field two peoples surpassed all others — the *Mochicas* in the northern coastal area and the *Nazcas* in the south.

Originating in the Moche valley, the *Mochicas* had within some six centuries extended their rule over the neighbouring valleys, from Piura in the north to Casma in the south. Huge adobe pyramids were erected to honour the gods, calling for the labour of many thousands of workmen: the most famous of these structures, the *Huaca del Sol*, contains no fewer than 50 million adobe bricks and is the largest monument of its kind in the world. Round these temples or holy places (*huacas*) clustered the adobe houses, roofed with reeds, of the ordinary people of the village — tillers of the soil, metal-workers, weavers, potters and other craftsmen — and the palaces in which the ruling classes, the priests and the warriors, received the homage of their subjects, took part in elaborate religious ceremonies or prepared to do battle with neighbouring peoples. All that we know of the Mochica people comes from their incomparable pottery, thousands of specimens of which are to be found in museums throughout the world, forming a kind of illustrated compendium of Mochica life. It is an art notable for its realism, producing pots which are like little pieces of sculpture in the round and culminating in the famous modelled heads, so varied and so true to life that they have been thought to be portraits.

In the southern coastal area the *Nazcas*, occupying the Chincha, Pisco, Ica, Nazca and Acarí valleys, largely maintained Paracas traditions. Their polychrome pottery, excellently fired and of marvellous delicacy, has a range of colouring unequalled in pre-Columbian Peru, with anything up to eight colours on a single piece. While the Mochicas handled clay like sculptors the Nazcas produced jars and dishes of very simple forms which they decorated with a teeming world of animals, plants and demons, including a strange kind of feline-headed millipede which is probably a reminiscence of the gods of Chavín. The pottery continued, however, to develop during the six or seven centuries of

Nazca culture: the designs, very simple at the outset, became increasingly abstract and elaborate, with complicated scrolls and appendages which make them increasingly undecipherable, while modelled jars became commoner.

The Nazca and Mochica peoples, like other less notable peoples in the coastal region (in particular the Lima area, with considerable centres at *Cajamarquilla*, *Maranga* and *Pachacámac*, the last of which was to become the country's leading religious centre), had many points in common. Both were peoples of peasant farmers, who tilled the soil with hoes and digging sticks (ploughs of any kind being unknown) and grew cotton, maize, groundnuts, manioc, peppers and potatoes, these last being an import from the Highland region. They were able to regulate the flow of rivers and convey water in aqueducts several kilometres long so as to increase the area of cultivable land and feed the constantly increasing population. They still fished and hunted seals, but they had long learned to domesticate llamas and guinea-pigs. In addition to the countless villages clustering round their temples there were now a few "towns" of larger size, like *Cahuachi* in the Nazca valley and *Pacatnamu* in the northern part of the Mochica territory. The system of government at this period seems to have been theocratic, and the pottery has many representations of warrior priests disguised as various fabulous creatures presiding over strange and cruel cults. Head-hunting was commonly practised, and the frequency of scenes of fighting shows the central place that war took in the life of the time.

We still know little of the cultures of the Highland areas during this period, though there seem to have been a number of brilliant cultural centres. In the *Cajamarca* basin a people about whom we are almost totally ignorant produced a very fine pottery made of white kaolin, with painted decoration noted for its delicate scrollwork. In the Santa valley (Callejón de Huaylas), and particularly in the *Recuay* area, numerous burials have been found containing pottery of complex shapes with "negative" decoration and some very fine stone sculpture. A number of towns were built in the Andes during this period, like *Tiahuanaco* (now in Bolivia), which was later to develop on such a considerable scale. Thus many small federations of tribes were being established and extending their domains, though none of them equalled the coastal peoples in magnificence.

Towards the end of the 9th century A.D. these brilliant cultures seem suddenly to have lost their energy and drive. The last works of the Mochica potters lack the earlier vigour and sobriety, and are mannered and over-ornate; their sense of form declines or becomes refined to the point of caricature. In the Nazca area new stylistic motifs appear, coming from the central Andes; for the whole country was now coming increasingly under the influence of a culture centred on *Huari*, near Ayacucho, which was soon to submerge all the small local confederations.

The Huari Empire (800–1200 A.D.)

Throughout the preceding centuries Andean society had been slowly developing and increasingly evolving distinctive regional characteristics; but now, suddenly, a revolution took place. As a result of the expansion of trade or the spread of religious ideas, or perhaps of a military conquest of which we have as yet no knowledge, there was a trend towards pan-Andean integration. The unification seems to have followed a period of crisis, or of wars between rival confederations seeking to achieve a precarious local hegemony. In the event a state centred on the large town of *Wari* or *Huari*[1], near Ayacucho, emerged victorious.

In its early days the Huari culture shows more affinities with the Nazcas than with the Tiahuanaco culture, which was long regarded as the starting point of this expansion. But soon influences clearly coming from Tiahuanaco begin to make themselves felt in the pottery—that essential landmark for the archaeologist: the geometric patterns and mythical beings with which it is decorated are similar to those carved on the Gateway of the Sun, the principal monument in the great Bolivian centre. Among them are animals, the serpents and birds of prey with angular features and triangular fangs and with eyes divided vertically into two halves, one white and the other black—a trait characteristic of Tiahuanaco. The sculpture of Huari is also similar to that on the massive monoliths found on the *altiplano*, while the delicate weaving and needlework show the same designs.

Around the year 1000 these features are found almost everywhere in Peru. The whole Andean region from the Cajamarca basin to Bolivia, previously split up into many small units, now

---

[1] *The form* Huari *is the traditional Spanish spelling;* Wari *is spelt according to the new phonetic orthography of Quechua now used by many writers. The new spellings are in general use for new sites and names which have only recently come into currency; otherwise the traditional spellings remain in common use.*

seemed to form a single state, obeying the same leaders and worshipping the same gods. This flourishing period, however, lasted only two centuries before falling into a sudden and in-explicable decline. The country then broke into pieces again, forming a multitude of small local states which reverted to their previous parochial attitudes.

The Age of Empires (1200–c. 1470)

Much had changed, however, since the days of the little theocratic states of the Nazcas and Mochicas. The power of military leaders had become preponderant; large well planned cities had been founded; and progress in technology—the making of bronze, the complete mastery of irrigation and water supply techniques—made the states stronger, though also more fragile. According to legend the most powerful of these states, the *Chimú* empire, fell when its enemies gained control of its water points and its principal water supply channels.

Thus about 1200 there emerged a number of well organised socio-political units, led by warrior chiefs who were always ambitious and sometimes successful. In what had once been Mochica territory, for example, the *Chimú* built their capital of *Chan-Chan*, a fabulous adobe city covering an area of almost 20 sq. kilometres, the most opulent if not the largest city in pre-Columbian South America. Its rulers, who claimed divine origin, surrounded themselves with a luxury and refinement of which we can gain some idea from the hundreds of pieces of jewellery, gold masks, necklaces of hard stones, sumptuous hangings and vast quantities of pottery found in their cemeteries. Art was now, however, mass-produced, and the Chimú pottery, rapidly moulded and almost always black, is frequently rather un-attractive. About the 14th century the rulers of *Gran Chimú* extended their authority towards the south and annexed some of the richest of the coastal oases. At one time the temple fortress of *Paramonga* marked the boundary of their territory, which was bordered by that of *Cuismancu*, in the Chancay area. In the southern coastal region there were probably one or more powerful chiefdoms centred on *Chincha* and *Ica*, and in the Sierra there grew up a number of small kingdoms—*Cajamarca, Huanca, Chanca*, etc.—which are known principally through their resistance to the Inca armies.

About 1465 the Chimú forces came into conflict with the equally thrusting forces of the *Inca* of Cuzco; and in this confrontation the Chimú empire, extending for some 1200 km along the coast but rendered vulnerable by its complete dependence on irrigation, was defeated. The last Chimú ruler, *Minchansaman*, was compelled to accept the overlordship of *Pachacuti*, the ninth Inca, who had been seeking for some 20 years to overcome the rival empire.

The Rise of the Inca Empire

We must now return briefly to the 13th century, when a small mountain tribe in the Cuzco basin, in the south of the country, began to emerge from its isolation. When in later days the Spaniards asked the Incas where they came from they were told that the founder of the dynasty, fathered by the Sun, had been born of the waters of Lake Titicaca or had come out of a cave near Cuzco. These legends, perhaps reflecting some memory of migrations in earlier times, were mostly fostered by the ruling caste in order to justify their power and their conquests. In fact the little Inca tribe, perhaps originally coming from Amazonia, seems to have had modest beginnings and to have taken a subordinate place among the other tribes which were in occupation of the Cuzco basin in the 11th and 12th centuries.

The eight rulers who followed *Manco Cápac*, the more or less mythical ancestor, gradually broke free of this subordination. *Sinchi Roca, Lloque Yupanqui, Mayta Cápac* and *Capac Yupanqui* undertook plundering expeditions against the neighbouring villages, and these successes paved the way for *Inca Roca's* seizure of power. His successors *Yahuar Huacac* and *Viracocha Inca*, the latter of whom reigned about 1400, consolidated their authority. The rule of the Incas still extended for no more than some 40 kilometres round Cuzco, but their power was about to enter a phase of rapid development which was to take it far beyond the status of one small state among many others.

The great days of the Inca empire began with a war against the *Chancas*, a powerful neighbouring confederation. *Inca Yupanqui*, son of Viracocha Inca, succeeded in saving his capital, then under siege, by winning a bloody battle at *Yawarpampa* (the Plain of Blood) around the year 1440 (if the evidence of the Spanish chroniclers is to be believed). He then deposed his father and had himself acknowledged as ruler under the name of *Pachacuti*,

"Reformer of the World". Helped by his brother and his son, he at once launched on a great campaign of conquest; and between 1440 and 1490 the frontiers of the Inca empire were extended northward into Colombia and southward to the Río Maule in central Chile. It also included Bolivia and north-western Argentina, giving it a total area during this period of over 900,000 sq. kilometres.

The Inca System

During the reign of Pachacuti the Inca Empire reached the peak of its power. Its immense territory was divided into four regions by two imaginary lines intersecting in the centre of Cuzco, the capital. The four regions — *Chinchasuyu* in the north, *Collasuyu* in the south, *Antisuyu* in the east and *Contisuyu* in the west — together formed *Tahuantinsuyu*.

The Incas maintained the cohesion of this vast empire by three principal means: large-scale transfers of population by the deportation of entire tribes (*mitmaj*), aimed at unifying this mosaic of different cultures and races; the imposition of a common language, *Runasimi* (Chechua), which — at any rate in theory — replaced the local dialects, now regarded as inferior; and the system of roads which covered the empire from north to south, running straight as a die over mountains (which were climbed with the aid of steps — for the Incas were ignorant of the wheel) and across torrents (which were spanned by suspension bridges). The Incas also imposed a state religion centred on the cult of the Sun God *Inti*, which — though not displacing the worship of the ancient pan-Andean god *Viracocha* — contributed to the spiritual unification of the empire.

The Inca, regarded as the son of Inti, was a mediator between the divine and earthly worlds, exercising absolute authority. His subjects approached him only with the profoundest adoration, in face of which he affected indifference. Following the example of his ancestor Manco, he always married his sister, who became his principal wife. His descendants in the male line formed the *panaca*, the royal lineage, charged to perpetuate his memory and watch over his mummy. The pattern was one of strict order and rigid organisation; and yet the end of each reign was marked by anarchy and violence, for the eldest son of the dead ruler did not necessarily succeed. The members of the royal family fought fiercely among one another, therefore, until one of the sons achieved victory over his brothers.

The Inca's apparently absolute power was exercised through a multitude of officials who ranged incessantly over the Empire, checking, counting, levying tribute, directing building work, watching over the maintenance of public order. The whole of this huge administrative network was centred on *Cuzco*, the capital. Originally a mere group of huts, Cuzco became during the reign of Pachacuti a splendid city of spacious squares surrounded by imposing buildings. "Cuzco, the city of the rulers of this country, is so large and fair that it could fitly be a city in Spain," cried Sancho de Hoz, one of Pizarro's companions. From the central square started the four great roads which linked the provinces with the capital, and the city was dominated by the cyclopean bulk of the fortress of *Sacsayhuamán* with its three tiers of walls.

Inca architecture is justly famous. The same accurately laid masonry, the same purity of line and the same regular layout are found in dozens of towns and fortresses along the whole length of the Andes from Chile to Ecuador and down to the very verge of the impenetrable Amazonian forest. Machu Picchu, although the most celebrated, is merely one example among many others. And yet the teams of thousands of men who transported and assembled these huge blocks and erected these walls did it all with tools of stone, bronze and wood. The arts of pottery and textiles fell short of these architectural achievements and failed to attain the perfection of the work produced by earlier peoples: the techniques and workmanship were excellent but the stereotyped shapes and decoration showed the effects of mass production. Only the craft of metal-working attained, and indeed surpassed, the technical standards of earlier times.

The End of the Inca Empire

The Inca world seemed permanent and unshakable; but this stability was merely apparent. The empire was a conglomeration of disparate and distant tribes whose chiefs (*curacas*), exercising local authority on behalf of the Inca, were inevitably tempted to rebel when opportunity offered.

About 1493 *Huayna Cápac* seized power after the murder of his father. The expeditions into distant parts continued, but the Inca armies had constantly to quell risings among peoples who had been conquered too rapidly and had not been completely subdued. Other troubles came to plague the Inca: the population was decimated by an unknown scourge (smallpox, brought by European discoverers), and messengers reported the appearance in the far north of bearded white beings, like the gods of ancient legend. *Huayna Cápac*, having been struck down by the dread disease, injudiciously divided the empire between his two sons *Huáscar* (or *Waskar*) and *Atahuallpa* and died, leaving the country plunged into fear at all these inexplicable prodigies.

A fratricidal struggle now took place between the two heirs. *Atahuallpa* had just overcome his brother, in 1530, when the ancient prediction was fulfilled: the white gods had returned, and this time they were advancing into the country in strength. In the divided and weakened empire the Spaniards found conquest easy. When at last the Indians realised that Pizarro and his companions were mere mortals it was too late: by then the invaders had made their way across the entire country. The Emperor was taken prisoner and executed: the last Inca had reigned over his vast empire for no more than a single day.

COLONIAL PERU

The Conquest

In 1532 a handful of Spaniards, coming from Panama, landed near Tumbes in northern Peru. Their leader, Francisco Pizarro, who is traditionally supposed to have been a former swineherd from the province of Estremadura, had been exploring the Pacific coasts for eight years in the hope of finding the fabulous land of gold (*El Dorado*), the name given by the Indians of South America to Tahuantinsuyu, the empire of the Incas. After making an alliance with the local tribes and founding the town of San Miguel de Piura in the centre of the coastal region he climbed into the first cordillera and entered Cajamarca, where Atahuallpa, one of the two claimants to the throne of Huayna Cápac, had established his headquarters.

The young Emperor, over-confident of the strength of his victorious army, allowed himself to be caught in a trap set by the Spaniards and was taken prisoner with the whole of his retinue. He gave the Spaniards the house full of treasure which they demanded as ransom, but in spite of this was executed in the following year after a mockery of a trial. Tahuantinsuyu, without its head, now fell to pieces. The large tribes which had chafed at Inca control now went over to the invaders one after the other, and the road to Cuzco was open. The conquest of the most formidable empire in pre-Columbian America seemed to be complete: in fact it took another forty years to bring it completely under Spanish control.

In 1536 the Inca people rose in revolt under the leadership of Manco, half-brother of Atahuallpa and Huáscar, whom the Spaniards had allowed to wear the old insignia of imperial power as a link with the country's past. With an army of 40,000 men Manco laid siege to Cuzco, in which the Spanish garrison was penned up for a whole year. Pizarro sent four relief expeditions from Lima, which he had just founded, but each in turn was wiped out. The rising spread throughout the whole of southern Peru and even threatened the new capital, when the arrival of timely reinforcements from Panama enabled the Spaniards to check the Indian advance. Thereafter a brutal policy of terror, involving the systematic destruction of crops, the burning down of villages and the massacre or mutilation of their inhabitants, finally drove Manco to evacuate the Sierra and take refuge in the wooded escarpments of the Amazonian flanks of the Andes, where he established a small Inca state which was to preserve its independence until 1572.

No sooner was the peril over than dissensions began to appear among the conquerors. In 1535 Diego de Almagro, one of Pizarro's companions, who had quarrelled with him over the distribution of the booty and believed that he had not been fairly treated in the territorial division of the country, had decided to mount an expedition into Chile, which the Indians of Peru claimed was the real El Dorado, hoping to divert the European invaders from their own country. After crossing the snow-covered passes of the cordilleras at the cost of great hardships and heavy losses he had reached Araucania, only to discover that the riches he expected to find there did not exist. Deeply disillusioned, he returned to Peru in 1537, skirting the Atacama coastal desert, with the firm intention of wreaking a long cherished revenge on Pizarro. His murder in the following year merely exacerbated the struggle between the "Pizarrists" and the "Almagrists", in which Pizarro himself was also killed (1541).

Hitherto the conquest had been a private enterprise which the Spanish Crown had merely encouraged from afar. The conquerors had divided up among themselves the treasures which they had systematically looted from temples, imperial palaces and the burial places of Inca rulers, and had split up the whole country and the whole population into *encomiendas*. These were independent fiefs whose holders could levy tribute freely on the local people, remitting one fifth (the *quinto*) to the royal exchequer. They were also entitled to exact all kinds of services in kind or in labour in order to meet their needs or satisfy their greed. In return they were merely required to maintain a priest on their *encomienda* and promote the conversion of the Indians.

Soon, however, the Spanish Crown began to intervene directly in the affairs of Peru, finding a pretext in the numerous and frequently horrifying abuses to which the *encomienda* system gave rise. In 1547 the *New Laws on the Indies* were promulgated at Barcelona, curtailing very considerably the exorbitant privileges which the Conquistadors had arrogated to themselves. They also prohibited the establishment of any further *encomiendas* and abolished the hereditary right of succession to those already in existence. Immediately they became known the New Laws led to a violent reaction among the Spaniards, who saw themselves as being ignominiously robbed of their due. Gonzalo Pizarro, Francisco's half-brother, who had at one time contemplated marrying an Inca princess and restoring the independence of Tahuantinsuyu with himself as Emperor, raised the standard of revolt. The Viceroy appointed by the Crown, Blasco Núñez Vela, who had just arrived in Lima, was compelled to flee to Quito. In 1546 the meagre forces which he had managed to rally to the royal cause were defeated in the battle of Anaquito, and he himself was taken prisoner and beheaded on the battlefield. Pedro de la Gasca, on whom fell the task of pacifying Peru, required to operate with both prudence and firmness to gain control of the situation and impose the authority of the Crown on the settlers, whom even the execution of Gonzalo Pizarro failed to quell.

This ruthless civil war left a lasting feeling of resentment among the Conquistadors and their descendants, which no doubt did something in later years to promote the emergence of Peruvian national feeling. The hostility to Spanish control was further increased in subsequent centuries by a policy of discrimination which excluded all Spaniards born in America from appointment to administrative posts in the colony and from the honours which went with such posts.

The restoration of peace enabled the Spaniards to complete the conquest. The still undefeated Incas in Vilcabamba, on the fringe of the immense Amazonian basin, were continuing to send pillaging expeditions against the colonial settlements and to threaten the vital Lima–Cuzco road. Negotiations were initiated with Sayri Túpac, Manco's son, who agreed to do allegiance to the Spanish Crown; but his brother Tito Cusi, who succeeded him as leader of the Indian resistance, was less forthcoming. Finally, exasperated by the interminable discussions which never produced any result, the Viceroy Francisco de Toledo, who had arrived in Lima in 1569, sent an army against Vilcabamba. The Inca state was occupied and its last ruler, Túpac Amaru, brought back to Cuzco as a prisoner and executed in the main square of the old imperial capital in 1572. There was now no further opposition to the authority of the Spanish Crown in what had once been the empire of Tahuantinsuyu.

The Organisation of the Colony

The real organiser of the colony was Francisco de Toledo, who now set about laying the foundations of the new Peru with the aid of a team of very competent officials; but the foundations were laid in an almost empty country. The bloody fighting during the conquest, the harsh treatment of the conquered Indians and the famines which had resulted from the destruction of livestock and crops and the "scorched earth" policy of the Spaniards had decimated the Andean peoples; and many more succumbed to diseases of European origin like typhoid and smallpox, as well as lesser scourges like measles, whooping-cough and influenza, against which the Indians were not genetically immunised. The great epidemics of 1546, 1554 and 1558, caused by the introduction of pathogenic germs hitherto unknown on the American continent, and the appalling pandemic of 1588–89 claimed hundreds of thousands of victims. Whereas the Andean region had probably between 8 and 10 million inhabitants at the beginning of the 16th century, the population a hundred years later was no more than a million. A demographic catastrophe on this scale had no precedent in the history of mankind and was equalled only by the comparable havoc wrought in Mexico during the same period and in similar circumstances.

The survivors were systematically removed from their villages, situated on the mountain tops at high altitudes, and concentrated in the valley bottoms, often more than a thousand metres lower down, where it was easier to secure their political control, economic exploitation and ideological manipulation. The new settlements to which they were transferred were built for the purpose by the colonial administration, laid out on the same regular plan with a grid of wide straight streets round a central square in which were the church and the prison, symbols of the new authority. Each village was assigned an inalienable area of land, the cultivable part of this being divided up each year into family plots which reverted to the common pool at the end of the farming cycle. A further area was held in common ownership and worked communally, the proceeds from the sale of produce from this land being paid into a fund from which the needs of the community were met. Timber, water and the mountain grazings were communal property to which all villagers had access. The affairs of the community were run by officials elected annually at a public meeting, subject to a double control by the former native chiefs (*curacas*) and by the Spanish official (*corregidor*) who administered the province (*corregimiento*).

Alongside the Indian villages were the great Spanish estates (*haciendas*). These were established towards the end of the 16th century by royal grant (*merced*) on land which had formerly belonged to the Inca state or had been abandoned by the decimated native population. Originally the grants had been of relatively small areas of land, but the holders steadily increased their estates at the expense of neighbouring Indian communities. The *hacendados* were less concerned to acquire land for its own sake than to gain control of the manpower required to work it: their aim was to deprive the Indians of their means of subsistence in order to compel them to hire their labour to the haciendas. By the beginning of the 18th century more than a third of the population of some areas were attached to the great estates as *peones*. The growth of this seigniorial system was promoted by the long economic crisis from which Peru suffered throughout the 17th century; and it was during this crisis that Peruvian society took on the fundamental characteristics which were to mark it so profoundly and so lastingly.

The *peones* on the estates did, however, enjoy certain counter-vailing advantages: they were exempt from the annual tribute payment, and they escaped the many obligations which bore heavily on the so-called "free" Indians in the villages. Of these obligations the cruellest was the *mita*, a native institution diverted from its original purpose to serve the interests of the settlers, under which the Indians were required to work for a period in the great mining centres from which Peru drew its (much exaggerated) reputation for wealth. Every year a seventh of the population living within a radius of 200 to 300 kilometres, selected in rotation, made their way in pitiable processions to Potosí to work in the silver mines or to Huancavelica to produce the mercury which was used in the treatment of the silver ore by the amalgamation process. Malnutrition, ill-treatment and the frequent collapse of mine workings produced such a high mortality among the silver-miners that the office for the dead was celebrated in the village churches when the annual contingent of workers left for the mines. In order to escape the *mita* many Indians fled to the in-hospitable surrounding areas which were still largely outside the reach of the Spanish authorities.

Another Spanish exaction which bore hard on the Indians was the system of *repartimientos*. The *corregidores* paid considerable sums to obtain their posts, which had a tenure of no more than five years, and they sought therefore to recover their investment and make substantial profits in addition by "distributing" (hence the term *repartimiento*, "distribution") to the people in their area of jurisdiction a variety of goods, many of them of poor quality and of no use to the Indians, but which they were com-pelled to buy. This system for the compulsory purchase, at exorbitant prices, of goods acquired from the Indians of some other region at absurdly low prices drained away the money that remained to the village communities after payment of the royal tribute. In one sense it integrated the local people in the colonial economy, but it also discouraged them from productive effort, which had to be stimulated by further constraints, thus creating a vicious circle of economic exploitation and social oppression.

The Spanish administration did at any rate bring about a considerable degree of cultural uniformity. The regional differences which the Incas had tried to reduce, without any great success, now began to disappear. The Quechua language came into general use from Colombia to the northern part of what is now Argentina, and the local dialects disappeared. A popular form of Catholicism centred on the cult of saints—who were often invested with the attributes of pre-Hispanic divinities—supplanted the native religions; the priests of these religions were driven away and their ceremonies vigorously repressed by the Spaniards in the name of extirpating idolatry. The elements taken over from Spain—very selectively—in both the material and the spiritual field profoundly modified Indian traditions and distorted their original character. A new culture now began to take shape, combining both Spanish and pre-Hispanic features, which was nevertheless radically different from both these constituent elements.

This new Andean world was dominated by Cajamarca, Huánuco, Ayacucho, the sumptuous city of Trujillo, the aristocratic Arequipa, the historic old city of Cuzco and many other towns proud of their coats of arms and jealous of their privileges. In them dwelt a powerful elite of landowners and a swarm of traders and craftsmen, many of them of mixed blood, who lived in their various parishes, in the shadow of innumerable church towers. Even the most prosperous of these towns, however, could not compare with Lima, which after the fall of Cuzco had become the capital of the colony. The proud "City of the Kings" was the seat of a Viceroy whose authority extended from the *audiencia* of Quito (now Ecuador) to the *audiencia* of Charcas (Bolivia). In its Andalusian palaces, with their balconies concealed behind intricately patterned lattice screens, lived a refined and elegant society made up of a constantly changing succession of officials of high lineage sent out by the Spanish court, with their swarming retinue of relatives, clients and dependants. Its plethora of religious houses and its churches, sometimes built in a rather

massive style made necessary by the possibility of earthquakes
in certain areas, were richly endowed by the piety of the wealthy
classes. Its port, Callao, was the largest trading centre in the whole
Pacific area; its university, San Marcos, was one of the most
illustrious in the New World. This splendid city, so often described in accounts of Spanish achievements in Peru, was no less
a part of the social picture than the hardships of the Indians of
the villages, which it could never outweigh or conceal.

Rebellion and Reform

At the end of the 17th century the Peruvian economy revived,
and the society which had been held back by its economic back-
wardness was moved by fresh impulses. Up till now the colonial
order had been based on the opposition between Indians and
Spaniards (whether the Spaniards were Creoles of local birth or
incomers from Spain); there was no place in it for those of mixed
Spanish and Indian blood. Since interbreeding had begun at a
very early stage and thereafter developed rapidly there were now
large numbers of people without any definite social status and
without legal recognition. From the beginning of the 18th century
onwards the process of interbreeding accelerated still further as
the result of the migration from Spain which now resumed after
a long interruption. The newcomers, mostly from the Basque
country and Navarre, could not be fitted into the structure of
urban life in Peru and settled in the country areas among the
Indians, in spite of the laws of residential separation which prohibited them from doing so. Within the villages they established
their own position by exploiting the Indian population and gain-
ing possession of the best land; and the Indians' holdings, already
threatened from outside by the nearby haciendas, were now also
threatened from within the village communities by the activities
of these "poor whites". The pressure on the available land
became even more severe at this period because after a long period
of decline the Indian population was now becoming stabilised
and indeed increasing slowly. The problems resulting from these
various factors grew more serious as time went on.

The old Indian nobility was not unaware of these problems.
Its ancient privileges had been respected and it had been granted
fresh honours. The heads of the main imperial families of Cuzco
led the lives of great Spanish noblemen on the estates which had
been allotted to them. Their sons were educated in the Prince's

College and the College of St Francis Borgia, and their daughters
were sought after as brides by illustrious Spaniards in America:
thus Captain Martín García de Loyola, nephew of the founder
of the Society of Jesus, married the daughter of Sayri Túpac. The
local chiefs had also found their place in the colonial system as
necessary intermediaries between the administration and the
people, from whom they exacted tribute on the government's
behalf. They had become great landowners or prosperous mer-
chants or entrepreneurs in the textile or transport industry. They
spoke Spanish and sometimes Latin, could read and write, and
wore European dress.

During the 18th century, however, this elite suffered a decline
in status. Their acceptance into the privileged classes of the
colony was no longer unquestioned; the colonial administration,
now much strengthened in numbers, tended increasingly to
exclude them from the responsibilities which had previously been
allotted to them. Thrown back towards the mass of the Indian
population from which they had previously been concerned to
distinguish themselves, the Inca nobles and local chiefs returned
to a tradition which they had earlier repudiated. They had their
portraits painted in the old imperial dress, along with their
families, and they wore these garments at ceremonies commemorating the great events of their pre-Hispanic history, which
now came suddenly into favour again. This enthusiasm for the
past was also reflected in art, in which European influence re-
ceded in favour of a trend towards the styles of the past. Similar
feelings were behind the great success of a Quechua verse drama,
"Ollantay", recounting the unhappy love affair between one of
Inca Pachacuti's generals and his daughter, and the popularity
of Garcilaso de la Vega's "Royal Commentaries of the Incas",
written a century earlier, which now found numerous enthusiastic
readers.

This interest in the Inca past inevitably took on a political
colouring. The leaders of the movement adopted an increasingly
critical attitude to the colonial regime as they were progressively
excluded from its benefits, and sought to give expression to the
aspirations of the native peasantry. In 1721 Vicente Mora Chimú,
the descendant of a line of chiefs from the coastal region, travelled
to Spain to represent to the king the grievances of his Indian subjects. In 1749 Calixto Túpac Yupanqui, who was descended
through his mother from Inca Túpac Yupanqui, also went to
Madrid to convey to the king a "Veritable Representation and
Humble and Lamentable Exclamation" of the Indian nation, of

which he claimed to be the representative. The Indians' grievances also found expression in a number of bloody risings. In 1742 Juan Santos, an Indian from Ayacucho who had taken the name of Atahuallpa, led the tribes of the area under the eastern slopes of the Andes in a rising directed against the Franciscan missions. The various costly military expeditions despatched against the rebels—who threatened to appeal for British help—were unable to quell the insurrection, and Spanish penetration into the Amazon basin was hampered for many years. In 1750, while the government was unable to assert its authority in the Sierra de Lima, it discovered a plot in the capital itself to assassinate the Viceroy. The Indian conspirators declared that they had been charged by St Rose of Lima to restore Tahuantinsuyu.

The most serious of the 18th century risings, however, was the one led by José Gabriel Condorcanqui, who called himself Túpac Amaru II after the last ruler of Vilcabamba, from whom he was descended. This broke out in the southern provinces of Canas and Canchis in 1780, but soon spread to the whole of the Peruvo-Bolivian high plateau; indeed its repercussions were felt all over Spanish America. Puno was captured, La Paz besieged, Cuzco threatened. Condorcanqui's aim was merely to establish the equality of Indians, half-breeds, Creoles and Spaniards from the Peninsula; but his followers were much more radical, and after his capture and execution in Cuzco they adopted a fiercely anti-white attitude. When the rising was eventually quelled it was followed by ruthless repression, the severity of which reflected the fear aroused among the Spaniards by the insurrection. The old imperial families were now deported to fortresses in Spain or in the *presidios* on the African coast; and the local chiefs, deprived of their status and reduced to ruin, were absorbed into the downtrodden peasantry.

In spite of these severe measures, a number of radical reforms were in fact carried through under the influence of the Enlightenment, which reached Spain during the reign of Charles III and Peru under the administration of Manuel Amat y Junient. The practice of *repartimiento* was prohibited; the *corregidores* were replaced by intendants; and new men and new methods were brought into the administration of the country. Intellectual life flourished and scientific activity developed. The emergence of a Peruvian press, the most notable representative of which was the "Mercurio Peruano", bore witness to the vitality of the ideas which came from Europe but were grafted on to the realities of Andean life. In spite of the occupation of the capital by

Napoleonic forces and the suspension of transatlantic trade which threatened the prosperity of the Peruvian economy the country remain loyal to the Spanish Crown. It could very properly be called the bulwark of the royal authority in Spanish America. It adopted the liberal Constitution of Cadiz (1812) without enthusiasm; and equally it accepted without bitterness Ferdinand VII's return to absolutism a few years later.

REPUBLICAN PERU

The Age of the Caudillos (1821–60)

Peru's participation in the great movement of American emancipation was both modest and late. The fear that a further Indian rising would lead to the extermination of all white men profoundly inhibited the national aspirations of the Creole elite, which in other Spanish possessions had been finding increasingly vigorous expression since 1810. It was in fact General San Martín's troops, recruited in Argentina and Chile, who, after landing on the coast and capturing Lima, proclaimed the independence of Peru on 28 July 1821, with San Martín as its "Protector". For another three years, however, the royalists remained in control of the whole of the mountainous hinterland, in which they were solidly established. It was only after the arrival of the "patriots" mobilised by Bolívar in Colombia that they were defeated on the Junín steppes and subsequently suffered an even more crushing defeat at the *battle of Ayacucho* (1824). This battle, the anniversary of which is still commemorated throughout Spanish America, marked not only the final emancipation of Peru but the end of three centuries of Spanish domination on the American continent.

Becoming the unchallenged leader of the victorious patriot forces after the withdrawal of San Martín, Bolívar dreamed of a close union between the young republics which had established themselves on the ruins of Charles V's Empire. In this union, founded on a community of language and culture, Peru — of which Bolívar had had himself appointed Dictator and later President for life — was destined to play a prominent part. But Bolívar's dream soon came up against a sudden revival of Peruvian national feeling, directed against the neighbouring countries which were equally jealous of their own sovereignty. After the collapse of a Peru–Bolivian Federation in 1825 war broke out with Colombia and Bolivia in 1828. A final effort to unify Peru and Bolivia in a confederation was made in 1835, but this too collapsed in the following year in the face of military pressure from Argentina and Chile, who felt threatened by the establishment of a large Andean state on their northern frontiers. The failure of this confederation, which was in any event strongly opposed by many in Peru, finally reduced the country to the boundaries of the old *audiencia* of Lima, as an independent state within a Balkanised Hispanic America.

Independence was the beginning of a period of great internal instability. Between 1821 and 1860 Peru had no fewer than nine constitutions and fifteen Presidents, five of them of foreign origin. No competent officials were available to take the place of the ponderous but reliable Spanish bureaucracy, and the government of the country fell to a series of military leaders, many of them of modest origin. Supported by the remnants of the liberating armies, who lived on the population as if in conquered enemy territory, these *caudillos* followed one another in rapid succession. In 1838 no fewer than seven of them claimed simultaneously to be the constitutionally appointed President. One or two of them had coherent and ambitious political plans, like Ramón Castilla, who established a national budget (1847), enacted a Civil Code (1852) and abolished slavery (1854). What they lacked was the means of putting their plans into effect. Without any popular backing in the country, their power rested solely on military force. Moreover the national exchequer was empty, and the loans periodically sought from other countries in order to pay the army, on which the government's authority depended, increased the national debt to a point where the country's sovereignty was mortgaged.

For the latent economic crisis of the closing years of the colonial period had now degenerated into an acute depression. The country's productive potential had been ruined by the war: thus the famous Huancavelica mines and the Cerro de Pasco mines, which the royalists and patriots had taken and retaken four times, had been taken out of production. In this economic situation, with the collapse of the market and a shortage of ready money, there was a restructuring of the economy centred on the large estates, within a neo-seigniorial framework. The landed aristocracy strengthened their position considerably by taking over increasing areas of land; and this trend towards the concentration of property in fewer hands, on similar lines to the movement which had developed in the 17th century as a result of the same factors, was promoted by new legislation based on the principles of European liberalism. In 1828 the abolition of mortmain brought into the property market the land held by the Church and the religious orders on this tenure, which in some areas amounted to anything up to a third of the availablel and. The Civil Code generalised these measures of *desamortización* of land, prohibiting disposals on copyhold tenure or long leases based on the mediaeval law which was still in force.

This extension of the large estates was achieved in the first place at the expense of the Indian village communities, whose special legal status—which had given them a limited but nevertheless real degree of protection—was now abolished. During a brief visit to Cuzco in 1824 Bolívar had decreed the abolition of the village community as an institution, the granting to the Indians in full ownership of the cultivated land which they held only on a life-rent, and the redistribution among them of the woods and grazings held as communal property. He saw these measures as contributing to the formation of a class of small independent landholders who would provide backing for a conservative government. The reality, however, was very different. The ignorant Indians, entirely under the thumb of the *mestizo* local officials, were robbed of their rights by the *hacendados*, who seized the land which had been granted to them in full ownership. Moreover the official recognition of the system of forced labour in payment of debts, which had been prohibited by the Spanish Crown but had been practised in clandestine fashion during the 18th century, reduced increasing numbers of Indians to a condition of *de facto* serfdom. The new regime had, at any rate as far as they were concerned, failed to live up to its promises of liberty and equality.

The Rise of Capitalism (1860–1919)

The economic situation took a turn for the better in the 1850s with the guano boom. The droppings of seabirds which had accumulated over many centuries on the islets of the coastal fringe, and which had been used to fertilise their fields by the Incas and before them by the Mochicas, now became a source of national wealth. European countries, particularly Britain and France, offered high prices for this valuable fertiliser, and in the year 1850 alone exports amounted to 140,000 tons, rising to almost 200,000 tons in the following year. Concessions for working this "grey gold" were granted to foreign companies (Gibbs, Montane, Dreyfus, etc.) and brought substantial revenues to the state. The national budget—which had been instituted to keep account of the large income now flowing into the exchequer—rose from 4,000,000 pesos in 1849 to 10,000,000 in 1855.

The guano boom also led to the accumulation of private savings, which were invested primarily in the large estates in the northern and central coastal areas. The new owners of these old colonial haciendas now abandoned the traditional subsistence farming to grow sugar-cane. The Cuban political crisis, which paralysed the island's sugar production and caused a steep rise in the price of sugar on the world market during the 1860s, provided the impetus for this change. By 1876 Peru was already exporting an annual 55,000 tons of sugar, and at that date 235 estates, mostly in the Chiclayo, Trujillo, Pacasmayo and Lambayeque areas, were devoted to sugar-cane. The plantations were worked by coolies from Macao and later by Japanese — the origin of the considerable Asiatic colony in present-day Peru. The cost of this labour force, however, was relatively high, and the planters turned therefore towards the use of steam power. The mechanisation of production now made progress, the first wholly mechanised sugar factory being opened at Casa Grande in 1871. On other plantations railways were built to speed up the transport of cane to the processing plants. This development led to a contrast, steadily increasing in later years, between the capitalist coastal regions, now in process of rapid modernisation, and the feudal Sierra, still living in its old closed world based on the serf labour of the Indians.

The two governments of General Ramón Castilla, which dominated the political scene between 1844 and 1860, brought a period of relative peace. The constitution promulgated in 1860, which remained in force until 1919, established a reasonable balance between the various sources of authority in the country, of which the planters on the Coast, now reduced in number, claimed the exclusive exercise, their demands becoming increasingly strident as the years went on. The Civil Party which they founded — the name itself reflecting their aims — argued for the establishment of a representative system of government directed by an oligarchy of money; and the victory of this party in the 1872 election, bringing Manuel Pardo to the Presidency, marked the end of the age of the *caudillos*. Henceforth the army was to be confined to its barracks, emerging at intervals thereafter, but always at the behest of the oligarchs, who had brought it entirely under their control, and in support of their economic interests: it now ceased to intervene on its own account in the political life of the country.

The development of capitalism and the consolidation of a representative political system were rudely interrupted by the

Pacific War of 1879–83, fought for possession of the nitrate deposits in the Atacama desert, where the frontiers between Peru, Bolivia and Chile had never been firmly defined. In 1879 Chile annexed the Bolivian part of the area, which had been developed by Bolivian labour and capital: whereupon Peru, which had a defence pact with Bolivia, went to the aid of its ally. The first engagements were fought at sea. The Peruvian fleet, commanded by Admiral Miguel Graú, flying his flag in the battleship "Huáscar", gained some initial successes but was then wiped out in the *battle of Angamos* on 8 October 1879. The Chileans were now able to land unopposed on the Peruvian coast and take their enemy in the rear. After successive victories at Iquique, Pisagua and Arica they launched an offensive against the capital, and on 17 January 1881 entered Lima after an ineffective defence by the makeshift forces raised by Nicolás de Piérola.

A provisional government led by Francisco García Calderón sought to achieve a compromise peace with the occupying forces, but Piérola fled to the Sierra and called for an out-and-out struggle against the enemy. He was succeeded as leader of the resistance by Andrés A. Cáceres, who directed the operations of Indian guerrilla forces from his base in the mountains while rebuilding an army. The new army was finally defeated, however, at Huamachuco on 10 July 1883; and the *treaty of Ancón* (20 October 1883), under which Peru ceded to Chile its southern provinces of Arica and Tacna, put an end ot the war, one of the bloodiest in the history of Latin America. The terms of the treaty, however, created lasting resentment in Peru, which was not dissipated by the return of Tacna in 1929, and a profound mistrust of Chile which has continued to manifest itself down to our own day.

In spite of the losses and the destruction it had suffered Peru recovered rapidly under the governments of Cáceres (1885–95) and Piérola (1895–99). Supported by massive investments of French and British, and later North American, capital, the oligarchy ceased to be based exclusively on sugar and diversified its interests in many sectors of the economy, which now took on a fresh lease of life. At the turn of the century cotton-growing was developed in the central coastal area, while the mining for which the country had been famed in the past was resumed in the interior, particularly in the Cerro de Pasco, where new metalliferous lodes were discovered. The banking system expanded, and the development of industry began (textiles, clothing, foodstuffs). A railway line was built from Lima to Huancayo in the heart of the Andes, surmounting the cordillera by extraordinary feats of engineering, and another line linked Cuzco with Lake Titicaca. The country's expansion was stimulated still further by the opening of the Panama Canal in 1914, which facilitated trade with Europe and the eastern United States, and the first world war, which led to a rise in the prices of the raw materials which Peru exported. For the oligarchy this was an age of prosperity, under the governments of Romaña (1900–04), Leguía (1909–12) and José Pardo (1904–08 and 1915–19). A different note was introduced in 1912 with the election of President Billinghurst, who tried to apply a social policy; but Billinghurst was rapidly removed from office by a military coup d'état.

The Oligarchy versus the People (1919–68)

The eleven years of Augusto Leguía's second Presidency (1919–30) marked the apogee of the oligarchy. During these eleven years (the *oncenio*) the highly centralised state, with all authority concentrated in Lima (now rebuilt and embellished to fit its role as capital), still further extended its control over the provinces of the interior, which were now served by a developing network of roads and communications by telegraph. The landed aristocracy in these provinces, now economically marginal, was destroyed, and the *hacendados* were steadily excluded from the positions of local authority, which they had hitherto seemed to occupy as of right, in favour of officials appointed by the government.

The world economic depression of 1929 was a devastating blow to a country whose prosperity was closely bound up with its international trade. It led to the fall of President Leguía and to an explosion of popular discontent among the mass of the population, who suffered directly from the cris. The Alianza Popular Revolucionaria Americana (APRA), a populist movement founded by Victor Raúl Haya de la Torre, made itself the mouthpiece for the demands of the agricultural workers of the coastal region, now threatened with unemployment, and expressed the aspirations of the lower classes in the coastal towns, whose conditions of life were deteriorating. APRA organised numerous strikes on the sugar-cane plantations, which frequently led to confrontations with the army. In 1932 there was an insurrection led by APRA at Trujillo, in the heart of the sugar-growing area, when the rebels captured the barracks in the town and massacred the officers of the garrison. Two years later a plan for a general rising was discovered a few days before the date fixed for the occupation of public buildings in the chief towns of all the provinces. In the ruthless repression carried out by the government of Colonel Luis Sánchez Cerro (1930–33) several thousand people were executed and tens of thousands were interned in the notorious Frontón prison (on an island off Callao) or in concentration camps in the depths of the Amazonian forest. After the assassination of Sánchez Cerro in 1933 Congress gave dictatorial powers to General Oscar Benavides, who wielded them until 1939 to enforce a return to the oligarchic order.

The second world war brought prosperity to Peru and contributed to the easing of social tensions. The revenue from the export of raw materials, which increased sharply in price, was now invested in the production of goods which Peru had previously bought from other countries but could no longer import because of the war. This policy of "import substitution", later to be recommended by United Nations agencies for under-developed countries, was behind the industrialisation which began during the Presidency of Manuel Prado (1939–45) and was accelerated in later years—though it remained confined to the narrow coastal strip of western Peru.

José Luis Bustamante, who was elected President in 1945, decided that the moment had come for a move towards the left, and made approaches to APRA, which had survived all persecution and indeed increased its popular support. The experiment failed. Alarmed at the presence of a party which still called itself revolutionary behind the scenes of government, the oligarchy put a stop to it three years later by bringing in General Manuel Apolinario Odría as President. Odría retained the Presidency for eight years and was then succeeded by Manuel Prado, a representative of the powerful industrial interests of the Coast, whose impressive programme of large-scale public works could not conceal the worsening of the country's social malaise.

This malaise was reflected in the increasing numbers of poverty-stricken peasants from the Andes who were now flocking down to the developing industrial towns on the Coast. The movement reached such proportions that it became known as the *wayqo serrano* (landslide or avalanche). Between 1940 and 1961 the population of the Sierra fell from 62% to 51.6% of the total population, while the population of the Coast rose from 25% to

39.9%. Round the coastal towns and particularly the conurbation of Lima–Callao (the population of which increased in twenty years from 600,000 to 1,600,000) there grew up rings of shanty towns (*barriadas*) providing squalid and overcrowded homes for the incomers from the Sierra.

The inarticulate aspirations of the rootless inhabitants of the *barriadas* now came together with the more specific demands of the middle classes created by the development of industry and the civil service, who were increasingly alienated from a social system which set limits to their ambitions. It was these middle classes who brought Fernando Belaúnde Terry to the Presidency in 1963, and the new President's programme was calculated to appeal to them. It provided for land reform, a building programme designed to get rid of the shanty towns, the bringing into cultivation of the virgin land on the Amazonian slopes of the Andes and a revitalisation of the old Indian village communities, which were to become cooperatives. But the carrying through of this programme was hampered by the opposition of Congress, which regarded it as too ambitious. Thus the land reform act passed in 1964 fell considerably short of the government's original proposals, excluding the coastal plantations and fixing such a high scale of compensation for the dispossessed *hacendados* that only a derisory area could be made available for redistribution to the peasants without risking inflation or bankruptcy. Disappointed in its hopes, the extreme left tried to force Belaúnde's hand by launching a guerrilla movement in 1965. This was quickly repressed, however, and merely had the effect of leading the government to seek a compromise with the conservative majority in both houses of Congress. The way to reform by democratic methods now seemed to be closed.

Belaúnde also came into conflict with the United States over the oil concession at La Brea and Pariñas held by the International Petroleum Co., a subsidiary of Standard Oil of New Jersey, which was due to expire. IPC sought a renewal of the concession, with increased privileges, and in a dramatic series of negotiations imposed its views on the government, now at the end of its tether. The army, seeing this as an affront to the national dignity, overthrew Belaúnde during the night of 3–4 October 1968 and seized power.

The 1968 Military Revolution

The coup d'état of October 1968 was fundamentally different from the earlier *cuartelazos* ("barrack risings") in that it was not carried out by a small group of influential officers but by the whole army acting as an institution. Moreover the generals who came to power were not concerned to defend the great financial and industrial interests which were now threatened: on the contrary the radical transformation of the country's social structures which was their objective implied the elimination of the oligarchy.

For some years the army, now increasingly officered by the middle classes and the lesser bourgeoisie, had been swayed by new trends of thought. Under the influence of North American advisers its staff officers had increasingly realised that Peru was not so much in danger from aggression on its frontiers as from internal subversion; and the young colonels and majors who had become aware of economic and social problems during their training at the Centro de Altos Estudios Militares realised also that the oligarchy and the poverty in which it maintained the mass of the population provided the soil in which subversion was bound to grow. The army's doubts about the viability of the existing system hardened into certainty when the guerrilla rising of 1965 broke out. The repression of this romantic episode, in which the army became involved against its will, had a traumatic effect, creating a feeling of lively resentment against a government which was so clearly incapable of making Peru into a modern industrial nation by peaceful means.

The "military revolution" led by General Juan Velasco Alvardo, taking the emblem of Túpac Amaru as its symbol, sought to be neither capitalist nor communist: it saw itself as a liberating movement concerned to maintain human values. The sharp and sudden changes carried through in Peru since 1968 have in fact amounted to a revolution. The establishment of exchange control and the nationalisation of the great credit houses and of foreign trade gave the government effective means of intervention in the country's economic life. The compulsory acquisition of sources of power supply like the International Petroleum Co and the principal mining company, the Cerro de Pasco Copper Corporation, a real state within the state, gave Peru control of the resources on which its development depended and which were now to be managed by public corporations. In the field of foreign policy links were developed with the socialist countries, in particular with Cuba, and a position of non-alignment was adopted in international affairs.

But the most ambitious and most novel reforms, reflecting most clearly the objectives of the regime, were in the field of land and industrial reform. The land reform which came into effect in 1969 applied to all the large estates, beginning with the sugar-cane plantations of the Coast, the ownership and management of which were handed over to the workers. In the Sierra the traditional haciendas were expropriated but not split up. Along with the surrounding village communities they were transformed into large production cooperatives known as "socialised agricultural societies" (SIAS), to which the government gave technical and financial assistance. The former owners were compensated according to the value of the land as declared for income tax purposes: since this was much below the real value the cost of acquisition was relatively low and the reform could proceed rapidly. Between 1969 and 1975 more than 6 million hectares were dealt with in this way.

The industrial reform was not confined to a few acts of nationalisation but provided for the transfer of half the shares of private companies to the employees, who were thus associated with management in both the profits and the running of the business, on an equal basis. Like the land reform, these measures were seen as part of a large-scale plan for the redistribution of power between different social groups at all levels of society. The "reformed" companies of this kind were designed to take their place alongside the nationalised enterprises and the completely "self-managed" companies which it was the government's intention to promote as one of the three great sectors of industry.

Many problems, of course, still remain. The most serious is to secure general acceptance of the changes and the participation of the mass of the population in their achievement, which the army has been unable to bring about on its own. As the self-proclaimed "vanguard of the people", the army sometimes seems to go too fast for the people. The riots in Lima in February 1975 reflected the difficulties which attend a revolution initiated from above: the mass of the people, for whose benefit the revolution is supposed to have taken place, may fail to understand all its objectives, but they are very sensitive to the constraints it inevitably imposes.

POPULATION

General

With a population of some 15 million, Peru takes second place among the Andean countries, coming after Colombia, and fourth place in South America as a whole. The population has more than doubled since 1940, and has multiplied fivefold over the past hundred years, from 2,700,000 in 1876 (6,208,000 in 1940). This rapid rate of increase (about 3.1% annually) is mainly due to natural growth, since immigration has now practically stopped. The birth rate is still high (an average of 47 per 1000) in all classes of society, while the death rate has fallen to around 16 per 1000, as a result of the progress of medicine rather than improved nutrition. Infant mortality, however, is still high in the poorer classes of the population, where one or two children per family still die in infancy. The government has a firm policy of encouraging large families, since it regards Peru, with 10.5 inhabitants to the sq. kilometre, as still being under-populated.

The population is very unevenly distributed. Much of the immense Amazonian territory has less than one inhabitant per sq. kilometre. In the Sierra and on the Coast there are pockets of very high density, with dramatic examples of local over-population, separated by vast expanses of *puna* or desert almost empty of inhabitants. In most of the coastal areas there are oases with a density of over 200 to the sq. kilometre. In the Vilcanota valley round Cuzco, at an altitude of 3400 m, there are densities of 50 to 80 per sq. kilometre. On the *altiplano* the density may exceed 100 to the sq. kilometre on the banks of Lake Titicaca, but may be as low as 5 or 6 on the large haciendas devoted to extensive stock-farming. Over-population has been aggravated in certain areas since the Spanish conquest by a pattern of land use in which large estates monopolised the best land and tiny peasant holdings occupied the rest.

In 1940 62% of the population of Peru still lived in the Sierra. Thus although its economic centre of gravity has moved to the Coast since colonial times the country still preserves a strongly Andean character. There are still high population densities between 3500 and 4000 m, meagre cultivated fields up to 4500 m and mining settlements at over 5000 m, so that the people have to be adjusted to living at high altitudes. The peoples of the Andes have respiratory systems adapted to the low atmospheric pressure and the reduced oxygen content of the air; the rib cage is wider, and the alveoli of the lungs have a larger area; the heart is larger, with a larger volume and a high count of red corpuscles. When an inhabitant of the Andes descends to the Coast or into the hot regions he has difficulty in adapting to the new conditions and is very vulnerable to pulmonary and intestinal affections — as a result of physiological changes (the destruction of antibodies which give relative immunity at high altitudes), alterations in diet and the influence of various socio-economic factors. In recent years there has been an increased movement of population to the Coast, which now has more than 60% of the population of Peru. This movement has been facilitated by the building of new roads, the improvement of existing roads and the steady increase in traffic using them. It is also stimulated by the over-population or poverty of the country areas, the attractions offered by the towns and the improved employment prospects held out by the development of commerce, the service trades and to a lesser extent industry. The effect of this trend is felt in all the *departamentos* in the Sierra, particularly Cajamarca, La Libertad and Ancash in the north, Junín and Huancavelica in the centre, and Ayacucho, Apurímac and Puno in the south.

The Towns

Most of the migrants have been attracted to the towns, and in consequence the urban population, which represented only 35% of total population in 1940 and 47% in 1961, now accounts for over 60% of the total. This, is of course, a feature characteristic of all developing countries, but in Peru it is a trend of long standing. In the pre-Columbian period there were large cities both on the Coast, in the Chimú culture, and in the Andes under the Incas, whose capital of Cuzco may have had a population of over 50,000. The Spaniards founded a network of towns and villages, both for their own occupation and later for the resettlement of the native peoples in the *reducciones*. In some cases they established themselves in conquered cities like Cuzco or Cajamarca, but as a rule they established new towns, sited for preference in the valleys (whereas the Incas in the Sierra had built their settlements on spurs of rock at altitudes around 3500 m). There are many examples of moves of this kind, in particular at Huánuco and at Pisar, near Cuzco, where the old Inca city with its formidable terraces can be seen above the village founded by the Spaniards on the banks of the Vilcanota.

The towns of present-day Peru have inherited from the colonial period their chequer-board plan, with a regular grid of streets laid out round a central square, the Plaza de Armas. Near the square are the Town Hall (*Cabildo*) and church, symbols of the Conquistadors' dual mission of ruling and evangelising. Every Spanish citizen (*vecino*) received an allotment of land (*solar*) in the town and an estate outside it. The *solar* usually occupied a whole "block" (*manzana*) with a street on each of four sides, the sides being known as *cuadras* and the corners (which were used as points of reference within the town and sometimes had names of their own) as *esquinas*. On this plot was built a house with a tiled roof and with one or more interior patios surrounded by arcaded galleries. Behind the house was a garden (which has now usually disappeared). The façades of the houses were similar to those of Mediterranean Europe, with high windows and often with balconies or carved wooden screens in front of the windows. Until very recently the towns, in addition to their administrative and religious functions, were also the residence of the local landowners, who held all economic and political power in the surrounding countryside. The commercial function of the towns was confined to the markets held on Sundays and a few shops in the arcades of the Plaza de Armas.

The recent growth of the towns has been particularly marked on the Coast, most of all in Lima. Unlike the other Andean countries, Peru has its political capital in the coastal region, and avoids the dualism found elsewhere—in Ecuador, Colombia and to a lesser extent in Chile—between a political capital in the Andes and an economic capital on the Coast.

During the colonial period Lima (and its port Callao) concentrated within itself all the main urban functions of the colony, and this primacy has been maintained since Peru achieved independence (see chapter 1, p. 109). With its population of 3,300,000 it far outdistances Peru's second city, Arequipa (pop. 300,000). Arequipa has established its position as the chief town of southern Peru, but since 1961 it has grown less rapidly than northern towns like Trujillo (pop. 241,000), Chiclayo (pop. 189,000), Chimbote (pop. 159,000) and Piura (pop. 126,000). The old Inca capital of Cuzco, which until 1940 took third place after Lima and Arequipa, ahead of the northern towns, has now fallen to sixth place with a population of 120,000. Just behind it comes Huancayo (pop. 115,000), with a more rapid rate of growth. These are the only two places of any size in the Sierra which have retained some of the migrants in this area in virtue of their commercial function, particularly as a junction on the roads leading to the *ceja de montaña* (see p. 18). The other Highland towns—places like Cajamarca, Huaraz (several times destroyed by earthquakes) and Ayacucho—are growing less rapidly, and none of them has a population over 50,000, in spite of their undoubted tourist attractions. In the south, Puno has suffered from the greater attractions of Arequipa and the growth of Juliaca, a mainly commercial town and an important railway junction.

The rapid growth of the urban population has brought profound changes to many Peruvian towns, introducing large modern blocks into the old colonial town centre and ringing the existing built-up areas with huge working-class suburbs—*barriadas* or, in the now fashionable term, *pueblos jovenes* ("new villages").

The other area which attracts peasants from the over-populated parts of the Sierra is the "hot lands" in the Amazon basin. The building of roads has promoted settlement in the Amazonian piedmont area and, to a much more limited extent, in the forest itself. The main areas of settlement are on the upper Marañón round Jaén and Bagua and on the Huallaga at Tingo María, Tarapoto and Yurimaguas. In the centre there is some pioneering settlement round San Ramón, La Merced and Oxapampa in the Chanchamayo valley and at Satipo. In the south, the Urubamba valleys (La Convención) and the Sandia and Caravaya valleys in the province of Puno were brought into cultivation during the colonial period, and in some places as early as Inca times. In the forest there are small and scattered groups of Indians and areas of settlement round some of the towns founded from the late 19th century onwards for administrative or commercial purposes. The largest of these towns are Iquitos (pop. 111,300), Pucallpa (pop. 57,500) and Puerto Maldonado in Madre de Dios (pop. 6400).

Elements in the Population

The fact that the population of Peru is no longer divided up into categories on the basis of race is a reflection of the extent to which, physically and culturally, it has been interbred. The only Indians of pure blood are the most isolated Amazonian tribes who are designated by the general term *selvaticos* or *nativos* (natives of the Selva). Throughout the rest of the country the Amerindian population has been in regular and constant contact with the white immigrants who have come to the colony from colonial times down to the present day, though never in very large numbers. At a very early stage, in the 16th century, negro slaves were brought into the country to work in the plantations in the northern coastal region where Indian labour had become scarce. This led to further interbreeding, and in the 18th century a whole range of different degrees of mixed blood were recognised, falling into three main categories: the *mestizos*, born of unions between whites and Amerindians; the mulattoes (between whites and negroes); and the *zambos* (between negroes and Indians). In the 19th century further elements were added to the racial pattern in the form of the Chinese coolies and the Japanese who came to live in the coastal oases and the Amazonian forest.

Nowadays the terms *mestizo* and Indian have no significance in physical terms and are mainly of importance in the cultural and even more in the socio-economic field. At most it is possible to distinguish a physical type characteristic of the Sierra in which Amerindian characteristics (brown skin, elongated eyes, prominent cheekbones, wiry black hair, little body hair, medium or small stature) are particularly marked, and a type characteristic of the Coast, the Creole (*criollo*) in which European or negroid elements are predominant. Some ethnologists apply cultural criteria, defining the Indian as a peasant speaking only a native language (Quechua or Aymará), illiterate, wearing traditional dress, chewing coca and either walking barefoot or wearing *ojotas* (sandals made from old tyres).

Traditional costumes vary considerably from one region to another, and this is one of Peru's great attractions to tourists. In the south they are still usually made of *bayeta*, a hand-woven woollen fabric, either untreated, black or dyed in vivid colours. The men always wear breeches reaching half-way down the calf, a poncho, a *chullo* (knitted cap) and a hat of raw felt (in Cajamarca a broad-brimmed straw hat). The women wear several ample skirts (*polleras*) on top of one another, kept up by a broad belt (*chumpi*), and a blouse and bodice. They invariably have a rectangular shawl (the *manta* or *lliclla*) in which they carry babies and miscellaneous burdens. On their plaited black hair they wear a *montera* (a type of hat of very varying form) or, in the Puno area, a brown felt hat.

When the Indians settle in towns they wear European-style clothes and give up the use of coca. An Indian of this type is classified by the sociologists as a *cholo*, able to speak Spanish and to read and write, extremely mobile as to place and type of employment, and already incorporated in the market economy. In the old economic structure of the great estates and the Indian village communities these various cultural features would have been insufficient to camouflage the Indian's situation of dependence in relation to the *mestizo*, and it would have been appropriate only to speak of peasants (*campesinos*). But even though the class of great landowners has now practically disappeared, particularly on the Coast, the situation of "internal colonisation" in which the Andean peoples were maintained from the Conquest onwards has left a profound imprint on Peruvian society.

ECONOMY

Unlike many other undeveloped countries whose economy depends on a single product, Peru can rely on its mineral resources (mining and, more recently, oil), the varied produce of its agriculture and stock-rearing (sugar, cotton, coffee, wool, etc.) and now on its recently developed industry (in particular fish-meal). This diversity of production and the country's rapid growth rate, with the GNP increasing at around 5–6% a year (compared with a population increase of 3%), should not, however, be allowed to obscure certain unsatisfactory features—the insufficient production of food, the social and regional disparities, and above all the situation of dependence in which the Peruvian economy finds itself in relation to other countries.

The end of the Spanish Colonial Pact left a clear field for European, and particularly British, capitalists (guano boom and trade in wool, 19th century) and later for their North American counterparts. The Americans were mainly interested in the mines and, in more recent times, in investment in banking and industry; and they were also involved in the loans made to the Peruvian government through the Alliance for Progress and the Interamerican Development Bank. This involvement of foreign interests promoted the development of the Coast, and particularly of Lima, at the expense of the inland regions, and reduced the Sierra, which had been the most populous part of the country in pre-Columbian times, to an economically marginal area. This dominance of foreign interests in the national economy was matched by a system of internal domination in which the towns established by the Spaniards controlled the administration, the land, the trade and the culture of the country areas, and the mestizos living in the towns controlled the destinies of the "Indians" in the country areas. These two patterns of dominance are now being challenged by the reforms undertaken by General Velazco Alvarado's *Junta Militar de Gobierno*, particularly the land reform and the various nationalisations that have been carried through.

Agriculture

The Peruvian economy has recently shown a sharp decline in the contribution made to the GNP by agriculture and an advance in commerce, the service trades and industry. Agriculture now employs 47% of the working population and accounts for 18.4% of the GNP, compared with 60% and 27.4% respectively in 1950. It has, however, shown a distinct improvement in its growth rate, which fell to a very low level from 1960 onwards, and particularly in 1965 (0.1%): after the land reform of 1969 the rate rose to 7.4%.

Peruvian agriculture is characterised by the opposition between the large estate (*latifundio*), formerly in private ownership but now collectivised, and the small holding (*minifundio*). In 1969 83.4% of holdings were under 5 hectares and accounted for only 4% of agricultural land, while at the other extreme estates over 1000 hectares, representing 0.2% of the total number of properties, accounted for 70% of the total area; for the middle range of holdings, between 5 and 100 hectares, the proportions were 15.3% and 8.8% respectively. There is a difference also in type of production between the small holdings, almost entirely devoted to subsistence farming, and the large estates which, particularly on the Coast, are often well organised and equipped for a market economy.

The large estates originated in the *repartimientos de tierra* or *mercedes* granted by the Spanish Crown or the Viceroy to Conquistadors, parishes, religious houses, hospitals, etc. The landowners continued to enlarge their properties over the centuries, and particularly after Peru became independent, at the expense of the native village communities, often using illegal and sometimes violent means to achieve their ends.

The *latifundios* in the **Sierra** used a system of controlling the labour force known as *colonado*. In return for working on the owner's land each *colono* received a plot of his own. In addition to working on the land, however, he had to perform certain other services — transporting the harvest, watching over flocks and herds or growing crops, supplying certain quantities of dung, maintaining roads and irrigation channels, performing domestic service in the landowner's house (*pongeaje*), etc. Often he was obliged to sell his scanty surplus to the landowner or to buy certain manufactured goods from him; his movements were controlled by the landowner; and the landowner also acted as intermediary between the government and the peasants, whom he kept in a state of illiteracy. The large estates, often inefficiently managed, had a very low productivity, and in recent times compared particularly badly with the results achieved by a number of modernised haciendas in the Sierra devoted to stock-farming for wool or meat (e.g. at Puno and round the Cerro de Pasco), to growing maize, barley for brewing, and potatoes, making much use of fertilisers.

On the **Coast** holdings of over 100 hectares occupy 80% of the irrigated land. They are devoted to export crops (cotton, sugar-cane), in the north to rice, round Lima to citrus fruits and dairy farming. They use intensive farming methods, with plentiful applications of fertilisers and chemicals and much use of machinery. The sugar-cane plantations are very large and modern estates with a paid labour force (*peones*). The cotton estates, which are much smaller, employ small numbers of paid workers, temporary workers from the Sierra and *yanacones*, share-croppers who give a fifth of their crop to the landowner and sell him the rest, while frequently working also as *peones*. The large estates were also found in the *ceja de montaña*, with both *colonos* and tenant farmers. Here they were traditionally devoted to the growing of coca, cacao and sugar-cane for the production of alcohol. From the end of the 19th century onwards tea and coffee also began to be grown (Convención and Chanchamayo valleys), together with rice and the oil palm or rubber in the Huallaga valley.

The **native village communities** are the descendants both of the pre-Columbian *ayllus* (clans, kinship groups) and of the *reducciones* granted by the Spanish Viceroys. They are particularly numerous in the Andes, but there are still some well organised communities in some of the northern coastal oases. The land is held in collective ownership, each *comunero* having only a limited tenure of his own plot. The periodic redistributions of land are, however, rarely carried out in practice, and the *comuneros* behave as if they did in fact own the land. They are allowed to pass their plot on to an heir but not to sell it. The grazings are usually communal property. The bonds between the members of the community are strengthened by arrangements for mutual aid known as *ayne* and *minka* and by certain tasks carried out in common (*faenas*), like the maintenance of roads and irrigation channels and nowadays also the provision of public services and utilities (schools, roads, drinking water supply, etc.).

The **colonos** on the haciendas, like the Indians in the communities, were relegated to the poorest land, and often had no more than a hectare to provide subsistence for their family. (The local unit was a *topo*, roughly one-third of a hectare). In the Sierra the land consisted of tiny plots scattered about on the hillsides, with a few rows of maize in the valley, a little square of barley, wheat or beans on the slopes above and a small field of potatoes higher up. The fallow periods necessary on the poor thin soil (usually one year for European cereals but as much as 5 to 15 years for tubers) reduced the area available for cultivation each year; and above 3300 m the crops were subject to the hazard of night frosts, hail and irregular rainfall. Techniques were still rudimentary: only the wealthy landowners in the valleys used wooden scratch-ploughs, while the hillsides were worked with the spade and above all with the *chaki-taclla*, a tool with a long wooden handle and an iron share. Harvesting was done with a sickle, after which the corn was trodden out by animals. Farming routines were, however, meticulously performed: the fallows were ploughed and the maize and potatoes were earthed up and weeded regularly several times a year. Only small quantities of dung (which was also used, dried, as fuel) were added to improve the soil. Yields were accordingly low—9 to 10 quintals per hectare of barley, 20 to 25 of maize, 90 to 100 of potatoes. In more recent times the introduction of nitrogen fertilisers and high-yield seed has brought some improvement, but the problem of inadequate yields could not be solved until the land reform of recent years. The livestock on a peasant holding consists merely of one or two cows, perhaps 20 sheep and a few farmyard animals.

The standard of living is still low, the average income being only 300 U.S. dollars per head. The diet consists mainly of soup, boiled beans or maize and *chuño* (a dish made with potato starch). Little meat is eaten, usually in the form of *charqui* or *sesina* (dried and salted meat) or the guinea-pigs (*cuyes*) which are eaten on feast days. The *comuneros* often eke out their meagre resources by various forms of craft production (*bayetas*, ponchos, blankets, woodworking, silversmithing, pottery) or by hiring themselves out as labourers in the hot lands or on building sites in towns during the off-season.

In the *puna* areas the growing of crops is even more precarious, but some crops are grown on east-facing slopes—*cañihua* (a cereal rich in proteins) and potatoes (with a fallow period of 8–10 years). Stock-farming is carried on extensively, with some improvements in the breeds of sheep and cattle but much less advance in the feeding of stock.

The *minifundios* on the Coast are in equally poor case. The staple of the peasants' diet is formed by maize, supplemented by pulses (*fréjoles* and *pallares*, kidney beans and Lima beans), sweet potatoes (*camote*), gourds, water-melons and various vegetables (in particular tomatoes) and condiments (pimentoes). In the *ceja de montaña* sweet manioc (*yuca*) is also grown. These crops are often grown in the shelter of fruit trees, which also provide fruit for marketing—avocados (*paltas*), pawpaws (*papayas*), cinnamon apples (*chirumoyas*), *lúcumas*, American plums, mangoes, bananas. The smallholders on the Coast are better integrated into the market economy, thanks to some market gardening crops and the growing of lucerne which makes possible some small-scale dairy farming.

Following the **land reform** of 1964 and the even more important measure of 1969 the maximum size of holding has been increased to 150 hectares of irrigated land on the Coast and ranges in the Sierra between 30 and 55 hectares (twice as much in dry farming areas). The *yanacones*, tenant farmers and share-croppers have been given possession of their land. The sugar plantations have become industrially organised agricultural complexes, and most of the large estates growing rice and cotton have been turned into cooperatives. Cooperatives have also been formed in the Sierra by amalgamating a number of haciendas and peasant communities. The former *colonos* and *comuneros* have been allowed to retain a life interest in their own plots of land and work for pay on the communally owned land. The "socialised agricultural societies" (SAIS), formed by the combination of institutions (*latifundios*, peasant communities, etc.) rather than individuals, form very large units indeed: for example the Túpac Amaru SAIS on the Cerro de Pasco has an area of 300,000 hectares. Agricultural output on the Coast has not been affected by these changes, but progress is slower in the Sierra, in spite of the effort devoted to increasing the cultivable area (only 1.5% of the total) by large-scale irrigation works in the north and at Arequipa and to new schemes for settlement in the hot lands.

Industry and Commerce

Since the Conquest Peru has been known as a mining country. To the export of gold (mainly obtained by looting) and the silver of Potosí was added in the 19th century the working of non-ferrous metals—lead, zinc and above all copper—which now account for 40% of the country's exports and 8% of GNP. The mines were mostly in the central Andes, round the concessions of the Cerro de Pasco Company and its refinery on the Oroya. After nationalisation in 1973 the mines came under the control of *Centromin*, which employs some 50,000 workers. More recently mines have been opened in the south, at Marcona, near Ica (9 million tons of iron), and at Toquepala near Tacna. Much is expected from the working of the copper at Cuajone and Cerro Verde near Arequipa and the nationalised concessions at Tintaya (Cuzco) and Michiquillay (Cajamarca). Thus alongside the foreign companies, which the government is now seeking to control more effectively, there is growing up a considerable nationalised sector.

Natural conditions in Peru are relatively favourable to industry. The abundant power supplies offered by hydroelectricity and oil (at Talara, and now in Amazonia) have hardly been tapped. The produce of agriculture and stock-farming is readily available, as are minerals. But, like all the countries of the Third World, Peru suffers from the years of dominance by the industrialised countries, which reduced it to the rôle of an exporter of raw materials, heavily dependent on foreign finance and technology and with a very limited domestic market in consequence of the low standard of living of its population. Heavy industry is represented only by the Chimbote steel-works (with an annual output of 150,000 tons), three cement factories and the oil refineries at Talara and Lima. The industries processing agricultural produce (sugar refineries, rice mills, cotton gins) and since 1960 the produce of the fisheries (fish-meal plants) account for over half the value of industrial production and largely produce for export.

The production of consumption goods began in the 1960s in a very liberal climate, using foreign (particularly American) capital and patents. It remains in the private sector but is now protected by customs barriers. The government is, however, seeking to promote worker participation in both management and profits through the establishment of "industrial communities" and "socially owned" firms, and to secure the decentralisation of industry from the Lima–Callao area, where it is too strongly concentrated. State intervention has also taken the form of nationalising sources of energy, the railways and some banks and of a tight control of the exchanges and credit through state banks.

Peru's foreign trade reflects its great dependence on other countries as an exporter of primary products (95% of exports) and an importer of equipment goods (37% of imports), foodstuffs (49%) and to a decreasing extent consumption goods (14%). Formerly very closely linked to the United States, Peru has sought since 1969 to diversify its foreign contacts by establishing relations with the European Community, the socialist countries, Japan and China. It also plays a leading rôle in the *Andean Pact*, the first step towards a Latin American common market.

Fishing

The abundance of fish off the Peruvian coasts is due to the meeting of the cold Humboldt Current with the warm equatorial counter-current, which promotes the growth of plankton. In the past, however, Peru had no tradition as a fishing country, apart from a few villages in the north, and the fish served mainly to provide food for the seabirds whose droppings were used in the form of guano. Industrial fishing began only in 1953, associated with the production of fish-meal for the feeding of poultry and stock in the industrialised countries. The main catch was *anchoveta* (*Engraulis ringens*), shoals of which swim near the surface in coastal waters, and the fisheries developed rapidly and successfully, so that by 1963 fish-meal accounted for a quarter of Peru's exports, equalling copper and cotton in importance.

All the little ports in the central coastal area, particularly Chimbote, were thus given a fresh lease of life. They now attracted peasants from the Sierra who, in spite of their previous lack of experience, became labourers and fishermen. Peruvian and, more rarely, foreign capital found a promising field for investment—in the purchase of boats (*bolicheras*, varying widely in tonnage), the establishment of factories and increasingly in shipbuilding. In 1970 Peru had the highest catch in the world with 12,600,000 tons, though in subsequent years catches have been markedly lower, a decline reflecting the fragility of an industry which had developed in a completely uncontrolled fashion, without thought for the protection of fish stocks. After suffering a temporary setback through the collapse of fish-meal prices in 1960–64, it is now threatened by falling catches, mainly due to an unpredictable increase in the volume of the warm current. The government has taken the opportunity to claim an extension of Peru's territorial waters to 200 miles from the coast and to nationalise the fish-meal industry; and it is also seeking to diversify the fisheries in accordance with the demand for fish for human consumption (e.g. by promoting tunny fishing).

DEPARTAMENTOS AND REGIONS OF PERU

PUBLIC LIFE

Government

Since achieving independence Peru has been a unitary republic. It is divided into 23 *departamentos* and the small *provincia constitucional* of Callao; the *departamentos* are in turn divided into provinces, which are subdivided into districts. Each *departamento* is administered by a prefect appointed by the government, each province by a sub-prefect appointed by the prefect, and each district by a governor appointed by the sub-prefect. The prefects, sub-prefects and governors are usually supporters of the party in power and not public officials (the public service of Peru being still in an embryonic stage). Their principal function is to maintain public order, a task in which they are supported by the *Guardia Civil*, a militarised police established in the 1930s on the model of the corresponding body in Spain.

The provinces and districts are financed by local taxes and annual grants from the State, and are run by provincial and district councils, headed by an *alcalde* (mayor). Since 1919 these councils, which are supposed to represent the local population, have been appointed by the government, apart from a short period between 1963 and 1968 when they were elected.

The constitution promulgated in 1933, which was suspended in 1968 but has never been repealed, provided for the separation of judicial, legislative and executive powers within the framework of a semi-Presidential system of a type common in South America. Judicial power rests with the Supreme Court, whose independence is guaranteed; legislative power is in the hands of a Congress of two chambers, the Chamber of Deputies and the Senate; and executive power is held by the President, who forms the government and appoints and dismisses ministers (also responsible, individually and collectively, to Congress). The President, deputies and senators are elected by direct universal suffrage for a six-year term; the President cannot be re-elected immediately on completion of his term. To the three traditional powers the constitution adds an "electoral power", vested in the *National Electoral Junta*, which draws up the voters' lists and supervises elections. All citizens over 21, both male and female, have the vote, provided that they can read and write: a restriction which disenfranchises the great mass of Indian peasants in up-country areas, who are frequently illiterate.

Since the coup d'état of October 1968 which overthrew President Belaúnde, dissolved the two houses of Congress and suspended the "electoral power" the country has been governed by a distinctly unusual regime. All government posts without exception are held by general officers in the three arms of the services, who are appointed according to their seniority, so that advancement in the government service depends on military promotion; when they retire from the service ministers also resign from the government, thus enabling fresh blood to be brought in at intervals. Only the Presidency itself is excluded from this provision, and it is one of the President's functions to hold the balance between the views prevailing in the different services, the army being traditionally more radical, the navy and air force more moderate. The President is assisted by an influential body of advisers, the *Committee of Assessors to the Presidency* (COAP), the members of which are all officers. This body lays down the main lines of policy, prepares legislation and carries out regular consultations within the armed forces, which operate a kind of "military democracy".

The highest posts in government departments and nationalised industries are also held by senior officers, and the more junior administrative posts are held by reserve officers rather than civilians, who are usually confined to executive functions. Thus the armed forces have taken over the whole apparatus of government, so completely that it is difficult to distinguish between civil and military functions; they carry out the tasks not only of government but of day-by-day administration, and indeed perform some of the functions of a deliberative body. They might in fact develop into a kind of political party were it not that their ideology leads them to reject any idea of full-blooded propaganda or regimentation of the population.

In 1971 the government established a "National System of Support for Social Mobilisation" (SINAMOS), aimed at directing popular support for their policies into useful channels. The local organisation of SINAMOS matches the military command structure, with regions, zones and sectors headed by the appropriate military commander. SINAMOS intervened tactfully and effectively in the disputes which arose over the expropriation of the large plantations in the northern coastal region, but it seems since then to have limited its ambitions, confining itself mainly to helping the local government authorities to develop. Its functions are, however, loosely defined, and there may be scope for expansion of its rôle in future.

The stability of a regime of this kind, which has no parallel among other military governments in South America, evidently depends primarily on the cohesion of the armed forces, on their united will to carry out the political programme which they have set before themselves.

Political Parties

Although the armed forces now hold a monopoly of political power, political parties have not been banned. Lacking any concern with government, however, many of the parties have lost such influence on public opinion as they formerly possessed, which in any event was usually fairly limited.

The limited importance of political parties in Peru resulted from the fact that they were always organisations built up round a single powerful figure, with the prime object of helping their leader to gain or to retain power. For the most part they were merely a kind of general staff whose function was to weave webs of influence throughout the country, based on the ties of kinship, friendship or social and business contacts. Hence their great instability and even greater ideological sterility: when their leader disappears they disappear with him, and their supporters seek a new patron. This was the case, for example, with the *Movimiento Democrático Peruano*, which was founded in 1956 to promote Manuel Prado's re-election to the Presidency and was dissolved at the end of his second term in 1962, when Prado, then an elderly man, announced his retirement from public life.

The *Alianza Popular Revolucionaria Americana* (APRA) is an exception to this rule. Founded in 1924 by a young Trujillo intellectual, Víctor Raúl Haya de la Torre, then in exile in Mexico, it is a populist party with a strong foundation of support among the mass of the population. Its programme, largely Marxist in inspiration, incorporates Bolívar's old dream of the political unification of Latin America and calls for the liberation of the sub-continent from North American domination; it is also strongly anti-imperialist and advocates the nationalisation of land and industry and the internationalisation of the Panama Canal.

In a country which had suffered severely from the world depression of 1929 APRA's policies at once attracted much support, and the party was thereupon subjected to fierce repressive measures. Between 1931 and 1945 and from 1948 to 1956 its members were denounced and persecuted as Communists in disguise. Haya de la Torre had a narrow escape from the fate suffered by thousands of the party's activists and took refuge in the Colombian Embassy, where he remained for six years imprisoned within the Embassy buildings, which were surrounded by troops. This was the period known as the "years in the catacombs", during which the party developed a centralised organisation well adapted to clandestine activity. The memory of these persecutions welded the members of the party together into a solidarity which has endured through the years—a solidarity so closely knit that the Apristas were frequently accused of sectarianism.

In 1956 APRA, realising that revolutionary methods were not producing results, decided to re-enter the Parliamentary arena and came out in support of Manuel Prado's re-election as President. By this means it obtained a foothold in Congress, and in 1963 its representatives actually formed a tactical alliance with the supporters of the former dictator, Odría, in common opposition to President Belaúnde. These compromises with the right, however, did not in any degree weaken the party's position in its traditional strongholds in northern and central Peru and in the coastal towns. Only a few younger members of the party broke away and founded the *APRA Rebelde*, which later became the *Movimiento de Izquierda Revolucionaria* (Movement of the Revolutionary Left) and took part in the guerrilla activities of 1965. The great mass of the militants followed Haya de la Torre, who has retained all his charisma: the birthday of the old "Jefe Máximo", 23 February, is still celebrated by large crowds every year in Lima. The *Confederación de Trabajadores del Perú* (CTP), an APRA foundation which is still the country's leading trade union organisation, has retained all its former influence in the plantations on the Coast and among teachers.

"El APRA nunca muere" ("APRA never dies") is a favourite battle cry of APRA supporters. It is at any rate a political force which the army—who robbed APRA of the power which had seemed within its reach in 1968—must still reckon with. These two opposing groups, which have developed in parallel with one another but in opposite directions, remain irreconcilable.

The pro-Soviet *Peruvian Communist Party* is the descendant of the Peruvian Socialist Party which was founded in Paris in 1928 by Eudocio Ravines and drew lustre from its association with the Marxist theoretical writer José Carlos Mariátegiu, author of the famous "Seven Essays in the Interpretation of Peruvian Reality". For long a party of intellectuals, it fought an unequal struggle with the Apristas, whom it denounced as "camouflaged Fascists". It began to achieve wider influence during the 1960s, when it seems to have acted partly under cover of the *Frente de Liberación Nacional*, led by a retired general and a priest who had come into conflict with the Catholic hierarchy. Since 1968 it has been active in support of the military regime. It has a solid base of support in the mining towns of central Peru. Its trade union organisation, the *Confederación General de Trabajadores Peruanos* (CGTP), embodies the great majority of Peru's miners and metal-workers.

In contrast the *Christian Democratic Party*, founded by Hector Cornejo Chávez, and Fernando Belaúnde Terry's *Acción Popular*, which worked together from 1963 to 1968, have lost the considerable support they formerly enjoyed among the urban middle classes and in the south of the country. Even before the coup d'état both these parties had split into a moderate wing opposed to the military regime and a radical wing which was favourably disposed towards the reforms initiated by the army. The *Unión Nacional Odriista*, a right-wing party which attracted support both from the fashionable districts of the capital and the underprivileged inhabitants of the shanty towns, did not outlive its leader.

The extreme left is represented by numerous splinter groups, including a (pro-Chinese) Marxist-Leninist Communist Party and various Trotskyite formations. These active minorities, mainly recruited from the universities, can on occasion wield an influence out of proportion to their numbers. A number of their leaders have come out in support of the military regime and hold posts in SINAMOS or in the government press.

Interest Groups

Peruvian political parties have always been too highly personalised to reflect accurately the competing interests of the various economic and social forces in Peru. It is true that at the turn of the century the ruling oligarchy expressed its views through the Civil Party, and more recently it found a mouthpiece in the *Unión Nacional Odriista*, to whose funds it contributed generously. In general, however, rather than linking its fate with a particular party, it sought to win the support of whoever was in government or seemed likely to win power. It remained outside the interplay of politics, while keeping a watchful eye on events, and on occasion, when they did not seem to be moving in the right direction, seeking to influence them by the use of military force.

The main economic interests are represented by their own associations and organisations. The *Sociedad Nacional Agraria* claims to represent all farmers, whether small, middle-sized or large; but in fact the society's management committee, which is elected by the "weighted" votes (i.e. weighted according to size of holding) of the members, represents the interests of the large landowners of the Coast, who have made it a pressure group for the sugar-growers and cotton-growers. Its influence, formerly considerable, has declined steeply since the land reform, which it sought in vain to oppose. The *National Chamber of Commerce* and *National Chamber of Industry* are still very active, but they have lost the favourable negotiating position with government departments which they enjoyed before 1968. They too seem to have little influence with a regime which is less accessible to particular interest groups than its predecessor.

Some sections of the middle clases have influential organisations to represent them: thus doctors, lawyers, accountants, agricultural scientists, architects, engineers and other professional groups have set up their own professional associations or *colegios*. These bodies are primarily concerned with the material and professional interests of their members, but they also take part in the great political debates, bringing their views to the notice of the public by taking large amounts of advertising space in the newspapers.

The organisations representing other classes of the population are less powerfully structured. The trade unions are grouped in four confederations — in descending order of size, the *Confederación de Trabajadores del Perú* (linked with APRA), the *Confederación General de Trabajadores Peruanos* (linked with the Communist Party), the *Confederación de Trabajadores Revolucioniaros* (set up by the military regime) and the small *Confederación de Trabajadores Cristianos*. In a country where trade union membership is relatively low, this division hampers the mounting of any large-scale action on behalf of trade unionists, which is in any case inhibited by the existence of massive underemployment. One or two trade unions, however, like the Federation of Bank Employees, show considerable combativity in the defense of the interests of their own members.

An important part is also played in the life of the country by various social clubs. The Cámara Junior, the Lions Club and the Rotary Club—the most prestigious of the three—have branches in even the smallest towns. These clubs recruit their membership by co-option of the leading people of the town, and gather funds for various good works in which they are interested by running charity sales, bingo evenings and lotteries. Their views on the management of local affairs have not inconsiderable influence with the provincial and district councils.

There are also many clubs in Lima catering for people who have come to the capital from country areas in the Sierra. There is hardly a village without its club in Lima to provide a meeting place for those of its inhabitants who have gone there in quest of work. These clubs provide a point of contact for newcomers and help them to find work and a place to stay, but they also look after the interests of those who have stayed in the village by conveying their requests (for the provision of a water supply, the building of a school, the construction of a new road, etc.) to the appropriate government department. This latter function is particularly valuable in the absence of any Parliamentary channel for putting forward such representations.

The Press

The Peruvian press is mainly centred in Lima. Although there are weekly, thrice weekly and daily publications in the larger provincial towns like Cuzco, Arequipa and Huancayo they are only concerned with local news: they supplement but do not compete with the Lima papers, which have a national circulation.

Peru prides itself on the possession of one of the oldest newspapers in Latin America, "*El Comercio*". Founded in the middle of last century, this paper is now owned by the Miró Quesada family and expresses views which are conservative in social matters and nationalist in economic matters. It supported the nationalisation of the International Petroleum Co., the re-establishment of Peruvian control over the country's mines and the protection of its newly established industry. Without abandoning their independence of mind or their obsessional hostility to APRA, the Miró Quesada family have made it the mouthpiece of the urban middle classes, sufficiently concerned for the national dignity to applaud the 1968 coup d'état but too prudent to support blindly the regime which it installed.

"*La Prensa*", founded by members of the ruling oligarchy at the beginning of this century, was edited for many years by Pedro Beltrán, who was Prime Minister during the Presidency of Manuel Prado. It has long been the voice of Peru's major economic interests, linked with international capitalism, and, as its leader page continually emphasises, is in favour of free enterprise, the free convertibility of the currency and the free circulation of capital and goods. It ran a vigorous campaign against Belaúnde's attempted reforms, which were supported in part by its great rival "El Comercio"; and the long and violent battle between the two papers played a part in forming public opinion.

"El Comercio" and "La Prensa", which have circulations of between 100,000 and 150,000, were expropriated in July 1974, together with "*El Correo*", a popular paper owned by the former fishing magnate Luis Banchero, and "*Ojo*", a paper specialising in miscellaneous news and scandal, both with circulations of between 50,000 and 100,000. The press law then introduced provided for their transfer to the "organised sectors" of the population: "El Comercio" to the peasants, "La Prensa" to the workers, "El Correo" to the liberal professions, "Ojo" to the intellectuals. Until these sectors are organised the papers were to be managed by temporary administrators appointed by the government.

This account of the daily press would not be complete without a mention of "*El Expreso*" and "*La Crónica*". "El Expreso" was launched in the early 1960s by the Mujica family, and supported the Acción Popular party. It was then bought by the financier Manuel Ulloa and subsequently taken over by the military government, who made it over to the staff of the paper. Under this new management it has followed a socialist and pro-Soviet line. "La Crónica" was also taken over shortly afterwards, together with the Banco Popular, on which it depended financially and which was itself part of the economic empire of the Prado family. Unlike "El Expreso", however, "La Crónica" is run by a public company.

The intervention of the State in the daily press has helped to raise the intellectual level of the papers concerned. The pages of social news, devoted to the marriages, the receptions and the movements of the fashionable world, have disappeared, and sport and miscellaneous news now take up less space, while much more space is now devoted to editorials, substantial articles and discussions of artistic, literary and cultural matters by the country's leading intellectuals. On the other hand there is less news of domestic political interest, and comment on matters of this kind is depressingly uniform.

Among the periodicals, "*Caretas*", a fortnightly which directed its ferocity against politicians, has had a chequered career, being in turn banned, allowed to appear and once again banned; since 1968, however, it has again been allowed to appear, though it has tended to play for safety by confining itself to frivolity and humour. "*Oiga*", a serious weekly reflecting the views of the moderate intellectual left, was suspended after its editor launched a vigorous attack on the new press law. The periodicals of the militant extreme left are not subject to difficulties of this kind, though they have small circulations and sometimes appear rather irregularly.

FOLK TRADITIONS AND FOLK ART

General

In a country so deeply imbued with legend and tradition as Peru almost all forms of artistic expression—not only arts and crafts but dancing and popular festivals—are reflections of folk traditions. It must be remembered, however, that those traditions are not exclusively of indigenous origin, and that the whole culture of Peru is profoundly marked by the effects of the Spanish conquest. Indeed it might have been thought that the swift and savage introduction of European culture would lead to the total disappearance of the cultural traditions of pre-Columbian Peru. The ruthless zeal of the Catholic priests combined with the greed of the Spanish soldiery and officials caused irreparable damage: temples and palaces were plundered and destroyed, religious rituals and practices were harshly repressed, and the native ceremonies and dances, addressed to the protective or maleficent divinities who ruled the universe, were either banned altogether or diverted from their original purpose to serve the ends of the Christian faith. All over the country churches were built, and the arts of Peru reflected the work of artists from the Iberian peninsula, and later from Italy.

And yet the native dancers, musicians and craftsmen, still profoundly imbued with the culture of Tahuantinsuyu, preserved their ancient beliefs and traditions in spite of the pressures exerted by the colonisers; and thus there developed during the 17th and particularly during the 18th century a new structure of folk traditions and folk art in which native and European features mingled to give birth to new and often very effective forms of expression.

Festivals and Dances

Almost all popular celebrations, whether festivals or folk dances, still reflect the universal submission of the human will to the natural forces personified by the spirits of earth and heaven. The old Inca calendar was linked with the movements of the sun, which determined the year's agricultural cycle. Most festivals took place in the period between sowing and harvest, a time of respite from activity which was used to honour the gods and

secure their benevolence. The same calendar still governs the
programme of the main festivals, which have so far as possible
been fitted into the calendar of the Catholic church. Some of the
pagan and Christian festivals coincide very satisfactorily with one
another, like the Corpus Christi celebrations in June, which
continue the ancient traditions of the *Inti Raymi*, the month of
sacrifices to the Sun.

The festival of Corpus Christi is celebrated at Cuzco with
several days of processions in which each saint is accompanied
by his *comparsa*, a group of dancers and musicians; and the
various parishes in the town vie with one another in the splendour and variety of their decorated floats, the dancers' costumes
and the displays of flowers. Unfortunately this festival is also
celebrated by the largest so-called folk parade in present-day
Peru, the *Inti Raymi* feast of Cuzco (24 June). This gigantic
pageant, which attracts all the peasants of the surrounding area
and thousands of tourists, is a tasteless and theatrical performance which bears no relationship to the Festival of the Sun as it
was celebrated in Inca times.

In the southern Andes, where the old traditions are best
preserved, the great festivals begin in the month of July, the
ancient *Anta-situa*, the month of harvest. At Pucará and elsewhere the celebrations begin on 16 July, when a great fair is held.
25 July is the feast day of Santiago or St James, who is identified
with Illapa, the thunder god. On 15 August is celebrated the
feast of the Virgin, who is in many respects an incarnation of
the old earth mother Pachamama.

Although the main festival season is from June to September
there are numerous festivals at other times of year. The *Carnival*
in February gives the peasants of the Andes an opportunity to
forget the hardships of their life for a few days: it is a time of wild
dances to the compelling rhythms of the *comparsas*, an explosion
of unrestrained popular rejoicing, but also a season of quiet
family celebrations in which traditional offerings are made to
Pachamama and the Wamanis, tutelary spirits of the mountains,
the rivers and the fields. In many towns, particularly in Ayacucho
and Cuzco, Holy Week is an occasion for great religious processions (*Semana Santa* in Ayacucho, the procession of the *Señor de
los Milagros* in Cuzco). Although Christmas is not a festival of
traditionally Peruvian origin it is an occasion for family cele-
rations, and in some towns there are very popular fairs, like the
Santoranticuy in Cuzco.

In all these festivals, except those of exclusively liturgical significance, dancing plays a prominent part, in the form of great parades or displays notable for the richness and variety of the dancers' costumes and for diversity of musical expression.

Some of the dances reflect old native beliefs, like the *choquelas*, in which the dancers are disguised as vicuñas or foxes, symbolising the mythical animals which protected the various *ayllus* (clans or kinship groups claiming descent from a mythical common ancestor), and are accompanied by flutes (*kenas*) and drums; the *Kena-Kena*, danced in the Lake Titicaca region, in which the ancestor is represented by a dancer clad in a jaguar's skin; or the *Sicuris*, dedicated to the condor as the symbol of strength and danced to the accompaniment of Pan pipes (*sicus*) and drums. Some dances of pagan inspiration like the *Kashua* and *Wifala* symbolise love and are danced mainly during the Carnival. Others again accompany ancient rites connected with hunting or farming, like the hunters' dance of the high plateau, the *Khajelos*, in which, after a symbolic hunt, an animal is sacrificed to the sound of flutes and its blood offered to the Sun, and the water dances in which couples dance all night long to the music of fiddles and harps, while the young unmarried men form a long chain winding to and fro.

There are a number of dances, clearly of later origin, which reflect a satirical intention, usually directed against the Spanish authorities, who are represented as grotesque old men or as arrogant and ridiculous functionaries dressed in 17th century Spanish costume.

But there are also dances of a more intimate family character: not merely a form of collective amusement but an occupation of some solemnity which accompanies all the occasions of life, whether grave or gay. No marriage or burial or house-warming is complete without the presence of a musical *conjunto* (group) playing the traditional *huaynos* to which couples dance untiringly for hours on end.

The festivals and dances so far discussed are those of the Andes, and particularly of the southern Andes, the most traditionalist part of the country. The Coast also has its own music and dances, strongly influenced by cultural features brought from Africa in the 17th and 18th centuries. The *marinera*, a favourite Creole dance mainly danced in the north, is directly descended from the old dances of black Africa.

Popular Arts and Crafts

In this field too a sharp break was brought about by the Spanish conquest and the upheaval which followed it, reflected both in new sources of inspiration and new techniques and forms.

There are a number of different types of handicraft, not always clearly distinguished from one another. On the one hand there are the domestic crafts, mainly devoted to the production of articles of everyday use (woollen or cotton garments, household pottery), on the other the more specialised trades, whose products may be either utilitarian or purely decorative, or both at the same time (leather articles, silver, tinware, weaving or carpets and blankets, art pottery, etc.). Thus there are families or whole villages of specialist craftsmen — the potters of Aco (*departamento* of Junín), Quinua (Ayacucho) and Pucará (Puno), the families of tinsmiths in Ayacucho and of silversmiths in Huancayo, the families in Cuzco (Mendivil, Olave) who specialise in the production of coloured figures of wood and plaster in the direct tradition of 18th century religious statuary.

Although the domestic crafts are practised in every village and household, the more specialised activities are frequently concentrated in particular villages or particular districts of towns (the Barrio Santa Ana in Ayacucho, the Barrio San Blas in Cuzco).

Textiles and Costumes

From one end of the Andes to the other the wool of sheep and alpacas (which were domesticated in pre-Columbian times) is spun and woven into fabrics. The making of carpets, blankets and hangings, woven on large looms of European type, is one of the main craft industries of central Peru (particularly at San Pedro de Cajas and Hualhuas in the *departamento* of Junín and at Ayacucho); in the south, round Puno, the principal activity is the working of alpaca furs and skins. Unfortunately the current efforts to stimulate traditional arts and crafts, though admirable in many respects, have frequently had unfortunate consequences: weavers now decorate their work with supposedly pre-Columbian patterns introduced for purely commercial purposes by outside interests, and use chemical dyes in place of the old traditional dyes made from local plants and minerals. Some craftsmen, however, still produce work retaining the simple, artless but highly decorative character of older products, like the carpets of Huaraz with their lozenge and check patterns in restrained pastel tints, the gaudy hangings of San Pedro de Cajas with their brilliant clash of colour, the fabrics of Hualhuas (near Huancayo) with their horizontal bands of small geometric designs on the white ground of the natural wool.

The traditions of the domestic crafts, devoted to the production of articles of everyday use, remain very much alive. In a corner in every *choza* (the hut dwelling of the Andes) is a small horizontal loom, directly inherited from pre-Hispanic times. Throughout the Andes the essential feature of male dress is the *poncho*, a large rectangular piece of cloth with a slit for the head, decorated with patterns and colours which vary from region to region. In the north of the country they are usually in a self colour (blood-red or brick-red at Cajamarca, often black in the Huánuco area, grey or white at Tarma, with brown stripes at Junín and Ayacucho), while the Cuzco region produces the finest ponchos in Peru, decorated with narrow bands of geometric patterns in many colours.

The poncho is not, however, of any great antiquity in Peru. The native costumes in use when the Spaniards arrived (for men a short-sleeved tunic known as the *unku*) were banned by the authorities after Túpac Amaru's rising in 1780. The present poncho is more closely related to the dress of Spanish peasants than to that of the Indians of Inca times. Older traditions are, however, represented by the *manta*, the square kerchief which women wear on their shoulders, keeping it in place with a brooch (*tupu*): this is the direct descendant of the ancient *lliclla*. The *ojotas* (sandals) still worn by the Indians—originally made of leather but now often cut from old tyres—are similar to those found in burials of the pre-Hispanic period. The headgear of the Indians shows the greatest diversity. Regrettably, however, men are increasingly tending to wear soft felt hats of European type, although women still wear the flat straw hats decorated with black velvet of the Cuzco area, the huge hats stiffened with maize starch of the central Andes and the fetching little bowler hats of the Lake Titicaca region.

Folk Art and its Sources

The last ten years or so have seen an extraordinary proliferation of popular art to meet the increasing demand from foreign visitors. Some traditional products have taken on a fresh lease of life, while other crafts have been established from scratch, some with happier results than others but all showing a tendency to diverge steadily from their original conception.

It is necessary at the outset to dispose of some commonly held misconceptions that the arts and crafts of Peru are based on traditions going back 5000 years, that the artists of the present day are following their pre-Columbian ancestors. It is true that certain techniques have changed little down the centuries; but in the field of design and pattern the return to pre-Columbian traditions is a very recent phenomenon, reflecting the demand from ignorant purchasers determined to take home something "typical", which must of course be something typically Inca.

Most of the artistic forms developed after the Conquest bear the mark of Catholicism, and it is no accident that the two areas where folk art is now most flourishing—Cuzco and Ayacucho—are both noted for their splendid flowering of colonial art in dozens of churches and religious houses. The sacred images, crosses, candlesticks and reredoses found in these areas reflect the expansion of the Christian faith, interpreted through the sometimes naive and often superstitious vision of the Indians of the Andes. Other works show traditions of pagan origin, also imported from Spain: for example the innumerable representations of bulls, or the decorative themes drawn from Mudéjar art.

The village of Quinua, some 20 km from Ayacucho, is a noted centre of pottery production, specialising in the making of small church models in beige terracotta, painted with brown or dark red patterns. Produced in an endless variety of shape and size, ingeniously decorated with pinnacled turrets and huge clocks, they are replicas, in varying degrees of fidelity, of the colonial churches of the region. The peasants set them up on the highest point of their roofs, so that they will protect the house and its inhabitants. They are often flanked by human figures— musicians playing the flute, the horn or the drum—or by vessels in the shape of a bull, a llama or a bird which fill with water and serve as bird baths. Originally produced entirely for local use, the churches and animals of Quinua are now among the most sought after products of popular art—a situation which has led to a distinct decline in their technical and artistic quality.

In the south, near Puno, another potters' village—Santiago de Pupuja—thrives on the production of thousands of the famous "Pucará bulls" and a crude local pottery decorated with fishes and flowers. For many centuries the peasants of this region have celebrated the marking of the cattle with a great festival called the *Senalacuy* during which the beasts' ears are clipped. After a long ceremony in which the finest bull in the herd is painted with ritual patterns, decked with flowers and ribbons and cut on the muzzle and nostrils, brandy is poured into its nostrils and a pimento stuck into its anus in order enrage it still further, and it is then released, its blood being collected and offered to Pachamama. The pottery bull, which is both a decorative and a ceremonial object (being dedicated to the *auquis*, the spirits omnipresent in nature), reproduces the massive bulk and the impression of strength and fury—with dilated nostrils, lashing tail and protruding tongue—of the real bull, maddened by pain and alcohol. Thus an animal originally alien to the Andean world is now fully integrated into the myths and traditions of the Indians, who were impressed by its majestic strength and quickly substituted it for their traditional totemic animals. Pottery bulls are produced in other parts of Peru (Quinua, Cajamarca), but none are so famous as the bulls of Pucará, which are certainly the best known products of Peruvian popular art.

The sculpture of Ayacucho, on the other hand, is of basically Christian origin. The wood and plaster reredoses and crosses and the alabaster Nativity groups produced here are copies of liturgical art which perpetuate the traditions of the Spanish and mestizo artists of the 17th century. The craftsmen of the present day, however, have adopted freer and more individual forms, and the objects themselves have sometimes become charged with a magical and pagan content.

The Indians who used to take caravans of llamas through the Andes carried with them a small wooden casket containing the image of a saint (St Anthony or, even more frequently, St Mark) to protect them and their animals from the hazards of the long journey through the Cordillera. These images were also used by the *curanderos* or witch-doctors in their consultations. The use of these "San Marcos" had almost died out when, around the year 1920, a group of artists at Huamanga (the old Quechua name of Ayacucho) who were interested in the native artistic traditions rediscovered their artless beauty and charm. Many craftsmen then set about producing "reredoses" containing a profusion of themes and figures, often quite unconnected with religion. Scenes from ordinary life (a hatter's workshop, a weaving shop, the gathering of prickly pears, a village festival), known as *costumbrista* themes, are now commoner in these works than representations of the Nativity, the Passion or the patron saints who protect livestock. The unchallenged master of this new style is Don Joaquín López Antay, who is famed for his huge reredoses, intricately modelled and painted, with their profusion of little figures enclosed by two wooden screens decorated with flowers and delicate scrollwork.

Another traditional product is the painted wooden "Passion Cross" which is fastened to the walls of houses, imitating the huge and heavy crosses bearing the instruments of the Passion which are set at the doors of churches or carried in procession.

Ayacucho is also noted for its carvings, in a very white alabaster known as "Huamanga stone", of the Magi or of small Nativity scenes enclosed in a casket. During the colonial period there was a flourishing school of alabaster carvers, whose work, often based on European themes (heraldic lions, shepherds and nymphs), adorned the sumptuous mansions of the provincial aristocracy. Alabaster working is now a minor art practised for the benefit of tourists, turning out mass-produced objects of poor quality.

We have left to the last the *mate*, the only product of popular art which is of genuinely pre-Hispanic origin. Indeed the oldest known objet d'art in Peru (from the Pre-Ceramic site of Huaca Prieta in the northern coastal area) is a *mate* with carved decoration. The term *mate*, the popular name for a gourd, is applied to a whole series of vessels or objects (depending whether or not the interior is hollowed out) made from gourds. All the various cultures of ancient Peru used *mates*, either plain or decorated, for ceremonial or everyday purposes. There are now three main centres or schools producing decorated *mates* — at Piura in the northern coastal region and Huancayo and Ayacucho in the central Andes. The *mate* of Piura, cut into a bowl or basin shape and decorated very simply with a frieze of red and black floral ornament, is commonly used for drinking the famous *chicha de jora*, a traditional drink made from fermented maize. At Huancayo, and particularly in the small village of Cochas, gourds of all shapes and sizes are decorated with a varied range of scenes — country life, popular festivals, military scenes, lorries and aircraft, even a portrait of the President. The artist covers the whole surface of the gourd with light-coloured paint and then engraves the design with a fine point and heightens the effect by burning. The finest *mates* are — or at any rate were until recent years — produced at Ayacucho, in a style dating from colonial times. Here, however, the design is produced by the champlevé technique, picked out in delicate lines against a ground which is later painted black. The decoration, covering the whole surface of the gourd, depicts scenes from country life or historical events, any empty spaces being filled with an exuberant ornament of scrollwork, garlands and flowers, in patterns inherited from the Mudéjar art of Spain. The most traditional form is the "sugar-bowl", with a delicately engraved lid which formerly had a knob of chased silver.

LANGUAGES

Although the Conquistadors imposed the Spanish language in Peru, the 1961 census showed that Spanish was spoken by only 60% of the population, with 20% using it as a second language. The use of Spanish is general on the Coast and in all towns; in the Sierra the country people speak Quechua or, in the Puno region, Aymará. To the Indians Spanish is a language used — sometimes rather haltingly — only in their dealings with mestizos or foreigners. Many of them, particularly women, do not speak it and understand it very imperfectly. In the Amazonian forest the Indians speak some thirty dialects belonging to the Arawak and Tupí-Guaraní language families.

The origins of Quechua (also called Runasimi, the "language of men") and Aymará are still not clearly understood. Some words and roots in Quechua have been found to show resemblances to the Maya languages and some Far Eastern tongues; and in its morphology affinities with Hungarian and other Finno-Ugrian languages have been detected. According to Garcilaso de la Vega the Incas themselves did not speak Quechua, which was the language of the Quechua people, occupying territory between the Apurímac and Urubamba rivers, who were conquered by the early Incas; it is not known whether they spoke Aymará, the language of the Collao region from which they originally came. They did, however, contribute to a limited extent to the spread of Quechua among the peoples of their vast empire; and the Spaniards continued the process by making Quechua the language of their missionary activity and, even more significantly, by codifying and devising an alphabet for a language which until then had been purely oral. This led to the disappearance of a number of old pre-Columbian dialects, in particular Chimú or Mochik, which was spoken all over the northern coastal region.

It was only very recently, at the Inter-American Indianist Congress at La Paz in 1954, that a simplified and systematic transcription of the Quechua language was adopted. Previously there had been wide scope for individual variations, given the abundance of consonants, the paucity of vowels and the frequency of guttural and glottal sounds. Thus the word *waman* ("falcon"), so written in accordance with the orthography agreed at La Paz, is found in older texts in the form *huaman* or *guaman*. Allowance must also be made for regional variations — for, according to Alberto Torero, there were at one time 31 Quechua dialects in use in Peru. The principal forms now distinguished — all much simplified — are the versions spoken at Cuzco (the most guttural), at Ayacucho (Quechua Chanka) and at Ancash-Huánuco. Outside Peru Quechua is spoken in part of Bolivia (Cochabamba), in north-eastern Argentina (the Tucumán area) and in Ecuador. Many Spanish words, particularly verbs and everyday terms, have been taken over into Quechua: *e.g. Cruzvelakuy*, "Festival of the Cross", *caballukuna*, "horses", and *Diospararasunki*, "thank you". Quechua has no distinction between masculine, feminine and neuter gender; the plural is formed by the addition of the suffix *kuna*. It has a large number of declensions, formed by the addition of suffixes to indicate number, tense, cases and the personal or possessive pronoun; the roots to which these suffixes are added are frequently of two syllables. Quechua is a vivid and poetic language which is fond of onomatopoeias and racy turns of phrase.

The intellectuals of the Sierra, particularly in Cuzco, take pleasure in speaking Quechua, and there is a literature of poems and stories in the language; there is also an Academy of the Quechua Language to which many of the authors belong. In the 18th century a popular play was written in Quechua, "Ollantay", based on a pre-Columbian legend relating the life of an Inca general. There are also many Quechua folk songs which reach a wide public on the radio and on disc. The use of Quechua has, however, declined with the advance of education and increasing urbanisation: in Cuzco, for example, many children no longer speak the language, although until quite recently they regularly learned it from Indian servants or from their grand-parents. Against this, it has made some progress in the *barriadas* of Lima, as Aymará has in those of Arequipa. The present educational reforms provide for the general adoption of bilingual teaching (Quechua and Spanish or Aymará and Spanish); and the government is also concerned to promote the cultural development of the native languages among the mass of the peasants by means of the radio and sometimes also the press.

Aymará shows considerable affinities with Quechua, but in view of the dominant position of Quechua under the Incas and during the colonial period it is difficult to know whether this reflects the original situation or the effect of later development. The roots of words are often the same, and syntax and sentence construction largely similar. Aymará has, however, a higher proportion of guttural, glottal or aspirate sounds than Quechua.

See Paul Rivet and Georges de Créqui-Montfort, *Bibliographie des langues aymara et kicua*, Paris, Institute d'Ethnologie de l'Université de Paris, 4 vols, 1951-56.

ART AND LITERATURE

Since the Spanish conquest—the pre-Columbian period having already been separately considered—Peru has shown extraordinary activity in the fields of art and literature, and can claim to be the oldest and undoubtedly the most varied artistic centre in the whole of America. The universities of Lima (San Marcos) and Cuzco were founded in 1553 and 1623 respectively, while the oldest university in the United States, Harvard, was not founded until 1636. The country is also notable for its numerous religious buildings, constantly rebuilt after earthquake damage, extended and embellished at the expense of generous donors, altered in accordance with changes in taste, and for the wealth of pictures which these buildings contain. Although the artistic models were Spanish, and in a lesser degree European, the art of Peru soon began to reflect a mingling of native and foreign cultures, giving expression to the elemental force of the American environment and the youthful vigour and spontaneity of its peoples, tinged at the same time with the melancholy of the defeated and oppressed and retaining some lingering memory of pre-Columbian techniques and traditions.

The Arts

Colonial art did not come into being in a vacuum: on the one hand it grew up in a country of very ancient, individual and diverse artistic traditions, and on the other hand it found inspiration in Spanish models and was guided in its early days by artists brought in from Spain. It is legitimate, therefore, to talk of an artistic conquest in parallel with the military conquest, to the extent that the works of art, both religious and civil, produced during the colonial period reflected the Spanish will to dominate the country and wholly rejected pre-Columbian traditions, which were regarded as works of the devil. Nevertheless by the end of the 16th century a hybrid art had developed, adapted to the geographical peculiarities of the conquered territories and leaving free play to the fancy, the naive manner and the cultural interbreeding of the local artists.

Colonial architecture followed artistic trends in Spain with a time-lag of some thirty years. To begin with it was very strongly influenced by Arab or at least Mudéjar art, as is shown by the

Santa Catalina monastery in Arequipa, opened only in 1970 after being closed for almost four centuries, which surprises visitors who are accustomed to the Baroque and have forgotten the profound imprint left by the Arabs in the Spain of the Reconquista. Few 16th century buildings survive in Peru as a result of the havoc wrought by earthquakes, but Mudéjar influence can be seen in many churches and religious houses, particularly in Lima, down to a fairly late period (cf. the church of San Francisco, the cloisters of Santo Domingo or the Torre Tagle Palace).

The Renaissance or Plateresque style is represented by few examples in Peru, for it soon came under the influence of the Spanish Baroque. This was predominant throughout the greater part of the 17th century and continued into the 18th, occasionally admitting some Rococo or Churrigueresque influences (cf. the tower of Santo Domingo in Cuzco). Many Iberian architects came to work in Peru, like the Spaniards *Alonso González Beltrán, Francisco Becerra, Juan Martínez de Arrona* and *Bartolomé Lorenzo*, who successively directed the building of Lima Cathedral; the Portuguese *Constantino de Vasconcellos*, who was responsible for the convent of San Francisco in Lima; *Martín de Aizpitarte*, who built San Pedro in Lima; and *Juan Manuel de Veramendi, Juan Correa, Francisco Domínguez de Chávez y Arellano* and *Diego Martínez*, who worked on the Cathedral and the Church of the Compañía in Cuzco. In the 18th century the building work was usually directed by the priests and monks themselves.

The style of building had to be adapted to stand up to the frequent earthquake shocks. The churches were, therefore, frequently massive, with huge piers in the interior, façades that were wider than they were high, low towers and flattened domes. Regional schools quickly grew up, skilled in the use of the materials available locally—in Lima bricks and sometimes *quicha* (cob), in Arequipa white volcanic stone, in Ayacucho alabaster and golden limestone, in Cuzco granite and andesite—but always leaving scope for the fancy of the builders (cf. the stone tracery of the doorways at Arequipa, Cajamarca and Juli). In Cuzco the Spanish builders contrived to use the stones and frequently the foundations of the Inca buildings destroyed during the Conquest: hence the hybrid structures to be seen in the streets of the old Inca capital, with the Spanish walls of whitewashed adobe brick, light and elegant with their carved balconies, superimposed on the massive and austere stone walls of the Incas, so solid that the Spaniards could not remove them.

The native or mestizo workers rapidly developed their ancestral stone-hewing techniques, particularly in Cuzco, and acquired extreme virtuosity in the carving of stone or wood. Hence the exuberantly decorated doorways and reredoses, the carved wooden pulpits and choirs, which the tourist may sometimes find a little overpowering but which illustrate the omnipotence of the conquering Catholic faith, the ostentatious wealth of the Spanish or mestizo donors and the vigorous faith of craftsmen recently converted to a new God and to new techniques. Everywhere we feel the desire to "lay it on thick", both on the part of the priests, anxious to impress their flock with their richly painted saints, their bleeding Christs, the profusion of gold (and of mirrors) which no doubt owed something to the glittering interiors of the pre-Columbian temples, and on the part also of the craftsmen, enthusiastic neophytes of a new religion. At any rate there is no monotony in these churches: consider, for example, the five main churches in Cuzco, widely different from one another although they were all rebuilt at about the same time, after an earthquake in 1650.

Colonial painting and sculpture were, even more obviously, imported arts, since the Inca civilisation had shown relatively little interest in these forms of expression. They were employed wholly in the service of religion, and representations of the saints, the Virgin and the Trinity soon drove out the pre-Columbian idols. Here again the artists followed European models, Italian or Flemish as well as Spanish. Gifts by Spanish sovereigns, viceroys and high dignitaries introduced Peru to the work of Velázquez, Zurbarán, Murillo, van Dyck, Rubens and many lesser painters. Charles V, for example, presented Cuzco Cathedral with the Christ now known as the "Señor de los Temblores" ("Christ of the Earthquakes") and two Virgins (La Linda and La Antigua). Many Spanish and Italian painters settled in Peru, setting up studios and even regular schools and sometimes moving from one town to another. The best known were *Juan de Illescas* and the Italians *Bernardo Bitti* (who lived in Peru from 1575 to 1610), *Mateo Pérez de Alesio*, *Angelino Medoro* and *Albano*.

Later a number of native painters came to the fore, and soon made important contributions to Peruvian art. Cuzco became a considerable cultural centre, whose influence extended throughout most of the Viceroyalty of Lima. The Cuzco school, much influenced by Bernardo Bitti, produced a number of notable native painters—*Pedro Loaiza* (who shows the influence of Bitti's mannerism), *Juan Espinoza de los Monteros* and his son of the same name, *Basilio Santa Cruz, Basilio Pacheco, Antonio Vilcas, Ignacio Chacón, Marcos Zapata, Juan Osorio, Antonio* and *Juan Sinchi-Roca*, and above all *Diego Quispe Tito* (who was active between 1634 and 1681: his main works are in the Cathedral, San Francisco and San Sebastián). The work of the Cuzco school is characterised by its use of gold dust (*pan de oro*) and the sumptuousness, sometimes carried to almost ludicrous excess, of the dress of its Virgins, archangels and saints, with faces rapt in ecstasy emerging from clouds of lace. Although the themes were copied from European paintings the faces of the figures very soon began to show Indian features, and homely local touches appeared (e.g. the Virgin suckling an Infant Jesus who wears an Indian cap). During the second half of the 17th century, particularly in the work of Diego Quispe Tito, landscape backgrounds began to play a considerable part in religious scenes, in the manner of the Flemish painters, but with scenery and a flora and fauna characteristic of the Sierra. There was also a profusion of work of lesser interest, often mass produced to meet the considerable demand which came from the remotest provinces of the Viceroyalty.

Among leading wood-carvers were *Martínez Montañés* of Lima and *Pedro de Vargas, Diego Arias de la Cerda, Luis Montes, Diego Rodríguez* and *Juan Tomás Tuyru Tupa*. Gold- and silversmithing, stone-cutting and weaving, which had long flourished in Peru, continued to develop. In these minor arts we frequently observe the continuance of Inca influences, in particular in the production of fabrics and *qeros* (painted wooden vessels), in a real transitional style to which there is no counterpart in architecture. This hybrid colonial style, originally evolved under Catholic pressure, had a marked influence on Peruvian popular art, both sacred and profane, which still shows extraordinary vigour in our own day.

The achievement of independence, the influence of Bolívar's liberal ideas and contacts with other European countries, particularly Britain and France, led to a sharp decline in religious art and a flowering of portrait painting, landscapes and genre scenes. *José Gil de Castro* is noted for his portraits of notable men of the day, *Pancho Fierro* (1803–79) for his water-colours depicting scenes of Lima life, usually satirical in tone, *Francisco Laso* for his landscapes and illustrations of popular legends. In the second half of the 19th century *Ignacio Merino*, a native of

Piura, travelled to Europe, as did *Daniel Hernández, Carlos Baca Elor* and *Lynch,* who had contacts with the Impressionists. In the 1920s and 1930s a school of painting influenced by the ideas of the *indigenista* literary movement (see p. 99) developed, its leading representative being *José Sabogal* and other members *Julia Codesido, Vinatea Reinoso, Camino Blas, Alicia Bustamente* and the self-taught naive painter *Mario Urteaga.* Their pictures reflect Indian life and the landscape of the Sierra, but are also strongly influenced by folk art. The various European artistic movements had their followers in Peru—for example cubism with *Carlos Quispez Asín* and surrealism with the collages of *César Moro,* a poet as well as an artist. Among contemporary artists are the painters *Ricardo Graú, Rodríguez Larraín* and *Fernando de Szyszlo,* who go in for abstract art; the fresco painters *Núñez Ureta* and *J. M. Ugarte Eléspuru; Alfredo Ruiz Rosas, Alberto Quintanilla* and *Manuel Zapata Orihuela,* practitioners of representational art; the engraver *Francisco Espinoza Dueñas; Delfín,* sculptor in metal; and *Tilse Tsuchiya.*

Music

Peruvian music is almost entirely folk music. On the Coast it is strongly influenced by Spanish and European traditions, with its waltzes, its *marineras* and its *tonderos,* but there is also a type of music showing negro influence, particularly in the north. In the Sierra the orchestras include both pre-Columbian instruments like reed flutes (*quenas*), Pan pipes (*sicus, zampoyas, antaras*), transverse flutes (*pinkuyus*), huge sea-shells (*pututus*), small drums (*tinyas*) and cow-bells, and European instruments brought in by the Spaniards, like guitars (and a variant known as the *charango,* a small instrument with a sound-box formed from the shell of an armadillo), harps, violins and trumpets. Pre-Columbian music was pentatonic, and the tradition of this music is still preserved by the groups of *zampoya* players who play three or four notes, one after the other, repeating the sequence interminably. The most popular tunes in the Sierra are the gay *huyno,* the slow and melancholy *yaravi,* the *kara chuncho,* which caricatures the war-dance of the forest Indians, the very lively *diblada* and the Carnival tunes, for which Puno in particular is noted. Among noted composers of chamber music on the Coast are *José Castro, Leandro Alviña* and *Teodoro Valcárcel.* In

Cuzco *R. Ojeda*, *Baltasar Zegarra* and *Policarpo Caballero* have successfully preserved much of the treasury of native and mestizo music.

Literature

There is still controversy among scholars about whether the Incas had a system of writing or some form of expression resembling a script. The Quechua language has a word *quilca* (Aymará *qelqa*) which means "writing"; and it has been suggested that the *quipus* used in the Inca empire were a form of writing. The *quipus* were clusters of string, some containing coloured threads, which were knotted in particular ways to form a system of decimal numbering used for statistical and record purposes. There were several types of *quipu* (for population counts, for economic or military purposes, etc.), whose care and interpretation was the responsibility of officials known as *quipucamayocs*. The chronicles also refer to *amautas* and *harawis*, who were "wise men" attached to the Emperor's court responsible for preserving historical tales and poems, mainly oral in character, and for reciting or singing them on the occasion of the great national festivals. There is also a tradition of Quechua oral poetry showing a profound love of nature, a high degree of sentiment and a genuine melancholy.

The written literature of Peru begins with the first accounts by the Spanish conquerors of their Conquest and the new world they had discovered. The first chroniclers were witnesses of the Conquest, like *Pedro Sancho de la Hoz*, who recounted the death of Atahuallpa and the taking of Cuzco, *Pedro Pizarro* and *Miguel Estete*, who recorded the travels of the Conquistadors in Amazonia in his "Noticia del Perú". Some years later the chroniclers began to give minute descriptions of the landscape of America and the way of life of the Indians — *Cieza de León* with his "Señorío de los Incas" and his "Crónica del Perú", *Juan Betanzos*, *Polo Ondegardo*, *Sarmiento de Gamboa* and the numerous religious chroniclers who were concerned to denounce Indian customs as works of the devil, like Father *Montesinos*, who lived in Peru from 1581 to 1663 and set out to write a "History of the Incas", Father *Calancha*, who was born in South America, the monks *Blas Valera* and *Cristóbal de Molina*, "El Cuzqueño", and in the 17th century Father *Cobo*, author of a "History of the New World". The vocabulary of these Spanish chroniclers rapidly incorporated terms and images from the Quechua language. The next stage was the emergence of two mestizo writers, *Garcilaso de la Vega* (1539–1616) and *Waman Poma de Ayala* (?–1613), marking the birth, by the end of the 16th century, of an authentically Peruvian literature.

Garcilaso de la Vega was the son of a Conquistador belonging to a noble Spanish family and of an Indian princess descended from Inca Huayna Cápac. He was thus a representative of a new phenomenon, the racial and cultural interbreeding of conquerors and conquered. The first Latin American writer, he abandoned his native town of Cuzco to seek voluntary exile in Spain. His literary career began with a translation of León Hebreo's "Dialogues of Love" and his "Florida del Inca", an account of the discovery of Florida by the Spaniards. His most important work, written out of his homesickness for America, is his "Royal Commentaries", a first attempt to lay the foundations for a history of Peru and of South America, still a magnificent account of the Inca empire. Although this has been criticised as a partial description which has helped to create an idyllic vision of the Inca state as an almost socialist conception, it is an interesting reflection of the ideas of a mestizo who was concerned to make known the past greatness of his ancestors.

In **Waman Poma de Ayala**, son of an Indian cacique and an Inca princess, we have a witness to the realities of life for the descendants of the Incas under their Spanish conquerors. Whereas Garcilaso, a cultivated mestizo who migrated to Europe, writes in a style which need not fear comparison with that of other Spanish writers of the day, Waman Poma uses a more colourful language which has a kind of primitive freshness and a certain naivety, occasionally tinged with irony. After collecting popular legends from all over Peru he described in his "Nueva corónica y buen gobierno" the social structure which the Spaniards destroyed in the Conquest and the misery and hardship suffered by the conquered peoples, illustrating his account with drawings when words seemed inadequate.

The Creole literature produced during the colonial period was very different. This was written by authors of European origin born in Peru who followed the models of the Siglo de Oro and imitated the language of metropolitan Spain. In the first half of the 17th century two writers stand out, a Lima woman who wrote under the pseudonym of Amarilis and the Cuzco writer Juan Espinoza Medrano. *Amarilis*, whose real name is unknown, wrote an epistle in Baroque style to Lope de Vega asking him to recount the life of St Dorothy. *Juan Espinoza Medrano* (1619–88), a mestizo poet, is remembered for a few pages (in particular an "Apology in Favour of Don Luis de Góngora") which imitate the Baroque style of metropolitan Spain but nevertheless reveal something of his native force and originality. In the second half of the 17th century a new genre more distinctively characteristic of Lima and of Creole literature came into being, often taking the form of satire, as in the case of *Juan del Valle Caviedes* (1652–96), a Spanish poet who had settled in Lima and records his ironical observations on the life of the capital of the Viceroyalty. In his principal work, "Romance sobre los dos terremotos que asolaron Lima", he casts off the melancholy of Spain and the Indians and shows something of the gaiety of Andalusia.

In the late 18th and early 19th century the Creole intellectuals took an interest in the new philosophical ideas of the French Encyclopaedists and reflected the values and principles of the French Revolution. Their mouthpiece was a periodical which claimed to give a new vision of South American reality, the "Mercurio Peruano", run by *Hipólite Unánue* (1755–1833), a doctor, physicist and mathematician, the poet *Baquijano y Carrillo* (1751–1818) and *Pablo de Olavide*. This was the organ of a group of intellectuals and scholars who called themselves the "Lovers of their Country" and gave expression both to the distinctive character of the Peruvian landscape and to the separate identity of the Creoles as Europeans born in the Spanish colonies. The first stirrings of Peruvian independence were voiced by *Mariano Melgar* (1790–1815) in his "Ode to Liberty". His patriotic fervour was mingled with an early romanticism in the poems addressed to his beloved ("Letter to Sylvia"). He was shot by royalist troops while taking part in the rising led by the Indian cacique Pumacahua. Along with *Carlos A. Salaverry* he represents the Romantic school in Peruvian literature.

After the agitated period of Independence and the first uncertain years of the Republic new writers came to the fore. Among them were two dramatists, *Felipe Pardo y Aliaga* (1806–69), a contributor to the "Nuevo Mercurio Peruano", and *Manuel Asensio Segura* (1805–71), author of "Sargento Canuto", who both continued the tradition of satire and the description of Lima life initiated by Juan del Valle Caviedes. *Abelardo Gamarra* (1850–1924), who write lucid accounts of life in Lima under the pseudonym of El Tunante, and *Leonidas Yerovi* (1881–1917), a humorous poet who also wrote plays and numerous articles in periodicals, are good representatives of *criollismo* in literature. The leading representative of this Creole literature of Lima was *Ricardo Palma* (1833–1919), who created a new literary genre in the "traditions" in which he sought to depict Lima's past as capital of the Viceroyalty. His "Tradiciones peruanas" mingle picturesque and often ironical descriptions with romantic tendencies and a touch of anticlericalism. Very different is the reality presented by the Cuzco woman writer *Clorinda Matto de Turner* (1854–1909), whose novel "Birds without Nests" was the first attempt to describe the conditions of native life and the scenery of the Sierra.

Flora Tristán (1803–44), a socialist writer and militant, belongs to Peruvian literature although she lived in France and wrote in French. Her "Peregrination of a Pariah" relates her journey to Peru in an attempt to recover her inheritance at Arequipa. She was closely associated with the early socialist militants and with Karl Marx, and was also the grandmother of Paul Gauguin. **Manuel González Prada** (1848–1918), in his early years a Romantic, later became an essayist who exercised great influence on the rising generation, and in particular on two leading statemen of the early 19th century, José Carlos Mariátegui and Victor Raúl Haya de la Torre. After Peru's defeat in the absurd "guano war" with Chile González Prada, a man of libertarian mind, sought to take a fresh look at the history of the Republic and to destroy some of the values established by Creole and mestizo culture. Declaring that the population of Peru was more mestizo and Indian than Latin, he demonstrated the need to integrate Indian culture more effectively into Peruvian culture. His two principal works are "Paginas libres" and "Horas de lucha". One of his poems became the battle-cry of APRA and the movement for university reform at the beginning of the century.

At the turn of the century *José Santos Chocano* (1875–1934) laid the foundations of a "modernist" poetry rooted in the space and many-sided reality of the American landscape, in the epic legends of the Incas and in the achievements of the struggle for independence. A man of adventurous disposition, he travelled widely in Central America, was a fervent supporter of Pancho Villa in the Mexican revolution, became an adviser to the Guatemalan dictator Estrada Cabrer and was finally murdered in Santiago (Chile) by a deranged assassin. Two of his works are particularly notable, "Alma América" and "Los Conquistadores".

The "post-modernists" rebelled against the formalism and intellectualism of the modernists, led by the Mexican poet González Martínez and the Peruvian symbolist *José Maria Eguren* (1872–1942), who was influenced by Mallarmé and Rubén Darío. A native of the Coast, he created a poetic universe devoid of any element of political or social concern, or even of literary "good taste" ("Simbólicas", "Canción de las figuras"). In the 1920s the literary group known as the Colónida came to the fore, following the leadership of *Abraham Valdelomar* (1888–1919), a poet born in Pisco who was also the real creator of the Peruvian short story. Modelling himself on the technique of Edgar Allan Poe, he described Lima as it was at the beginning of the century in his novel "La ciudad de los tísicos" and a short story, "El caballero Carmelo", which mingled tenderness, irony, intellectual scepticism and a concern to depict the realities of the life of ordinary people on the Coast.

Following a series of great events—the Mexican revolution of 1910, the movement for university reform which started in Córdoba (Argentina) in the same year, and the Russian revolution of 1917—two major political and intellectual personalities emerged who were to have a profound influence on Peruvian thought: *José Carlos Mariátegui* (1894–1930) and *Victor Raúl Haya de la Torre* (b. 1895). **Mariátegui,** a mestizo born in Lima, was the first Marxist essayist, a self-taught man who was identified with a great variety of causes on behalf of the people. He began his career as a critic and journalist and was associated both with the Colónida literary group and with González Prada, in whose house he met Vallejo and Haya de la Torre. He travelled in Europe, where he discovered Marxism, and in the Soviet Union, where he became a communist. His "Seven Essays in the Interpretation of Peruvian Reality" (1928) reflect the first attempt by an intellectual belonging to the lower middle classes of Lima to interpret the social realities of Peru in the 1920s. In these essays he touched on all Peru's problems—the problem of the country's economic dependence on the United States, the problem of integrating the Indians who made up 70% of the population (and here Mariátegui was the first to link the difficulties of the Indians with the question of land ownership, which led him to call for land reform), the necessities of university reform, the problems of painting, literature and culture. He edited an avant-garde magazine, "Amauta", and was the founder of the Peruvian Communist Party (1928). Until the end of his life, despite increasing infirmity, he devoted himself to the interests of the working class, becoming the repository of their hopes for the transformation of Peru and exerting a powerful influence on several generations of intellectuals and politicians.

Although the ideas of **Victor Raúl Haya de la Torre** were fairly close to Mariátegui's at the outset, they led him in 1928 to the foundation of APRA (the American Popular Revolutionary Alliance). Following the anarchist radicalism of González Prada and setting as his early objectives economic independence of the United States and a confederation of the Latin American countries, Haya de la Torre, who had a very active life of militancy, wrote many books and articles, including in particular "El anti-imperialismo y el APRA" and "Espacio-Tiempo Histórico". His ideas, although claiming to accept "native values", remained profoundly mestizo and Creole, and can be categorised as populist. The party he founded owed its success more to the personality of its leader and his commanding position in the opposition than to the intellectual rigour of his ideology. He succeeded in bringing together under his banner a number of intellectuals (including *Luis Alberto Sánchez* and *Ciro Alegría*), much of the urban middle class and the workers in the plantations on the Coast. The ideas of Mariátegui and Haya de la Torre, particularly the former, were opposed by *Victor Andrés Belaúnde Díez Canseco*, who published in 1930 "The National Reality", reflecting the extraordinary ferment of political ideas in Peru during the 1930s.

These political ideas had their literary and artistic counterpart in a very productive movement known as *indigenismo*, which had considerable influence on the political parties just mentioned. This was a radical movement of reaction against the traditions of Creole and Spanish-influenced literature which were particularly well established on the Coast. It reflected an awareness of the realities of Indian life in the Sierra and of the oppression to which they were exposed by the large landowners and by officials, and looked back to the Inca past, promoting the idea of the Inca state as based on socialist principles which now rapidly became fashionable.

The works of the *indigenista* school frequently took on the aspect of a literature of combat with little concern for literary form, considering the ideas of *indigenismo* as sufficiently revolutionary in themselves. The magazine "Amauta" opened its columns to the poets, short story writers and novelists of this school. Among the novelists a leading place was occupied by *López Albújar* (1872–1966), who, although born on the Coast (at Chiclayo), used his experience as a magistrate and set out his view of the unjust treatment accorded to the Indians of the Sierra in "Cuentos andinos" and "Nuevos cuentos andinos". His novel "Matalaché" is a denunciation of the racialist attitude of the large Creole landowners to the negroes on the Coast. *Luis Valcárcel* (b. 1893) strengthened the *indigenista* movement, bringing to it his training and his skills as a historian. Apart from his historical works ("From Ayllu to Empire", "History of the Early Culture of Peru") and his sociological studies ("Cultural Development of Peru", 1945) he also wrote a novel, "Storm over the Andes" (1927). As a professor in Cuzco he gathered round him a very active group of intellectuals and artists, prominent among whom was the Cuzco writer *Uriel García*, author of "El nuevo indio".

César Vallejo (1892–1938), a member of the *indigenista* movement, was the great poet of international reputation whom Peru had hitherto lacked. Born in a poor country family on the Coast, he studied literature and law at Lima University. His first and second collections of poems, "Los heraldos negros" (1918) and "Trilce" (1922), showed the influence of symbolism, but his novel "El Tungsteno" (1931) reflected his allegiance to *indigenismo*. He went to live in Paris, and travelled in Spain during the Civil War, and his subsequent poetry gave expression to the sufferings and the homesickness of exile, as well as to his political commitment to communism: "España , aparta de mi este cáliz", "Poemas humanos" (1939).

Alberto Hidalgo, a poet who belonged to the Colónida group, also became a communist, although showing a rather anarchic individualism ("Biography of Myself"). *César Moro* (1903–56), *J. Eduardo Eielson* and *Adolfo Westphalen* were influenced by surrealism. During this period also there were two noted novelists: *César Falcón*, a committed writer, author of "People without God" and "The Good Neighbour, Sanabria U.", and the solitary and mysterious *Martin Adán*, who was influenced both by Góngora and James Joyce ("La casa de cartón", 1928).

Ventura García Calderón (1886–1959) was mainly a literary critic, writing in both Spanish and French. *Riva Agüero y Osma*, *Basadre*, *Aurelio Miró Quesada* and *Raúl Porras Barrenechea* were historians and essayists, who produced a series of important works during the first half of the 20th century.

The writers of our own time have both extended their field of observation of Peruvian society, particularly in the towns, and enlarged their professional skills through their contacts with European literature—English (Joyce), Italian, French (Camus, Sartre, the *nouveau roman*) and North American (Faulkner, Hemingway, etc.). Although often living abroad, most of them feel a profound commitment to the economic and social problems of their country and the Third World. Two writers, Ciro Alegría and José María Arguedas, lie on the boundary between *indigenismo* and more modern literary trends. *Ciro Alegría* (b. 1909), son of a large landowner in northern Peru, is conscious of the Indian problem but treats it in a paternalist manner in his novels and short stories ("Serpiente de oro", 1935; "Los perros hambrientes", 1938; and his most important work, "El mundo es ancho y ajeno", 1941). José María Arguedas (1911–69) brings to his studies of Indian life the experience and sensibilities of a poor mestizo brought up among the peasants of Apurímac and Ayacucho, whose first language was Quechua, together with his training as an anthropologist and an authority on the Quechua language. His principal novels are "Agua" (1935), "Diamantes y pedernales", "Yawar fiesta" (1941), "Los ríos profundos" (1959), "Toda la sangre" (1964) and "El sexto" (1960), in which he describes life in a prison in Lima. In his last novel, "El zorro de arriba y el zorro de abajo", he extends his range to take in the proletariat of Chimbote, swollen by the influx of Indians from the Sierra. Another heir to the traditions of *indigenismo* is *Eleodoro Vargas Vicuña* (b. 1924), with his "Tales of Nahuín" (1955). The peasant movements of the 1960s provided material for the journalist *Hugo Neira* and the novel by *Manuel Scorza* (b. 1928), "Redoble por Rancas". The poetry of *Gustavo Valcárcel*, *Alejandro Romualdo*, *Luis Nieto* and *Washington Delgado* ("Days of the Heart", "To Live Tomorrow") also has a marked political and social commitment. At the other extreme is the work of *Blanca Varela*, *Javier Sologuren*, *Carlos Germán Belli* and *Juan Gonzalo Rose*, which is much more intimate, evocative and often of magical effect.

Life in the *barriadas* (shanty towns) of Lima has been described by Enrique Congrains Martín (b. 1932) in "Lima, hora zero" and "No uno, sino muchos muertes" (1958) and by *Julio Ramón Ribeyro* (b. 1929) in "Vulture without Feathers". Ribeyro also criticises middle class urban society in "Crónica de San Gabriel" and "Los genecillos dominicales". *Sebastián Salazar Bondy* (1924–65), a poet and dramatist as well as a novelist, seeks in his novel "Lima la horrible" to show up the often sordid realities of life in the capital, as does *Osvaldo Reynoso* in his "En Octubre no hay milagros". The most important and most prolific of contemporary writers, **Mario Vargas Llosa** (b. 1936 in Arequipa) also describes urban and mestizo society in his novels. His first works, "Los jefes" (1957) and "La ciudad y los perros" (1963), are based on memories of his adolescence and student days. "La casa verde" (1966) is a work of extraordinary complexity which reflects the complexity of life in present-day Peru. In his "Conversaciones en la Catedral" (1972) he describes life under the dictatorship of Odría. The younger school of writers includes the novelist *Alfredo Bryce Echenique* ("Mundo para Julius"), the critic *José Miguel Ovideo* and the poets *Naranjo*, *Arturo Corcuera*, *César Calvo*, *Antonio Cisneros*, *Mirko Lauer*, *Rodolfo Hinostroza* and the youthful *Javier Heraud*, who was killed at the age of 20 in the guerrilla fighting in the Madre de Dios.

BIBLIOGRAPHY

Works in English

G. Arciniegas, *Latin America: a Cultural History*, New York 1967.

L. Baudin, *A Socialist Empire—the Incas of Peru*, New York, 1961.

L. Baudin, *Daily Life in Peru under the Last Incas*, London, 1961.

H. Baumann, *Gold and Gods of Peru*, London, 1963.

W. C. Bennett, "The Andean Highlands: an Introduction" and "The Archaeology of the Central Andes", in *Handbook of the South American Indians*, vol. 2, Washington, 1946.

W. C. Bennett, *Ancient Arts of the Andes*, New York, 1954.

W. V. Bennett and J. B. Bird, *Andean Culture History*, London, 1965.

E. P. Benson, *The Mochica*, London, 1972.

C. A. Burland, *Peru under the Incas*, London, 1967.

G. H. S. Bushnell, *Peru* (Ancient Peoples and Places), London, 1963.

G. H. S. Bushnell, *Ancient Arts of the Americas*, London, 1965.

W. Byford-Jones, *Four Faces of Peru*, London, 1967.

S. Clissold, *Latin America: a Cultural Outline*, London, 1965.

J. Descola, *Daily Life in Colonial Peru*, London, 1968.

E. Dew, *Politics in the Altiplano*, London, 1970.

F. J. Dockstader, *South American Indian Art*, London, 1967.

H. U. Doering, *The Art of Ancient Peru*, London, 1952.

T. R. Ford, *Man and Land in Peru*, Gainesville, Fla, 1962.

V. W. von Hagen, *The Incas: People of the Sun*, Cleveland, 1961.

V. W. von Hagen, *The Desert Kingdoms of Peru*, London, 1965.

J. Hemming, *The Conquest of the Incas*, London, 1970.

A. Kendall, *Everyday Life of the Incas*, London, 1973.

G. Kubler, *The Art and Architecture of Ancient America*, Harmondsworth, 1962.

E. P. Lanning, *Peru before the Incas*, Englewood Cliffs, 1967.

R. Larco Hoyle, *Peru* (Archaeologia Mundi), Geneva, 1966.

R. Larco Hoyle, *Checan: an Essay on Erotic Representations in Pre-Columbian Art*, Geneva, 1971.

Sir Robert Marett, *Peru* (Nations of the Modern World), London, 1969.

J. A. Mason, *The Ancient Civilization of Peru*, Harmondsworth, 1957.

A. Metraux, *The Incas*, London, 1965.

B. Mishkin, "The Contemporary Quechua", in *Handbook of the South American Indians*, vol. 2, Washington, 1946.

H. Osborne, *Indians of the Andes: Aymaras and Quechuas*, London, 1952.

R. J. Owens, *Peru*, Oxford, 1963.

J. H. Parry, *The Spanish Seaborne Empire*, London, 1966.

J. L. Payne, *Labor and Politics in Peru: the System of Political Bargaining*, New Haven, Conn., 1965.

G. Pendle, *The Land and People of Peru*, London, 1966.

Peru: Challenge and Response, Portrait of a Resurgent Nation, Lima, 1971.

F. B. Pike, *The Modern History of Peru*, London and New York, 1967.

W. H. Prescott, *The History of the Conquest of Peru*, New York, 1847 (frequently republished).

W. H. Prescott, *The World of the Incas*, London, 1970. (The introductory section of Prescott's *History*, illustrated with photographs.)

D. A. Robinson, *Peru in Four Dimensions*, Lima, 1964.

J. H. Rowe, "Inca Culture at the Time of the Spanish Conquest", in *Handbook of the South American Indians*, vol. 2, Washington, 1946.

G. Savoy, *Vilcabamba, Last City of the Incas*, London, 1971.

G. Woodcock, *Incas and Other Men*, London, 1959.

T. R. Ybarra, *Lands of the Andes: Peru and Bolivia*, New York, 1947.

Works in Spanish

J. Basadre, *Historia del Perú*, Lima, 1963.

Bravo Bresani, Cotler and Matos Mar, *El Perú actual*, Mexico City, 1970.

Dominación y cambios en el Perú rural, Instituto de Estudios Peruanos, Lima, 1969.

Estudios sobre la cultura actual del Perú, Universidad San Marcos, Lima, 1958.

E. Fioravanti, *Latifundio y sindicalismo agrario en el Perú*, Lima, 1974.

Instituto Nacional de Planificación, *Atlas del Perú*, Lima, 1970.

L. Lumbreras, *De los pueblos, las culturas y las artes del antiguo Perú*, Lima, 1969.

L. Lumbreras, *El origen del estado en el Perú*, Lima, 1972.

Neiva Moreira, *Modelo peruano*, Buenos Aires, 1974.

C. Peñaherra, *Geografía general del Perú*, Lima, 1969 onwards (several volumes in course of publication).

Perúhoy, Instituto de Estudios Peruanos, Lima, 1971.

J. Puglar Vidal, *Los ochos regionales naturales del Perú*, Lima, 1967.

E. Romero, *Geografía económica del Perú*, Buenos Aires, 1960.

A. Tamayo Vargas, *Literatura peruana*, Lima, 1965.

Tosi, *Zonas de vida natural en el Perú*, Bol. No. 5, 1947 (Zona andina, Programa de cooperación técnica UNESCO).

L. Valcárcel, *Historia del Perú antiguo*, Lima, 1969.

F. Vargas Uarte, *Historia general del Perú*, Lima, 1966.

Virgilio-Roel, *La economia agraria peruana*, Lima, 1971.

A. Weberbauer, *El mundo vegetal de los Andes del Perú*, Lima, 1945.

F. Yepez, *Perú 1820-1920: un siglo de desarrollo capitalista*, Lima, 1972.

Description
and Itineraries

1. LIMA

Situation

Plan in colour: beginning of volume.

Lima was founded by Francisco Pizarro on 5 January 1535, two years after the capture of the Inca capital of Cuzco. The site was chosen because of its proximity to the sea, replacing Pizarro's first capital at Jauja, in the Mantaro valley; and Peru is thus the only one of the Andean countries which has its capital on the coast. It is admirably situated in the centre of present-day Peru, 1300 km from the northern and southern frontiers and 1100 km from Cuzco, in one of the largest oases of fertile land on the Peruvian coast, well watered by the Rímac, a river which flows throughout the year. The city lies on the left bank of the river some 12 km from the sea, at the foot of the Cerro San Cristóbal. It occupies an extensive Quaternary alluvial fan which ends at the sea in an impressive shingle cliff 60 m high, slashed by a number of short ravines called *malecones* (the Malecón Cisneros in Miraflores, the Malecón Pérez Armendáriz or Osma at Barranco, etc.). The Rímac fan is continued on the north side by the alluvial plain of the Chillón and at its upstream end is caught between desertic slopes at the foot of the Andes. This large area of flat ground, with only the most gradual slopes, is eminently suitable for the development of a large city. There is an abundance of water, but this is now proving inadequate to meet the needs of the expanding population. Lima's port, Callao, also enjoys an excellent situation, sheltered from the ocean swell by the tombolo of La Punta and the islands of San Lorenzo and El Frontón.

Lima has a climate which is both tropical, with a mean annual temperature of 18°C (6° lower than the normal temperature for lat. 12°S) and a narrow range of temperature, and desertic, with an annual rainfall of only 40 mm. In spite of this low rainfall, however, Lima has a very high humidity and a low average of sunshine. Except during the three months of summer (January to March) the weather tends to be dull, damp and rather enervating.

History

When the Spaniards arrived the oasis seems to have been a long settled and densely populated area, as is evidenced by the remains of a number of *huacas* (temples, sacred places), some of which have been buried under later building. Visitors can still, however, see the pyramids of adobe bricks which represent the Huaca Juliana (in San Isidro, seven blocks west of the 27th block in Av. Arequipa), the Huaca Huayamarca (2nd block, Av. Rosario, San Isidro), with an attractive site museum, and the Huaca Maranga (near Callao, Av. Progreso), the largest surviving example. The shrine of Pachacámac, an important pilgrimage centre, was also near the river Rímac.

Pizarro laid out his new town on a regular grid plan, with 117 lots for houses of substantial size which were distributed between 60 Spaniards. He named the town Ciudad de los Reyes ("City of the Kings") in honour of the Epiphany, but this soon gave place to the modern name of Lima, a corruption of the Quechua word Rímac ("He who speaks"—probably an allusion to the oracle of Pachacámac or to the murmur of the river flowing down through the coastal desert).

As capital of the Viceroyalty, Lima had important political and religious functions, and contained numerous churches and religious houses, all generously endowed with land. Since its port had the monopoly of trade with Spain it was also a busy commercial town. Twice a year the Spanish fleet arrived in Callao, bringing goods of all kinds from Spain, and these were then redistributed not only within the present territory of Peru but also to the territories now known as Chile, Bolivia, Argentina and Ecuador. In return Callao exported the produce of the country's mines, particularly silver from Potosí, which was then much more important than its agricultural produce.

The town's economic heyday was in the 17th century. It went through more difficult times in the 18th century, particularly after an earthquake in 1746 which caused 4000 deaths out of a population of 60,000, and suffered further setbacks some time later with the closing down of the Potosí mines and the establishment of the independent Viceroyalty of Buenos Aires, which met the desire of the Spanish colonies on the Atlantic coast of South America for emancipation from control by Lima. In 1614 Lima had a population of 26,700, including 13,400 Spaniards, 10,300 negroes and 2000 Indians—reflecting the early and rapid development of the slave trade to Peru. In 1782 it was still the largest town in America, with a population of 63,000. Between 1640 and 1647 it had been surrounded by walls to protect it from attack by British or Dutch pirates. The walls, built under the direction of the Marqués de Mancera when Viceroy, had a total length of 11.8 km and enclosed a total area of 505.9 hectares, of which 358.3 were built up. The line of the walls, which were destroyed in 1868–70, is marked by the present Av. Alfonso Ugarte and Av. Graú; a fragment of the walls can be seen in private grounds in Jirón Comandante Espinar. There were originally 35 towers and eleven gates, including five principal gates.

Independence considerably reduced the status of the capital by withdrawing from its jurisdiction the territories which now became part of other new Andean states. Within Peru itself, however, its dominant position was enhanced by the centralising tendencies of the Republican governments and the economic development of the Coast, while the Sierra tended to become economically marginal. Situated as it was in an oasis given up to cotton-growing, the town was linked with the port of Callao by the first railway line in South America, constructed in 1851; and in 1870 a line connecting it with the mines of the central Andes was opened. Until around 1930, however, its growth remained slow: from 87,000 in 1810 the population increased to 100,000 in 1876 and 273,000 in 1931. The built-up area expanded mainly westward in the direction of the port of Callao, which nevertheless remained a separate entity until quite recently, and southward towards the bathing resorts of Magdalena and later Miraflores, Barranco and Chorrillos, with which it was linked by two railway lines.

From 1930 onwards Lima, like most of the South American capitals, grew very rapidly—to 645,170 inhabitants in 1940, 1,845,910 in 1961 and 3,317,650 in 1972. Whereas it had only tripled in the 120 years between 1810 and 1930, it increased threefold in the next 20 years and then almost doubled in another eleven. There were two reasons for this expansion—the population explosion and the large-scale movements of population from all over Peru, particularly from the Sierra, to a city whose predominance was steadily increasing; for Lima was not only the political capital of a country with a long tradition of highly centralised government but also Peru's economic capital. By 1963 it provided 49% of the total number of jobs in the service trades, 53% of jobs in commerce and 61% of all office jobs; it possessed 64% of the country's industrial establishments, representing almost 60% of its total industrial output; and it handled 70% of Peru's bank deposits and loans. Lima is preeminent by a very considerable margin over all other Peruvian towns, the second largest (Arequipa) having a population of only 300,000.

Anatomy of the City

In recent years Lima has expanded in all directions, particularly towards the Andes in the north and along the coast to the east, and now extends to the Chillón valley in the north and the Lurín valley in the south, with a total area of some 40,000 hectares, 15,000 of them built up. Its expansion has taken two forms — private development (more rarely State or municipal development) for the well-to-do and the middle classes and the *barriadas* occupied by the poorer classes, which originally grew up on a spontaneous and unplanned basis. The better-class development monopolised the best land, the well irrigated cotton plantations, while the *barriadas* invaded the sandy slopes of the Cerro San Cristóbal and Cerro San Cosme to the north, El Agustino to the north-east and the bed of the Rímac, and are now spreading on to the hillsides round Comas in the west and Villa Maria del Triunfo in the south-east. At first the dwellings erected in these areas were of the most makeshift kind — shacks of plaited straw or cob (*quincha*) built without authority and without any kind of services; but gradually these local communities began to achieve a measure of organisation, their right to occupy the land was recognised, streets were laid out and some services like water and electricity were provided. Gradually also more substantial houses were built, in adobe brick or concrete, many of them of two floors and containing several rooms. In spite of these improvements, however, the *barriadas* have still very high densities of building and population, ranging from 100 people to the hectare in the large settlements on the outskirts of the city to as much as 1500 on the cerros near the centre.

The centre of Lima has lost much of its colonial character except in the immediate neighbourhood of the Plaza de Armas. Large numbers of high buildings, particularly office blocks, have been erected in the city centre, and from their roof terraces fine views can be had of the immense sprawling city, largely consisting of small low individual houses. The roofs of these houses offer curious glimpses of Lima life, for since rain is practically unknown in Lima they are used for a variety of domestic purposes — as open air store-rooms, for drying the family washing, as children's playgrounds, sometimes for the keeping of poultry, often nowadays as additional living accommodation, forming what can only be described as penthouse slums. The city centre itself is steadily declining as a residential district, being increasingly occupied by shops, offices, the imposing headquarters of the banks, and business buildings of all kinds. Round the quadrilateral area of the original town, the principal buildings in which are described below, are the outer districts built in colonial times (the Barrios Altos to the east and Rímac beyond the river) and at the beginning of this century (La Victoria and Breña). These densely populated areas tend to be dilapidated and squalid, with much slum property. Frequently the interior patios (*corralones*) of older houses have been partitioned to produce small one- or two-roomed dwellings; elsewhere cramped little houses are huddled along both sides of narrow blind alleys (*callejones, quintas*). Water-taps and lavatories are frequently shared by several families. Numbers of craftsmen's workshops and small factories are squeezed in between the houses.

The districts lying beyond these slum areas, towards the sea, are better structured. They are residential in character, with a limited provision of shops. Between Av. Arequipa, Av. Salaverry and Av. del Brasil and beyond this last street are Jesús María, Pueblo Libre, Magdalena and Bellavista, middle-class districts of fairly high population density, with many houses of modest standard and some 5- and 6-storey blocks of flats. Round Av. Javier Prado and Av. Salaverry, in San Isidro and, farther out, in Miraflores, are the better class districts, with handsome houses in a variety of styles, well cared for parks and gardens and a lower population density. Miraflores, to the south, has a modern shopping and cultural centre which is both very European, with its restaurants and its boutiques, and very North American. Along the coast to the east are Surquillo, Barranco and Chorrillos, in which a few remaining elegant 19th century mansions, often much dilapidated, mingle with better-class housing development and areas of slum property. All round the city are the extensive slum developments of the *barriadas*. Industry — mainly producing consumption goods and some equipment goods — has developed in four favoured areas — along the railway line from Lima to Callao, north of Callao (with many fish-meal plants), along the North Panamerican Highway and on the Carretera Central.

(Note the use of the Peruvian term *jirón* for *calle*, "street".)

1. The Plaza de Armas

As in all Peruvian towns, the Plaza de Armas is the centre of urban life, surrounded by the principal public buildings. On the north side of the square is the *Presidential Palace* (rebuilt 1931), the former Viceroy's Palace, itself originally established on the site of Pizarro's house. On the east side are the *Cathedral* and the *Archbishop's Palace* (1924). On the west side is the *Municipality* (rebuilt 1945), successor to the old *Cabildo*, the Council of the town's leading citizens.

The Plaza de Armas has lost its former commercial importance. The market has long been held elsewhere, and the square retains only a few shops under the arcades on the south side and in the Olaya Gallery (formerly the Callejón Petateros). In the past much used for religious processions and even for bullfights, the Plaza de Armas now shares its rôle as a centre of public life with the Plaza San Martín, a square to the south laid out in 1920 with which it is connected by two busy and populous streets, Jirón de la Unión and Jirón Carabaya.

Most of the buildings round the Plaza de Armas were rebuilt at the beginning of this century and fitted with wooden balconies with lattice-work screens, often of massive construction and out of keeping with the colonial tradition. The arcades on the south and west sides of the square were rebuilt in 1945. The small corner house facing the Presidential Palace and the Cathedral is the only surviving colonial building (18th c.). In the centre of the square is a bronze *fountain* (1650).

The **Cathedral** surprises the visitor by its large size and massive aspect, designed to display the power of the Catholic church in the conquest of America. The construction of the Cathedral started at a relatively late stage and proceeded slowly. The first chapel was built in 1555, and thereafter a number of architects were concerned in the work, the last of them being Francisco Becerra. The Cathedral was consecrated in 1625, but the towers were not completed until 1649.

It suffered severe damage from earthquakes in 1687 and 1746 and was subsequently rebuilt.

The *façade* has two Baroque doorways decorated with statues of saints and columns. The towers have curious conical roofs with pinnacles.

The **interior** is imposing, with three huge aisles in neo-classical style. In the first chapel on the right is the *sarcophagus of Francisco Pizarro*. In the second is a magnificent reredos by *Martínez Montañés* (mid 17th c.). The central altar has handsome gilded columns. The 17th century choir was the work of a Catalan, *Pedro Noguera*. The ivory crucifix on the wooden pulpit was presented by the Emperor Charles V. There are some fine paintings, including a "St Veronica" attributed to *Murillo*. At the far end of the choir, to the left, is a small religious museum.

Between the Cathedral and the Archbishop's Palace is the small *Capilla del Sagrario* (beginning of 17th c.), beautifully decorated with ceramic tiles, and with wooden balconies formerly occupied by the Viceroy and the Cardinal.

2. East of the Centre (round the Plaza Bolívar)

The visitor's sightseeing programme in the rest of the town can conveniently begin with the area to the east of the centre and the Barrios Altos district (see plan, pp. 120–121). After the Cathedral he can see the nearby church and convent of San Francisco, and then cross the wide Av. Abancay (one block away) to reach the Plaza Bolívar (also called the Plaza de la Inquisición), in which are the Parliament Buildings (*Congreso*).

The church and convent of **San Francisco** (one block east of the rear part of the Presidential Palace, near the river Rímac and the Central Station) were founded in 1546 but after being destroyed in an earthquake in 1656 were rebuilt (1672) by a Portuguese architect, Constantino de Vasconcellos. They are of strikingly massive aspect, both externally with their high walls of rusticated stone and internally with the huge piers supporting the three aisles which have enabled the structure to withstand later earthquakes.

On the north side of the square outside the church are the
Capilla de la Soledad and the *convent doorway*, with two windows
in the upper part and a niche containing a statue of St Francis.
The *main front of the church* has a late 17th century **doorway**
(1674) flanked by two tall square towers. The doorway consists
of three registers, the first with cylindrical columns framing the
door, the second with statues of the Virgin and saints, the third
with an oval *oeil-de-boeuf* window. The towers have balustrades
round the base and two low upper storeys, also with balustrades,
and are topped by pinnacled domes; the corners are strengthened
by square pilasters.

The **interior,** surprisingly, is in Mudéjar style, the vaulting and
columns being covered with stucco ornament in geometric designs.
Above the entrance is a *choir* of carved wood (1673), entered
from the upper gallery of the convent. The side *chapels* are
interesting, though rather dark. There is a *museum of religious art*,
established in 1968, containing silver liturgical utensils, embroidered chasubles, wooden balconies and furniture, and a
very fine collection of paintings by *Zurbarán* representing apostles
and saints, replicas of the series in the National Museum in
Lisbon.

The **cloisters,** on the north side of the church, were rebuilt in
the late 17th century (1669–74) and consist of two galleries in
very different styles. The upper gallery shows clear Arab influence,
with its horseshoe arches alternating with *oeil-de-boeuf* windows,
and the walls are covered with magnificent *ceramic tiles* in the
Sevillian Mudéjar tradition. Above are early 17th century
paintings relating the life of St Francis.

Under the church are three levels of brick-built *catacombs*
which were used for burials until 1808.

Opposite San Francisco is the *Casa Jarava* or
Esquivel (also known as the *Casa Pilatos*), of the late
16th and early 17th century, now occupied by the
House of Culture.

The house has a doorway of grey stone surmounted by a small
corbelled balcony. The patio, paved with cobblestones, has an
upper gallery reached by a central staircase. Very fine glass
lamps and pictures of the Cuzco school.

On the far side of Av. Abancay, in Plaza Bolívar with its
gardens and its equestrian statue of the Liberator, are the National

Congress and the House of the Inquisition. The **Congress Building,** which housed the Peruvian Parliament, was built between 1906 and 1939 on the site where the first Constituent Assembly met in 1822. The Renaissance-style entrance is framed in a peristyle of twin Doric columns. The **House of the Inquisition** (17th c.) has the aspect of a Greek temple, with its six Doric columns and pediment.

A long chamber with a magnificent coffered ceiling and five windows decorated with ceramic tiles now houses the *Congress Museum*. It was formerly occupied by the *Court of the Inquisition*, which operated in Peru from 1569 onwards. Adjoining it are various rooms which were used for storing records, as a prison and a torture chamber. They are entered through a small door known as the Puerta del Secreto. Under the Republic the hall was for many years the meeting place of the Senate.

In a block facing on to the Plaza Bolívar, in Jirón Ancash, is the *Casa de las Trece Monedas*, a charming Rococo mansion of the mid 18th century which now houses one of Lima's most fashionable restaurants, noted for its Peruvian cuisine. Nearby, almost at the junction of Jirón Ancash and Jirón Pasco, are the ruins of the **Royal College of San Ildefonso** (built 1606 onwards), which was for some time a Catholic University. It was destroyed in an earthquake in 1687 and rebuilt in the early 18th century. The best preserved part has been restored and now houses the *National School of Art*.

The **Barrios Altos** quarter, originally one of the outer districts of the colonial town, is full of life and colour. Wandering about in the crowded streets, visitors will find many remains of aristocratic mansions and numerous restaurants in which they can sample typical Lima dishes like *cebiche*, *anticuchos* or *mazamorra morada*.

Going south from here and then turning right into Jirón Capón or Ucayali, famous for its Chinese restaurants, we cut across Av. Abancay to see, immediately beyond it, the church of San Pedro and opposite this the Torre Tagle Palace, at the corner of Jirón Ucayali and Jirón Azángaro.

San Pedro is the only 18th century church in Lima which has remained intact, having been little affected by successive earthquakes. Founded by the Jesuits, it was built by Martín de Aizpitarte and consecrated in 1638.

The **façade** and the **altars in the inner chapels** (four in each of the lateral aisles) are notable examples of Baroque architecture, showing great virtuosity in the carving of stone and, even more strikingly, in the carved woodwork gilded with *pan de oro*. The altars, decorated with a profusion of twisted columns richly carved with conches and small arches, contain numerous niches with polychrome statues or paintings. Each chapel is roofed with a small dome borne on massive columns.

The central altar is set between two handsome galleries of gilded wood for the Viceroy and for monks. Several Viceroys are buried in the church.

To the right of the entrance is the *Penitenciaria Chapel*, roofed with several domes, which contains some fine pictures. It leads into the vestibule of the Sacristy, which contains a notable Virgin by *Bitti* (late 16th c.). The **Sacristy** itself (17th–18th c.) contains a number of magnificent paintings of saints and a "Coronation of the Virgin" by *Bitti*.

From the vestibule we can enter the chapel of the **College of San Pablo**, the most celebrated in Lima, founded by the Jesuits in 1586. It was largely destroyed by the construction of Av. Abancay, but part of its huge library (which in the 18th century contained 40,000 volumes) is now occupied by the *National Library*. The college was closed when the Jesuits were expelled in 1767. Its memory is perpetuated in the names of some of the neighbouring streets — Estudios, Cascarilla ("quinine"), Botica de San Pedro (the two latter names recalling the Jesuits' famous pharmacy).

The **Torre Tagle Palace,** which now houses the Ministry of Foreign Affairs, was built in 1735 for Don José Bernardo de Torre y Bracho, Marqués de Torre Tagle. It was restored in 1956–58.

The façade is two-storeyed with a roof terrace surrounded by a wooden trellis. The grey stone *doorway* on the ground floor contrasts harmoniously with the white stucco of the upper floor, the pink roughcast walls and the imposing openwork wooden balconies. The door is studded with huge bronze nails. The *patio* is in the Andalusian style, with a vestibule clad in ceramic tiles, a paving of cobbles and an upper gallery with cusped arches supported by slender columns. On the first floor are a small chapel with a Baroque altar, a drawing room with family portraits and the *Treaty Hall*, with paintings by *Teófilo Castillo* (19th c.) and artists of the Cuzco school. Note the fine wood-carving on the underside of the upper gallery and the lions in the patio.

3. The Rímac District

The Rímac district, on the other side of the river, can best be reached either by the *Ricardo Palma Bridge* (Av. Abancay) or by the *Puente de Piedra* (Stone Bridge) built during the Viceroyalty of the Marqués de Montesclaros (1607–15). Millions of whites of egg are supposed to have been used as mortar in the building of the bridge.

The old *Barrio de San Lázaro* is one of Lima's most populous districts. In colonial times, however, it was

---

 1 Presidential Palace
 2 Municipality
 3 Archbishop's Palace
 4 Cathedral
 5 Torre Tagle Palace
 6 San Marcos University and Pantheon
 7 Church of Merced
 8 Church of Santo Domingo
 9 Church of San Pedro
10 Church of San Marcelo
11 Church of Jesús María
12 Church of Las Nazarenas
13 Santa Rosa de Lima
14 San Francisco
15 Municipal Theatre
16 Segura Theatre
17 Art Gallery
18 Central Station
19 Law Courts
20 Museum of Peruvian Culture
21 National Library
22 Civic Centre

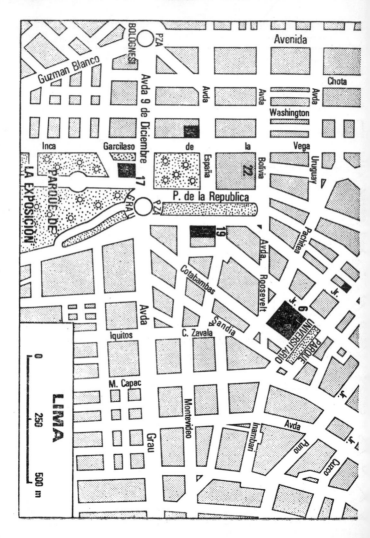

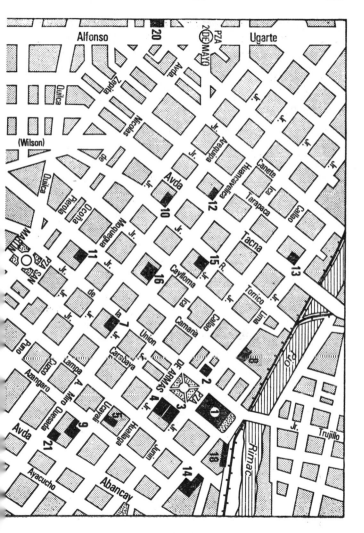

a favourite place of resort and recreation for the Creole aristocracy, with the *Plaza de Acho*, a bull-ring built by the Viceroy, Manuel de Amat, in 1768, the oldest in America, with accommodation for 8000 spectators (bullfights from October to December), and two beautiful promenades, the *Alameda de los Descalzos* and the *Paseo de Aguas*.

The **Alameda de los Descalzos** was laid out in 1611 by the Marqués de Montesclaros, with wide avenues, fountains and shady trees. After being practically abandoned in the middle of the 18th century it was restored by Manuel de Amat, who held great festivities here in honour of his favourite, the actress Michaela Villegas, known as La Perricholi. In 1768 he extended it in the direction of the Plaza de Acho by laying out another promenade with fountains, the **Paseo de Aguas.** In the middle of the 19th century most of the trees in the Alameda were felled and the present high wrought-iron railing and the twelve statues representing the signs of the zodiac erected in their place.

At the far end of the avenue are the quiet little *church and convent of the Descalzos* (Discalced Friars), founded by Antonio Corso, a Franciscan, in 1592: a humble structure of adobe brick which has stood up well to successive earthquakes. It consists of a small church, a house of retreat and a convent with its cloisters, all in simple rustic style.

In the western part of the Rímac quarter, in Jirón Presa (4th block, Jirón Francisco Pizarro), is the **Quinta de Presa,** which houses the *Museum of the Viceroyalty*. This is a large 18th century mansion, formerly belonging to the La Presa family, with handsome rooms and a gallery to the rear opening into the garden. To reach it, cross the Santa Rosa Bridge, which continues the line of Av. Tacna. See p. 131.

4. The Western Part of the Old Town

This itinerary, starting from the centre of Lima, takes in the western part of the old town between the Plaza de Armas, Jirón de la Unión, Av. Tacna and Av. Nicolás de Piérola, familiarly known as *La Colmena*, the "Beehive", because of the swarming crowds which fill the busy shopping streets in this area.

In the narrow Jirón Palacio, opposite the western entrance to the Presidential Palace, is one of the oldest houses in Lima, the **mansion of the Aliaga family**, which descended from one of Pizarro's companions, Gerónimo de Aliaga y Ramírez.

The house was built in the 16th century on the site of a pre-Columbian place of worship. The first patio, with pink rough-cast walls, has a central staircase and is decorated with a stone urn, statues and a beautiful window with lattice screens. With the owner's permission visitors are admitted to the drawing rooms, the chapel and a rear patio with old fig-trees.

In a small square opposite the *Head Post Office*, with its busy shopping arcade, is an *equestrian statue of Francisco Pizarro* by the American sculptor Charles Ramsey, a replica of the one in Pizarro's native town of Trujillo in Spain.

The **Convent of Santo Domingo,** to the west of the Post Office, occupies the *solar* (plot of land) granted to Father Vincente Valverde by Pizarro when the town was founded. The building of the convent extended over the whole of the second half of the 16th century. It stood up fairly well to Lima's various earthquakes, but the main nave vaulting was rebuilt in the 18th century and the interior completely reconstructed in neo-classical style.

There remain only **three cloisters** out of the five which the convent originally possessed. The first (early 17th c.) is in Mudéjar style, with horseshoe arches borne on slender colonnettes in the first-floor gallery, a beautiful decoration of ceramic tiles and pictures relating the life of St Dominic. The **chapter house** is in Baroque style, with very fine *carved wooden stalls*, a beautiful *pulpit* and pictures relating the life of St Thomas. To the right of the doorway is the entrance to a crypt in which two Peruvian saints are buried—St Martin Porres (a dark-skinned saint who is represented holding a broom as a reminder of his very modest

origins) and St Rose of Lima. The second patio also shows
Mudéjar influence but is more rustic in style.

To the left of the entrance to Santo Domingo is the
Veracruz Chapel, so called because it was said to possess
a fragment of the True Cross, which was the home of a
confraternity founded by Pizarro in 1540. In the little
square in which the chapel stands are a number of
19th century houses with handsome wooden balconies.

Continuing along Jirón Conde de Superunda
(formerly Jirón Lima), we pass the *Casa de Oquendo*,
a beautiful late 18th century mansion, with a fine
doorway and five graceful balconies, in which General
San Martín stayed. It now contains the offices of
Enturperú (Corporación de Turismo del Perú), where
bookings can be made for all government-owned
hotels. Farther down, at No. 341, is the *Fernando
Berkemeyer Bullfighting Museum*, in a 17th century
colonial house with a large balcony.

Crossing Av. Tacna, we come to the **Shrine of St
Rose of Lima.**

The church, founded at the end of the 17th century and rebuilt
in the 19th, is of no great interest apart from the miraculous
image of the Infant Jesus known as "El Doctorcito". In the
adjoining garden are a small hermitage of adobe brick and a
well into which worshippers throw written petitions to St Rose of
Lima, patron saint of Peru and the whole of Catholic America, a
Dominican nun named *Isabel Flores de Oliva* (1586–1617) who
was canonised in 1670.

Returning towards Jirón de la Unión along Jirón
Callao (one block south), we can see in the second
block on the left a handsome colonial mansion with
four patios and many beautifully furnished rooms.
One block farther south, at Jirón Ica 426 (returning
towards Av. Tacna), is the **Mansion of the Marquès de
la Riba** (18th c.), with beautiful balconies and two

graceful patios, which now houses a number of cultural associations, including some foreign associations. Continuing along Jirón Ica in the direction of Jirón de la Unión, we come (No. 323) to a single-storey 17th century house, now occupied by an association of artists. In the following block, at the junction of Jirón Ica and Jirón Camaná, are the **church and convent of San Agustín.**

This is a massive 19th century building which preserves the *Churrigueresque doorway* and the sacristy, with carved wood panelling on the walls, of the first church, founded by the Augustinians in the 17th century. The beautiful sculpture symbolising Death is by the 18th century Lima sculptor *Baltazar Gavilán*. The vestibule has a fine coffered ceiling. In the cloisters are paintings by the Cuzco artist *Basilio Pacheco* (1742).

Turning right along Jirón Camaná, we see, opposite the church, the *Riva Agüero Institute*, in a 17th century colonial house which belonged to the family of that name. Behind the church, in Jirón Huancavelica, are the *Manuel Segura Theatre* and, on its left, the *Alcedo* concert hall, on the site on which the town's principal theatre was built in 1662.

At the corner of Jirón Huancavelica and Jirón de la Unión is the **Church of the Merced.** This is the oldest convent in Lima, which has been much altered and rebuilt.

The building of the first church, which succeeded a modest earlier chapel, began in 1541, and a tall tower was added at the end of the 16th century. A new church was built from 1628 onwards, but this suffered heavy earthquake damage in 1687 and again in 1746 and was rebuilt in altered form on each occasion.

The present **façade** dates from the second half of the 18th century, and is built over the earlier Baroque front. It suffered much mutilation during the 19th and early 20th centuries, but was restored in the years following 1939. It is in the Churrigueresque style, with carved stonework of exceptional quality.

The church has three aisles and many *chapels*, sumptuously decorated through the munificence of wealthy donors. The *central altar*, covered with silver, contains the image of the Virgen de la Merced, who bears the title of Grand Marshal of the Peruvian army. Above the entrance is a wooden choir. In the sacristy are fine furniture and pictures of the colonial period. The *principal cloister* has arcading showing Mudéjar influence on the upper floor and pictures recounting the history of the Mercedarian order. There is also another cloister.

Near the Plaza San Martín, at the corner of Jirón Moquegua and Jirón Camaná, is the little **Convent of Jesús María,** which is open to visitors only on Tuesdays, Wednesdays and Saturdays from 9 to 10 a.m.

The Community of Jesus, Mary and Joseph was founded at the end of the 17th century by an Indian couple who received poor girls into their home. This little community of enclosed nuns dedicated to poverty formed a striking contrast with other religious communities in the town, who were celebrated for their vast wealth. The church was completed in 1726 and restored after earthquake damage in 1746.

Returning towards Av. Tacna, we see at the corner of Jirón Riva Agüero and Jirón Rufino Torrico the little **church of San Marcelo,** founded by the Augustinians in the mid 16th century, rebuilt at the beginning of the 17th century and again after suffering earthquake damage in 1687 and 1706. At the beginning of this century it was restored on the model of a church at Palca, near Nazca. The gilded reredoses are 18th century.

Beyond Av. Tacna is the **church of Las Nazarenas,** seeming rather isolated from the others. It was built in the second half of the 19th century to house a *miraculous painting of the Crucifixion*. The painting was the work of a negro who lived in what was then merely a cluster of adobe huts, and acquired great reputation when it survived an earthquake in 1665 undamaged. A copy in oil was painted in 1747, and the fresco itself was restored in 1954.

Every year on 18 October a procession organised by the Brotherhood of the *Señor de los Milagros* (Christ of the Miracles) leaves the church carrying the much venerated image, which is taken to another church where it remains for some days before returning to the Nazarenas. The procession is followed by a multitude of worshippers, some of whom have worn during the preceding month a purple robe or a mourning band in token of penitence. The image, in its gold frame, is carried on a huge silver litter weighing over a ton by members of the brotherhood, wearing purple robes, one group relieving another at intervals. The procession moves forward very slowly, stopping every ten minutes or so, to the accompaniment of funeral music, religious chanting, clouds of incense and a rain of flowers. At intervals along the route are stalls which dispense food and drink to the crowds following the procession.

5. Other Features of Interest

Two blocks south of the Plaza San Martín is the **Paseo de la República,** a wide but rather neglected promenade with some handsome bronze statues. On the east side are the imposing *Law Courts*, built in 1938, on the west side the massive new *Civic Centre*. From the Paseo leaves the new motorway to the coastal resorts south of Lima: officially a *via expresa*, it is popularly known as the *sanjón* ("trench").

Between the Paseo de la República and *Av. Inca Garcilaso de la Vega* (formerly Av. Wilson) are two small parks, the Park of Neptune to the north and the Exposition Park to the south, separated by the *Paseo Colón*, which runs from the Plaza Graú in the east to the Plaza Bolognesi in the west. On the side of the Exposition Park facing the Paseo de la República is the *Museum of Art* (p. 129).

Two other parks near the city centre may be of interest to visitors: the *Reserva*, near the new National Stadium (5th block in Av. Arequipa), and the *Campo de Marte*, the starting point of Av. Salaverry. The Campo de Marte has a spacious esplanade for military parades and an open-air auditorium for concerts and theatrical performances.

The other districts of Lima also have their central squares, with the church and town hall situated in or near them in accordance with Spanish tradition. Among them are the main squares of *La Victoria*, with a monument to Manco Cápac; *Magdalena* (or *Pueblo Libre*), dating from the colonial period; and *Miraflores* and *Barranco*, more recently laid out, with attractive gardens. In the fashionable district of *San Isidro* is a small grove of olives (El Olivar), the first trees in which were brought from Spain by Don Antonio de Rivera, son of one of the founders of Lima; concerts are sometimes given here. Nearby is the Country Club with its golf course. There are also beautiful gardens in the two main avenues which run through this district, Av. Salaverry and Av. Javier Prado, one at right angles to the other.

Rather farther from the centre, in Av. de la Marina, is the *Park of Marvels*, with a zoo, a small botanic garden and an amusement park for children. Nearby are a market selling craft goods and the exhibition grounds of the International Pacific Fair (see below).

Entertainments

Visitors to Lima can enjoy excellent **bathing** from December to March. The most popular bathing places are the beaches of *La Herradura* and *Agua Dulce* at Chorrillos, *Barranco* and *Miraflores*, and *La Punta* at Callao. There are **bullfights** in October-November and January-March in the *Plaza de Acho* (Rímac). On Saturdays and Sundays there is **horse-racing** at the *Monterrico* racecourse. Every Sunday morning there are displays of **folk dancing** in the *Coliseo Chacra Ríos* (Av. Venezuela, 22nd block). In another hall at Jirón Sandia 150 there are **cock-fighting** contests, and in the National Stadium (built 1952) **football** matches—both very popular sports in Peru.

The *International Pacific Fair* is held in October, coinciding with the *procession of the Señor de los Milagros* (see above, p. 127) and the opening of the theatre and concert season. On 24 June the Festival of the Sun (*Inti Raymi*), harking back to the Inca period, is celebrated in the suburb of Amancaés, at the foot of the Cerro San Cristóbal; it is accompanied by a great folk dancing and singing contest. Another folk contest held in the Campo de Marte at the beginning of November, the *Inkari*, brings together the best folk groups in the country.

6. Lima's Museums

For visitors with only limited time at their disposal the **Museum of Art** (Paseo Colón) 125) offers a comprehensive survey of the different periods in Peruvian cultural history. The museum occupies an old exhibition hall built in 1872 on the model of exhibition pavilions designed by Gustave Eiffel, constructor of the Eiffel Tower; it was opened in 1961.

On the ground floor can be seen some very fine examples of **Chavín pottery**. On the first floor are several rooms devoted to **colonial art,** with furniture, silver, ivory and tortoiseshell articles (particularly crucifixes and fans), leather boxes and a very fine collection of paintings, including works by *Bernardo Bitti* and artists of the Cuzco school. The rooms devoted to **pre-Columbian art** display pottery of the Mochica, Nazca, Tiahuanaco, Chancay and Inca cultures, very beautiful fabrics from Paracas, Chimú and Mochica gold and silver jewellery, mummies, etc. Finally there are rooms devoted to **19th and 20th century art,** including work by *Ignacio Merino* (1817–76), *Pancho Fierro* (1803–79: some 300 watercolours) and *Carlos Baca Flor*.

Visitors with more time available must not omit a visit to the **National Museum of Anthropology and Archaeology** (Plaza Bolívar, Pueblo Libre or Magdalena Vieja district). Founded in 1938, it contains material formerly in the museum of San Marcos University, together with objects recovered by excavation or presented by donors, and offers a panoramic view of the pre-Columbian period, with almost 85,000 pieces of pottery. Among its chief treasures are the *Tello Obelisk* and the *Raimondi Stone* (Chavín culture) and the splendid *fabrics from Paracas* (3rd–1st c. B.C.). The gold and silver objects are kept in an underground room (open only from 10 a.m. to 1.30 p.m.).

Near the National Museum, at Av. Bolívar 1115, is another museum devoted to pre-Columbian art, the **Rafael Larco Herrera Museum.**

This is a fabulous private collection (some 55,000 pieces of pottery), originally assembled in a hacienda at Chiclín in the Chicama valley. It consists mainly of material belonging to the cultures of the northern coastal region — Cupisnique, Mochica, Salinar, Virú and Chimú — including pottery, textiles, articles in precious metal, wooden objects, etc. One room contains a collection of erotic pottery of the Mochica and Chimú periods.

Also near the National Museum of Anthropology and Archaeology is the **National Museum of the History of the Republic,** housed in a colonial mansion in which Bolívar and San Martín lived during the 19th century. It contains a wide range of material relating to the period of Independence and the subsequent history of the Republic, including furniture, uniforms, flags, weapons and manuscripts. A particular feature is its collection of material on the battle of Ayacucho and the surrender of the San Felipe fortress. There are two *galleries of portraits*, one of the Viceroys, the other of Presidents of the Republic.

Near this museum is the little church of **Santa Maria Magdalena,** founded by the Franciscans in 1557. It is in Churrigueresque style, with beautiful altars of gilded wood and eight windows decorated with "Huamanga stone" (a kind of alabaster).

The **Museum of Gold** at Chacarilla (reached by following the line of Av. Primavera), which is privately owned, is one of the world's leading museums in its field. It can be seen by arrangment with its owner, Sr Miguel Mujica Gallo (telephone before visiting; closed Saturday afternoons and Sundays). The ground floor room contains a very fine *collection of weapons* of various periods from the 15th century onwards and a *collection of silver stirrups*.

The main collection of **gold objects** is in the basement and consists of some 10,000 items belonging to all the pre-Columbian cultures and in particular to the Chavín, Vicus, Chimú and Nazca cultures. Among the finest items are an *uncu of the Chimú period* (a kind of cotton poncho embroidered with almost 13,000 pieces of gold), several *Chimú necklaces*, including one with eight human heads and a gold idol inlaid with turquoises, Chimú *tumis* set with turquoises, Chimú *masks* with eyes made of emeralds or lapis-lazuli, articulated *funerary hands* of the Mochica period, *gold bags* for oca representing stylised animals (Frías culture), three curious Nazca balances of copper, silver and gold with gold scales, a Chimú *litter trapping*, a length of wood covered with gold and silver, with six niches decorated with turquoises and small gold and silver bells containing 18 idols in gold garments and masks, and a *Lambayeque vase* with four stags and three divinities on the stirrup handle. There are also numerous garments, headdresses and crowns decorated with multi-coloured plumes, pointing to contacts between the coastal peoples and the Amazonian forests from which these plumes came (Nazca, Chimú, Tiahuanaco and Chancay cultures).

The **Amano Museum** at Jirón Retiro 160, Miraflores (seen by appointment; closed on Saturdays, Sundays and public holidays) has a small collection of pottery, including items from Chavín and Cupisnique, but is mainly notable for its material from Kotosh (a temple near Huánuco) and a variety of material belonging to the Chancay culture (pottery, magnificent fabrics of all kinds).

For those interested in colonial art there is the **Museum of the Viceroyalty** (*Museo Virreinal*), in the Quinta de Presa (barracks of the Guardia Republicana), Rímac. In this 18th century mansion and its garden are displayed furniture, clothing, jewellery (belonging to La Perricholi), portraits and a carriage which belonged to the Conde de Torre Velarde.

Two interesting private collections in the Barranco district are the **Lavalle Collection** (Pedro de Osma 348), with fine pictures by artists of the Cuzco school, and the **Pedro de Osma Collection** (Pedro de Osma 421), with a splendid display of silver.

The **National Museum of Peruvian Culture** (Av. Alfonso Ugarte 650) is mainly devoted to ethnography and folk traditions, but also puts on temporary exhibitions of archaeology and history. It has an important library and publishes a journal.

The **Natural History Museum** (Av. Arenales 1256) is attached to the San Marcos University. It contains varied collections of Peruvian plants, animals and minerals, including the herbarium formed by Antonio Raimondi during his travels in the 19th century. The 18th century chapel of the old San Marcos University, in the Parque Universitario, has been since 1924 a **Pantheon of the Heroes of Independence** (the "Próceres"). The dome is decorated with frescoes by the *indigenista* painter *José Sabogal*.

Those interested in military matters will want to see the **Museum of Military History** in the Real Felipe Fortress (second half of 18th c.) in Callao and the *Naval Museum* in Plaza Graú, Callao (open Mondays, Wednesdays and Fridays, 9 to 12 and 3 to 5).

In the **Casa de la Tradición** (Av. Salaverry 3052), a large mansion with a colonial patio, visitors can see, by arrangement with the owner, a scale model of the Plaza de Armas in Lima as it was in the 19th century (around 1860).

Finally there are two small **bullfighting museums,** one in the *Plaza de Acho* (open Monday–Friday 9 to 1 and 3 to 6, Saturdays 9 to 2), the other the privately owned *Fernando Berkemeyer Museum* (Jirón Conde de Superunda 341: tel. 27 54 31 for an appointment to visit).

SURROUNDINGS OF LIMA

1. Pachacámac

The principal excursion in the surroundings of Lima is to the **sacred city of Pachacámac** ("Lord of the Earth", from *pacha*, "earth", and *camac*, "master"), some 30 km from the capital on the South Panamerican Highway (leave by Av. Javier Prado, Primavera or Benavides and then take the motorway to the southern coastal resorts). This was a very ancient cult centre with a celebrated oracle which was conquered by the Incas in the reign of Pachacuti and converted to the cult of the Sun God. Open 9 to 5; closed Mondays.

The **temple** is a typical example of the huge adobe-brick pyramids of the Coast, in which the Inca structure can be clearly seen to be overlying an earlier temple built of smaller bricks. The Inca temple has a base of dressed stone and walls of clay bricks, with a system of terraces on the west side and spacious esplanades for ceremonies to the east. Below these are the **remains of a town,** partly dating from pre-Inca times, regularly laid out with streets and squares, with the remains of houses, etc. There are traces of various secondary temples, no doubt dedicated to the subsidiary divinities worshipped by the Incas—the moon, the stars, thunder, the rainbow, etc. At the entrance, near a small pine-wood, is the house of the *Mamaconas* (Virgins of the Sun), where girls selected from all over the country for their beauty and accomplishment lived a life of seclusion in the service of the Sun God. This adobe-brick guilding has, unfortunately, recently been restored in concrete.

It was said that the oracle of Pachacámac warned the Incas of the coming of white men to the Andes and foretold the fall of the empire—a prophecy which undoubtedly aided Pizarro and his men to achieve the Conquest. When Atahuallpa was arrested by the Spaniards his ransom came from the fabulous treasure of gold and silver contained in the temple.

To the south of Pachacámac is the village of *Lurín*, with a beautiful colonial church (18th c.).

2. The Bathing Resorts

The motorway to the south provides easy and rapid
access to a series of beautiful bathing beaches, some of
them undeveloped, like *Conchán*, below the sacred city
of Pachacámac, others belonging to private clubs. The
finest lie beyond Pachacámac, at *Punta Hermosa*
(Waikiki Club, with surf-riding, 45 km from Lima),
Punta Negra, Santa Maria and *San Bártolo*. 70 km from
Lima is the picturesque fishing port of **Pucusana,** with
a beautiful beach, two underwater fishing clubs and
good restaurants specialising in fish and seafood.

To the north are the two beautiful resorts of *Ancón*
and *Ventanilla*. They are reached from the centre of
Lima by the North Panamerican Highway (via Av.
Alfonso Ugarte, over the Ejército Bridge, then Av.
Zarumilla and the *barriada* of Comas) or from Callao
by way of Av. del Emisor and, after crossing the Rímac,
the "old road" to Ancón (which joins the Panamerican
Highway in 28 km, soon after Puente de Piedra).

The bathing resort of **Ancón,** 38 km from Lima, was established
in the 1870s during the Presidency of Pedro Balta, and developed
rapidly after it was connected with Lima by rail at the end of the
century. It is now a mingling of beautiful villas and pleasant
sea-front promenades of a distinctly aristocratic air with tall
blocks of very recent construction. There are excellent facilities
for sailing. Ancón is also noted for its archaeological sites,
including in particular a *Chavín cemetery* (1200 B.C.). To the
south of Ancón, 30 km from Lima on the old road, is the very
modern resort of **Ventanilla,** which has been developed since the
1960s. Between these two resorts is **Santa Rosa,** which also has
good bathing and archaeological excavations.

A short distance beyond the Puente del Ejército a road
branches off the Panamerican Highway for *Canta* and continues
over the *Viuda pass* (4760 m) to Cerro de Pasco. This provides
an opportunity of seeing a very beautiful coastal valley, the
Chillón or *Carabayllo* valley, with good hotels at *Santa Rosa de
Quives* (62 km: Hotel Turistas) and *Canta* (102 km, alt. 2832 m:
more modest hotels).

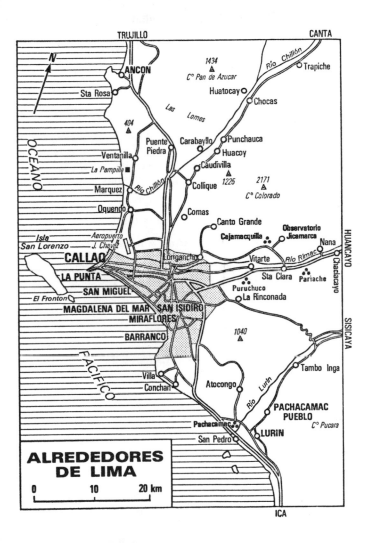

ALREDEDORES DE LIMA

0   10   20 km

3. The Rímac Valley

The *Carretera Central*, running east from Lima, leads up the valley of the Rímac, with its archaeological sites bearing witness to the antiquity of human settlement in the valley and its pleasant holiday resorts on the lower slopes of the Cordillera (alt. 350 to 600 m), above the fogs of the coastal area. Public transport services to Chosica throughout the day from the Parque Universitario.

8 km from Lima, after passing through the *barriadas del Augustino* and a large industrial suburb, we come (on right of road) to the site of **Puruchuco** (in Quechua, "plumed helmet": open 9 to 11.30 and 2.30 to 5; closed Mondays).

This was the residence of a *curaca* (a tribal chieftain and a functionary of the Inca empire); it was restored in 1953. The building is small but of great interest, with its windowless walls of pink adobe bricks, its triangular niches and its labyrinthine plan. In the large entrance courtyard, which has excellent acoustic properties, displays of folk singing and dancing are given on Wednesday evenings. The small *museum* contains very beautiful fabrics, garments adorned with plumes, mummies, pottery, jewellery, weapons and various everyday objects. In an enclosure at the entrance are llamas, alpacas and vicuñas.

In 12.5 km, beyond *Vitarte*, a road goes off on the left (5 km) to the ruins of **Cajamarquilla,** an ancient pre-Inca town (7th c.) of adobe brick.

In 16 km, after passing on the right the famous *Granja Azul* restaurant (roast chicken), we see the remains of **Pariache,** in the Hacienda San Juan. They are similar to the Puruchuco remains, and were restored by the same architect (A. Jiménez Borja).

3 km away, also near the highway, is **Huaicantambo,** the first Inca posting station (*tambo*) on the road from the lower Rímac valley to the Sierra, one day's march from the coast. There are the ruins of a citadel of

labyrinthine plan, with *colqas* (round store-rooms or granaries) and the remains of a town laid out on terraces on the mountain-side.

At Vitarte (alt. 350 m), and sometimes even as early as Puruchuco, we emerge from the fogs of Lima into a region which is sunny and dry throughout the year, providing an agreeable surprise for the visitor. As a result of irrigation the country is very fertile, with many trees (eucalyptuses, willows, figs, flam-boyants, etc.), bougainvilleas, oleanders, etc. On the slopes above are the organ-pipe cactuses characteristic of the *yunga* vegetation zone.

In this area are a number of residential and holiday centres much frequented by the people of Lima, like *Ñana* (22 km from Lima), **Chaclacayo** (30 km, alt. 5670 m) and **Chosica** (42 km, alt. 860 m). In these places are numerous handsome villas, most of them occupied only at weekends and during the winter holidays (the summer being spent on the beaches). With the improvement of road communications with central Lima, however, they are developing into places of permanent residence for commuters. There are a number of very pleasant clubs. At Chaclacayo there is the private El Bosque club, but also the *Huampani* holiday village, run by Enturperú, where visitors can enjoy the facilities offered by its parks, swimming pools and conference halls and can rent comfortable holiday chalets. Chosica was developed at the end of the 19th century round the railway station, and caters for those looking for either an active or a restful holiday with its numerous hotels, guest-houses and convalescent homes (Hotel San Jorge, in the main square, or Villa del Sol, on the other side of the Rímac opposite the station). From Chosica a road runs up the narrow *Santa Eulalia* valley, with attractive villages which grow maize, lucerne to provide fodder for their dairy cattle, and fruit for the Lima market. The scenery is very similar to that found round the Mediterranean, with its terraced fields and low stone walls, its irrigation channels lined with agaves or eucalyptus and its adobe houses with tiled roofs.

# 2.	NORTHERN PERU

Some visitors to Peru, for whom pre-Columbian Peru means only the Inca empire, tend to forget that there were much older cultures in the north, at Chavín in the Ancash mountains, and in the coastal oases, from the Vicus culture which flourished round Piura to the Chimú empire of Chan-Chan (Trujillo). This northern coastal area, extending from Lima to the frontier with Ecuador, a distance of 1325 km, is now Peru's region of greatest economic development, with a number of large and rapidly growing commercial and industrial towns.

1. LIMA TO TRUJILLO

This first stage of the journey to the northern towns (556 km) is covered by the communal taxis (*colectivos*) from Lima in about 7 hours. It follows the Panamerican Highway, which runs through the coastal desert, usually keeping fairly close to the sea. In the more southerly oases cotton is grown, and farther north, beyond Pativilca, sugar-cane. The region's good connections with Lima have recently promoted the development of market gardening and fruit-growing (particularly citrus fruits) and the growing of lucerne as fodder for dairy cattle. The towns in these valleys, with populations of perhaps ten or twenty thousand, are administrative centres and active commercial centres with populations largely engaged in agriculture. Formerly staging points for the mule-borne traffic of the Sierra, they now benefit from their position on the Panamerican Highway. The little harbour towns specialise in the *anchoveta* fisheries and in the manufacture of fish-meal; among them are Chancay, Huacho, Supe, Huarmey and *Chimbote*.

All these little towns, with a population of mixed negro blood, attract the Indians down from the high valleys, and often provide them with a temporary stopping place before they move on to Lima. They are all very similar to one another, with their low houses of cob or interwoven straw, with roof terraces, straggling along both sides of the road.

The first oasis is that of **Chancay,** 75 km from Lima.
Before reaching it the new road goes over an impressive
bridge at *Pasamayo*, on a sandy escarpment rising
300 m above the Pacific and often shrouded in mist.
At the entrance to the oasis is *Boza*, with a thermal
spring.

In this valley, between the 12th and 15th centries, there
flourished an interesting culture which produced large white
pottery jars, often anthropomorphic or zoomorphic in shape,
and a wide variety of very beautiful fabrics, particularly lace
and gauze (to be seen in the Amano Museum, Lima).

The road runs past the two towns in the valley, the harbour
town of *Chancay* and the commercial centre of *Huaral*.

At about km 123 a road goes off on the left to salt-
pans which have been worked since pre-Columbian
times and to *La Yesera* with its thermal springs.

Huacho, at the entrance to the Huaura oasis (140 km
from Lima), was destroyed several times by earthquakes
but has nevertheless preserved a beautiful colonial
church. There is a good hotel. Near the town is the very
picturesque little fishing port of *Carquín*.

The road then runs through **Huaura,** famous for its
pilgrimage to the Virgin of Carmen.

From the balcony of a house in the town General San Martín
proclaimed the independence of Peru in 1821. Visitors can see the
"Liberty Bell", the first to celebrate the occasion.

After a further stretch of desert the road enters the
three oases formed by the rivers Supe, Pativilca and
Fortaleza, which are excellent examples of the historical
and economic development of the northern coastal
oases. The first to be encountered is the *Supe* oasis,
whose port, with its fish-meal factories, illustrates the
economic dynamism of present-day Peru. 9 km beyond
this is *Barranca*, which was a busy commercial centre
in the days when goods travelled on mule-back (i.e.

until the beginning of this century) and is still an important staging point, with numerous restaurants and modest hotels. *Pativilca*, 8 km farther on, is a colonial town with a beautiful church and imposing old houses, in one of which Bolívar stayed for some time when ill. Finally at **Paramonga** is the fortress (or perhaps temple) which marked the southern boundary of the Chimú empire and was besieged by Pachacuti.

With its terraces of adobe brick the fortress looms over the sugar-cane plantations of the large Paramonga cooperative (8000 hectares), formerly a hacienda belonging to the American company of Grace. Adjoining the sugar refinery is a large paper-mill using bagasse (dried cane stalks) from the refinery. Here, 200 km from Lima, a road goes off to the *Callejón de Huaylas* (see next itinerary, p. 143).

Between Pativilca and Huarmey (287 km) the road runs close to the shore, passing many beautiful lonely beaches, usually very easy of access. The *Huarmey* oasis is one of the poorest in the northern coastal region; the town, situated half way between Lima and Trujillo, has a comfortable hotel (limited accommodation). 370 km from Lima is **Casma,** severely damaged by an earthquake in 1970, which controls the second route to the Callejón de Huaylas.

Near Casma are **three pre-Columbian sites** of considerable interest, rarely visited by tourists. The first of these, which is very easily accessible, is **Sechín,** 5 km from Casma in the valley of the same name. The remains consist of five buildings laid out round two plazas, the whole group being surrounded by an adobe wall. The main building is partly in adobe and partly in stone. The latter part of the structure, some 50 m long, is decorated with carvings of warriors surrounded by dead bodies, in a posture which has earned them the name of *danzantes*. The carvings have certain affinities with Chavín, but may belong to an earlier culture.

15 km south-east of Casma, in the valley of the river Casma, are the ruins of **Chanquillo,** also known as the *Castillo de San Rafael*. This curious structure, occupying the summit of a hill,

consists of three concentric rings of walls on an ovoid plan. On the uppermost platform are three small enclosures, two of them rectangular and the third circular, each containing a number of separate rooms. Lower down, on the rim of the plateau, is a row of thirteen square structures aligned towards the east. They are rather crudely built of irregularly shaped stones bound together with mud, though there are remains of a decorative surface coating with anthropomorphic, zoomorphic and geometric patterns on a yellow ground. The purpose of this complex, which is contemporary with the Mochica culture, has not been established with certainty. Some authorities believe it had a defensive function; others see it as having an astronomical purpose, the thirteen "towers" being related to the thirteen months of the lunar calendar.

30 km north of Casma in the Nepeña valley, 8 km off the Panamerican Highway to the right, is the **Huaca de Pañamarca**, the most southerly of the Mochica temples or tombs. It contains astonishing *frescoes* of warriors, unique of their kind, which were discovered only in 1958.

425 km from Lima is the town of **Chimbote** (pop. 160,000), which is of no great tourist interest, although its excellent hotels (particularly the Hotel Chimú) make it a good staging point for travellers.

Nevertheless this is one of the most exciting towns in Peru. Formerly a modest fishing port, with a population of only 4200 in 1940, it was selected in 1958 as the site of the *first iron and steel plant in Peru*, the choice being determined by the presence in the vicinity of a small coalfield and the hydroelectric station at Huallanca on the river Santa. Thereafter the town also developed into *Peru's leading fishing port* and one of the main centres for the manufacture of fish-meal. These developments attracted large numbers of incomers, who built the huge *barriadas* of which the town is largely composed. In his novel "El zorro de arriba, el zorro de abajo" J. M. Arguedas gives an excellent description of the atmosphere of Chimbote, a city full of life and vigour in spite of the unpleasant smells from its factories and the damp air of the surrounding swamps.

There was formerly a railway line from Chimbote to the Callejón de Huaylas, but this was destroyed in the 1970 earthquake.

On the old hacienda of *Guadalupito*, beyond the river Santa (the river with the largest volume of water on the whole Peruvian coast), can be seen the remains of a Mochica irrigation system. Also in the lower Santa valley are the remains of the "Great Wall of Peru", some 50 km long, which dates from the Chimú period. Along its course are a series of town sites, forts and agricultural terraces.

Beyond the Santa there is another stretch of desert extending to Trujillo, with remarkable fields of crescent-shaped dunes. There are two valleys: the *Chao* valley, which is arid and very poor, and the *Virú* valley. At *Virú* (510 km from Lima) is an important archaeological site which has yielded material belonging to the Chavín (Guañape), Saliner (or Virú) and Mochica cultures. **Trujillo:** see p. 158.

2. TO THE CALLEJÓN DE HUAYLAS

The Callejón de Huaylas is the name given to the middle valley of the river Santa, enclosed between the White Cordillera to the north and the Black Cordillera to the south. 150 km long and lying at an altitude ranging from 3800 m to 1800 m, its great attractions are its temperate climate, the beauty of its scenery, set against a background of snow-capped peaks, and its wealth of archaeological remains. It was devastated by the 1970 earthquake and the avalanche of mud and ice which accompanied it, in which 70,000 people lost their lives, but is now the subject of a large-scale rehabilitation and development scheme.

The Callejón de Huaylas can be reached by road, leaving the North Panamerican Highway at Pativilca (196 km from Lima) or Casma (370 km from Lima); the former is recommended. Since 1970 there has also been an airport at Huaraz, the chief town in the valley, and there is an older airport at Caraz (daily connections with Lima). The railway line from Huallanca, below Caraz, to Chimbote was destroyed in the 1970 earthquake.

From Pativilca the road (not asphalted but in good condition) runs up the valley of the Fortaleza. As it

climbs out of the coastal desert it enters the semi-
desertic *yunga* zone, then the Quechua zone (here
much narrower than elsewhere) and finally the *puna*.
56 km from Pativilca is *Chasquitambo*, once an Inca
posting station (restaurants). After Cajacay (98 km)
the road goes over a pass (4080 m) and then runs down
to the *Conococha Lagoon*, in which the river Santa
rises. A road goes off on the right to the village of
Chiquián (32 km), at the foot of the beautiful *Huay-
huash Cordillera*, little visited by tourists. The road to
Huaraz runs north down the Santa valley, passing
through a wide depression with a landscape pattern
characteristic of high-altitude tundra, to which the
peasants of the middle Santa bring their herds every
year during the rainy season. At *Catac*, 50 km beyond
the lagoon (180 km from Pativilca), a road goes off to
Huari and the site of Chavín de Huantar, described
below (p. 147). Near the village is an important pre-
Inca excavation site.

Recuay (alt. 3400 m) is the first village in the valley,
with a few modest hotels and restaurants. It has given
its name to a culture characterised by white or red
pottery and large stone statues.

28 km down the valley is **Huaraz,** chief town of the
departamento of Ancash (218 km from Pativilca, 156
km from Casma, 417 km from Lima). Situated at an
altitude of 3060 m, it had until 1970 the typical aspect
of the little Sierra towns founded by the Spaniards,
with its regular plan, its narrow streets, its whitewashed houses with blue-painted shutters and balconies and its imposing *Cathedral*. After being damaged
by an avalanche of mud in 1945 it was half destroyed
in the 1970 earthquake, in which some 20,000 people
were killed.

The **Archaeological Museum** is one of the most interesting and attractive in Peru, noted in particular for its collection of *carved monoliths* and material belonging to the Chavín culture.

Near the town can be seen the remains of the *Pumakayan* temple.

Huaraz is the starting point for climbs in the White Cordillera, in particular the ascent of Huascarán. Advice and information can be obtained locally, or from the Club Andinista Cordillera Blanca (Nicholás Alcázar 256, Pueblo Libre, Lima) or the Club Andino Peruano (Casilla 1963, Lima).

7 km below Huaraz is *Monterrey*, a considerable holiday resort with a thermal spring and an excellent hotel. Near Mancara is *Chancos*, where there is another thermal spring; but although it is beautifully situated it is too far from the main road and inadequately equipped to cater for visitors. The Chancos road continues to a hacienda, *Vicos*, formerly belonging to the Huaraz Public Assistance Department, where an important anthropological programme was carried through in the 1960s.

Carhuaz, 34 km from Huaraz at the foot of Hualcan (6125 m), has a number of inns. Shortly before coming to Yungay the road passes between the huge blocks of stone brought down by the avalanche which submerged the village of Ranrahirca in 1962, causing 5000 deaths. In 1970 the town of **Yungay** itself, with 20,000 inhabitants, was completely destroyed by another avalanche set off by an earthquake.

Yungay was one of the most attractive towns in Peru, with its colonial houses, its agreeable climate (alt. 2500 m) and the striking contrast between the palms in its Plaza de Armas and the twin snow-capped peaks of Huascarán, Peru's highest mountain, towering over the town. Now only the tops of the palm-trees emerge from the mud, providing landmarks for the setting up of the thousands of crosses which mark the position of the vanished houses.

3 km from the main road a track suitable for motor vehicles goes off to (26 km) the two lagoons of *Llanganuco*, of glacial origin, situated at altitudes of 3600 m and 3850 m, with a fine forest of *geñoas* and magnificent views of the glaciers of the White Cordillera — Huandoy (eastern peak 6160 m) to the north, Huascarán to the south, with Chacraraju and Chopicalqui

behind it rising to over 6000 m. The track continues over a pass (4767 m) to *Piscobamba* on the eastern slopes of the cordillera.

Caraz, 16 km beyond Yungay, also suffered severe damage in the 1970 earthquake. From here there are fairly difficult climbs on a nearby mountain, Tunaspampa, from which, at an altitude of 3200 m, there is a splendid panoramic view of the northern mountain chain, particularly towards the *Parón* lagoon (4185 m).

North of Caraz is the *Cañón del Pato*, at the far end of which are the *Huallanca* hydroelectric station (113 km from Huaraz; alt. 1382 m) and the railway which before the 1970 earthquake ran from this little town to Chimbote, on the coast. There is also a track off on the right to *Corongo*, continuing via Sihuas and Pomabamba to Piscobamba, on the Amazonian slopes of the mountains.

There is also a *road from Huaraz to Casma* (156 km, c. 5–6 hours) through the **Black Cordillera** (so called because it has no snow or glaciers).

From the first bends in the road there are fine views of the valley and the peaks in the White Cordillera, particularly Huantsán. The fields of barley and potatoes extend up the mountainside to a height of almost 4000 m. Near the *Punta Callán* pass (4225 m) note the round herdsmen's huts, built of stone with conical thatched roofs. The road then runs down the ravine of the river Casma on the Pacific side of the range, with many steep and dangerous stretches. From *Yautan* (40 km before Casma) there is a tarred surface.

The Callejón de Huaylas was one of the earliest parts of Peru to be settled. As a result of the differences of altitude there is scope for growing and exchanging crops appropriate to cold, temperate and even, in the Yungay-Caraz area, tropical climates; and water is abundant everywhere. All too often, however, death and devastation have been caused in the valley by terrible avalanches. The contrast between large estates and small farm holdings was very marked in this area, and there were frequent peasant revolts, as at Atusparia in 1885. Emigration, which in earlier times had occurred on a temporary basis for the collecting of guano on the Coast, took place on a massive scale in the first half of this century, and increased still further from 1950 onwards, with the development of Chimbote and the activities connected with fishing and commerce. The *departamento* of Ancash thus has one of the highest rates of movement away from the land in the Peruvian Sierra.

Chavín de Huantar

Chavín de Huantar is on the road from *Catac* (180 km from Pativilca) to *Huari*. This road runs alongside the Qeros lagoon and cuts through the White Cordillera in the *Kawish Tunnel* at an altitude of 6700 m. The village of *Chavín* (pop. 1600) lies 104 km from Huaraz (c. 3 hours by car) at 3180 m. There are daily services by bus, lorry and taxi from Huaraz. Pending the construction of more comfortable accommodation there are two or three modest hotels and restaurants.

The **ruins of the temple** are 200 m from the village, near the river Mosna, a tributary of the Marañón. The first excavations were carried out by the Peruvian archaeologist J. C. Tello in 1919 and subsequent years, and the exploration of the site is still

1 Grand Plaza (500–200 B.C.?)
2 North Platform
3 Alba Staircase
4 South Platform (500–200 B.C.?)
5 Altar of Choqe Chinchay
6 Jaguar Staircase
7 Atrium of the Stone Slabs
8 Great Pyramid (500–200 B.C.?)
9 Portico of the Falconidae
10 *Cabeza-clave* in situ
11 Gallery of the Doorway
12 Gallery of the Double Bracket
13 Gallery of the Columns
14 Gallery of the Decorated Beams
15 Gallery of the Carved Stones
16 Gallery of the Captives
17 Gallery of the Bats
18 Gallery of the Niches
19 Temple of the Lanzón (1500–1000 B.C.)
20 Atrium of temple
21 Gallery of the Lanzón
22 Gallery of the Labyrinths
23 Gallery of the Madman
24 Gallery of the Offerings
25 Gallery of the Rocks
26 North Pyramid (beginning of Christian era?)

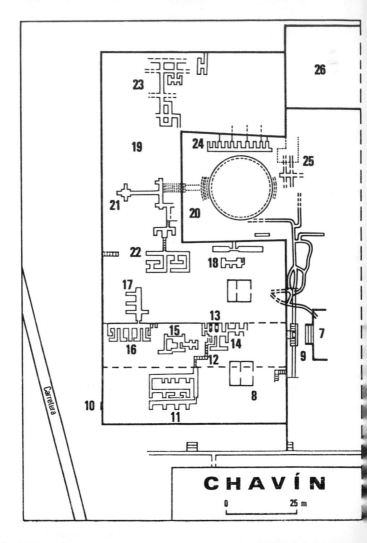

CHAVÍN

0   25 m

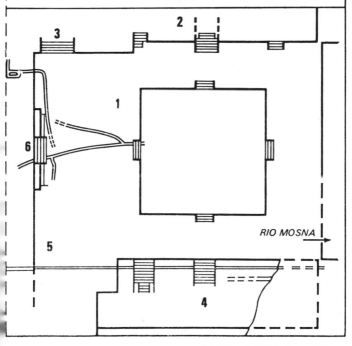

1 Grande Place (500-200 avant J.-C. ?)
2 Plateforme Nord
3 Escalier Alba
4 Plateforme Sud (500-200 avant J.-C ?)
5 Autel de Choque Chinchay
6 Escalier des Jaguars
7 Atrium des Dalles
8 Grande Pyramide (500-200 avant J.-C. ?)
9 Portique des Falconidés
10 Cabeza-clave in situ
11 Galerie de la Portada
12 Galerie de la doble mensula
13 Galerie des Colonnes
14 Galerie de las vignas ornamentales
15 Galerie des pierres sculptées
16 Galerie des captifs
17 Galerie des chauves-souris
18 Galerie des Alacenas
19 Temple du Lanzon (1500-1000 avant J.-C. ?)
20 Atrium du Temple
21 Galerie du Lanzon
22 Galerie des Labyrinthes
23 Galerie « du fou »
24 Galerie des Offrandes
25 Galerie des roches
26 Pyramide Nord (début de notre ère ?)

RIO MOSNA

Legend in English : see page 147

by no means complete. Work was interrupted in 1945 by a large flow of mud which partly covered the remains. The excavations have revealed a culture dating from about 1000–1200 years before Christ whose sphere of influence seems to have extended to Ayacucho and Ica in the south and Piura and Cajamarca in the north. Two alternative derivations have been suggested for the name Chavín—either from the Quechua *chawpin* ("middle, centre") or the Carib *chavi*, meaning a feline (lion or tiger).

On the site as we see it today it is possible to distinguish structures belonging to later cultures overlying the specifically Chavín remains. The chronology of the site can be followed without difficulty in the atrium of the Temple of the Lanzón, near the archaeologists' encampment. Under the black earth left by the 1945 flood can be seen fragments of pottery and the remains of simple rustic dwellings belonging to the Callejón de Huaylas culture, set in brown earth. Below this, in soft red earth, are the *Mariash culture* and the *Huaraz culture*, which is comparable with the culture evidenced in the temple at Pumakayan, near Huaraz. The northern pyramid of the temple seems to have belonged to this culture. Finally, in red earth of rather harder consistency, there are the remains of buildings belonging to the *Chavín culture*, completely demolished, and the remains of temples. The temples seem to have been destroyed, although we do not know by whom or in what circumstances. The Chavín culture itself appears to have gone through four phases, corresponding to different stages in the building of the temples.

The tour of the site can most conveniently start from the archaeologists' encampment, going east towards the river Mosna.

The first feature encountered is the **Main Plaza** in which the pilgrims gathered. It is square, measuring about 50 m each way, and is on two levels, linked by four steps. It is bounded on the north, south and west sides by massive platforms; the platform on the east side has been destroyed by the erosional action of the river Mosna, which has also caused much damage to the south terrace. The *North Platform* is the largest, and apparently the oldest. It has four staircases, the

best preserved of which, the *Alba Staircase*, is the one
farthest from the river.

In the south-west corner of the Main Plaza was found the
Tello Obelisk, evidently reflecting a cult of the celestial gods,
which was sent in 1919 to the archaeological museum of the San
Marcos University. The obelisk stood near the *Altar of Choqe
Chinchay* ("Altar of the Seven Kids"), a flat-topped rock with
seven cavities in the upper surface arranged in the pattern of
the stars in the constellation of Orion, and at the same time
representing the feline which is characteristic of the Chavín
culture.

The *East Platform*, which serves as the base of the
Great Pyramid, is reached from the Grand Plaza by
the **Jaguar Staircase.** This led up to a portico, the
columns and lintels of which were decorated with
jaguars, but nothing of all this is left but a few carved
stones and a much dilapidated cylindrical column. The
staircase is formed of white stones on the south side
and black ones on the north side.

This alternation of colour is found also in the small
courtyard in front of the pyramid, called the *Atrium
of the Stone Slabs* (Atrio de las Lápidas) on account
of the large slabs which surround it on the north, south
and west sides. These slabs seem to have supported
another course of carved stones, some fragments of
which were found in the courtyard; they are now to be
seen in the galleries of the Temple of the Lanzón. They
represent anthropomorphic beings, birds and various
stylised animals.

From the courtyard we approach the **Great Pyramid**
(sometimes called the Castillo de Chavín), which stands
some 10 m high, with a square base measuring 70 m
each way. The three stages of construction of the
temple can be clearly distinguished. To the north (the
visitor's right) there is a sharp break between an older
building, the Temple of the Lanzón, and a more

recent structure which ends at the central portico. The break is made more evident by the staircases and an area of collapse in the upper part. The southern part of the pyramid (to the left of the central portico) is more recent, belonging to the third building phase. The front of the pyramid has a blind portico with staircases on either side leading to two upper landings surrounded by carefully dressed slabs of stone which from below look like windows. From these landings other staircases lead up to the top of the pyramid.

The **Portico of the Falconidae** has recently been rebuilt. Preceded by black and white steps, it consists of two cylindrical columns of black stone supporting a lintel of black and white stone. The columns are carved with various stylised birds of the falcon family (in Spanish and Quechua, *halcón huamán, cernicalo killincho, gavilán anka*). The lintel is also carved with falcons, seven of them looking north and seven south. (The best time to visit the temple is in the morning, when the sun is in the right position for seeing the carvings). On either side of the portico are *large square stone slabs*, again showing the alternation of colour characteristic of the temple—seven white ones (very well preserved) on the south side, seven black ones (unfortunately incomplete) on the north side. As in the atrium of the temple, there seems to have been an upper row of carved stones protecting the internal staircases. The number seven, like the alternation of black and white, seems to have had a magical significance.

The final element in the decoration of the façade of the pyramid was a row of **cabezas-claves** (carved stone heads set into the wall along the top. In these heads human characteristics are mingled with feline elements (muzzle, fangs) and with serpents writhing in the hair or on the cheeks. This row of heads was probably surmounted by a cornice decorated with carved birds. Only one example of the *cabezas-claves* is left in situ at the southwest corner, with a head very different from the others; the other remnants of the frieze are badly dilapidated and barely identifiable.

The structure of the pyramid can best be seen by walking round the south side. It is built up of a mass of small irregularly shaped stones and earth, only the visible parts being faced with dressed stone laid in horizontal courses. The later parts of the structure have two courses of smaller stones alternating with one course of large blocks, some of which are as much as 3 m long and 60 cm thick. The stones are bound together by a kind of coarse mortar made of pebbles (*pachilla*). On the south side of the pyramid are various platforms and passages which are at present being excavated.

The **top of the pyramid** can most conveniently be reached from the south-west corner. Here there are two platforms, one 2 m higher than the other. On the upper platform are the bases of two quadrangular buildings, which seem to have been at the top of the two staircases flanking the portico. From this point there is an excellent general *view* of the whole temple. The platforms give access to the *internal galleries*—a complex network of corridors, cells and staircases built at different periods and on different levels, only some of which can be entered. (In most of these there are electric lights which the keeper will switch on if requested, but visitors may find it useful to carry a torch or candles).

At the south-west corner of the pyramid we enter the **Gallery of the Doorway** (Portada), which seems to have been the main entrance to the temple from the south front. It has a trapezoidal doorway of accurately dressed stone.

From here a small staircase leads up to the *Gallery of the Double Bracket* (Doble Ménsula), running north and south. This belongs to the third building period, with rather roughly dressed and coursed stones. At a higher level is another corridor running from east to west, with four cells opening off it on the south side. There are similar cells, of unknown function, in part of the Gallery of the Doorway. Note in this corridor the system of rectangular tubes providing ventilation between the different galleries and between the galleries and the south and west fronts of the pyramid.

To the east of the Gallery of the Doorway is the *Gallery of the Columns* (second building period), the roof of which is supported by four cylindrical columns of stone and adobe. The line of cells in this corridor is interrupted by a roof fall, and in order to reach the eastern end, in which is the **Gallery of the Decorated Beams** (Vigas Ornamentales), it is necessary to go round the outside. In this last gallery are fine carvings, mainly of fish and crayfish, with traces of polychrome painting.

On the north side of this gallery the difference between the first two building stages can be clearly distinguished. To the second stage belong also the *Gallery of the Carved Stones*, to the west, and the *Gallery of the Captives*, built against the south front of the older temple. The Gallery of the Captives—a name which reflects a local tradition about its function—has stone projections in the upper part of the walls and seven cells, four of them L-shaped, on the south side. In this gallery an obelisk carved with geometric designs was found in 1956. From here a doorway and staircase on the north side lead into the *Gallery of the Bats* (first building period), a high corridor in an excellent state of preservation with three cells on the west side and one on the east side. Finally in the north-east corner of the pyramid is the small *Gallery of the Niches* (Alacenas), very difficult of access, in which various objects, apparently offerings, were found.

The Great Pyramid is merely the south wing, the last part to be built, of the **Temple of the Lanzón,** which is U-shaped, with the open end to the east. In front of the entrance is a small atrium bounded by well built walls, in which many carved heads and engraved stones were found.

The temple seems to have been formed of a number of platforms. A central staircase leads up to the *Gallery of the Lanzón*, access to which presents no difficulties. A short vestibule running north and south, with two cells in the west wall, leads into a corridor in the centre of which is the **"Lanzón"**. This is a monolith of blackish stone 4.53 m high, in the form of a knife with the point stuck into the ground and the edge facing east.

The Lanzón represents an anthropomorphic divinity with feline attributes. It stands looking towards the east, with the right arm raised to shoulder height and the right hand level with the forehead, and the left arm hanging down its side. The handle of the knife rests on the figure's head. Its hair is in the form of writhing serpents, and from the mouth emerge two curved fangs; the ends of the lips are turned up in what appears to b expression of wrath. The divinity wears ear-rings, a necklace and bracelets, and is dressed in a fringed garment with a belt from the back of which two serpents are suspended. The figure stands in a cruciform cell with three apse-like recesses which seem originally to have had an upper level.

The Temple of the Lanzón contains a number of **underground chambers.** The one on the south side, known as the *Gallery of the Labyrinths,* has a vestibule containing three cells, the most southerly of which opens into a staircase and a system of corridors in the shape of the letter G. Also on the south side, in the wall of the main pyramid, can be seen the entrance to another gallery, much dilapidated, with a staircase leading up to the top of the temple. On the walls of this gallery are fragments of a mud coating and of red colouring: the interior walls seem to have been covered with several coats of fine mud to a depth of 8 cm and painted in red, yellow and other colours. In the north wing of the temple is the *Gallery of the Madman,* a maze of corridors and cells. Under the courtyard is the *Gallery of the Offerings,* running from east to west, with nine cells in the north wall. In this gallery, which appears to be later than the temple (750 B.C.), were found large quantities of pottery and bone and stone objects, all broken. Finally, in the north-east corner of the courtyard, there is the *Gallery of the Rocks,* the oldest part of the structure (1200 B.C.), built of rough angular boulders. In this gallery also broken pottery was found, mingled with animal bones. The *Gallery of the Cobblestones,* which runs across the central plaza, dates from the same period. Traces of other underground structures have been found, extending as far as the village of Chavín.

3. TRUJILLO

Like Cuzco, Trujillo preserves evidence of a history reaching far back into the past, with the remains of the important pre-Columbian city of Chan-Chan and a sumptuous heritage of colonial buildings. It is now also a busy industrial and commercial city.

Archaeological Sites in the Area: Chan-Chan

The antiquity of human settlement in this area is demonstrated by a number of archaeological sites in the valleys of the Moche (Santa Catalina valley) and the Chicama, north of Trujillo.

The oldest of these sites (1200 B.C.) appears to be the **Huaca de los Reyes,** on the Hacienda Laredo to the east of the town, which shows Chavín influence. This is a U-shaped temple with large patios for the performance of ceremonies, decorated with friezes of felines in adobe or stone and carved figures of birds with the remains of red and white colouring.

The 3rd century B.C. saw the rise of the Mochica culture, centred on **Moche,** whose influence extended to Jequetepeque in the north and the Nepeña valley in the south. It is noted for its pottery, fine examples of which can be seen in the Archaeological Museum of Trujillo University (Calle Bolívar), and for the *Huaca del Sol* and *Huaca de la Luna* at Moche. These are funerary structures in the form of huge rectangular truncated pyramids of adobe brick. The Huaca del Sol is 48 m high, 228 m long and 135 m wide, the Huaca de la Luna 27 m high and 80 m long. On the large open space between the two pyramids and in the immediate surroundings the remains of houses were found.

For visitors interested in economic matters the Moche valley is an excellent example of a coastal oasis showing the contrast between the *latifundio* or large estate, here represented by the Hacienda Laredo (8000 hectares), which is now a cooperative, and the *minifundio*, the small peasant holdings worked by the Indian community of Moche. (Moche can be reached by frequent bus and taxi services).

In the 6th century the Mochica culture gave place to one centred on Tiahuanaco, and this in turn was succeeded, about the 12th century, by the Chimú empire, which was conquered by the Incas shortly before the arrival of the Spaniards.

Chan-Chan, capital of the Chimú empire, is a huge city of adobe brick covering an area of some 20 sq. km. It can be reached by bus or taxi (services to Huanchaco), and visitors flying to Trujillo can see it from the air. Some estimates put its population at 50,000, others at 300,000. The Spaniards found it practically abandoned and much dilapidated, following its capture by the Incas about the year 1470 after nearly three centuries of existence. Thereafter its destruction proceeded apace, largely as a result of the activities of treasure-hunters looking for gold and other valuables. The heavy rain-storms which periodically ravage the northern coastal region, and which were particularly violent in 1925, have also contributed to the devastation of the site. Nine "palaces" or "citadels" have been identified, with a rôle which was largely ceremonial and administrative. The restored Ciudadela Tschudi gives some idea of what its architecture was like.

Each citadel is surrounded by an adobe wall some 10 m high and separated from its neighbour by a distance of 200 or 300 metres. There is only one entrance, leading into a spacious walled *plaza* for political or religious gatherings. Adjoining the plaza is a *ceremonial hall* with an altar for idols. Then come a series of small **shrines,** all on the same plan—a rectangular chamber containing an altar with six cavities for idols. The decoration of the plaza and the shrines is on marine themes: stylised pelicans, *guanays* (*piqueros*), at rest, flying or sleeping, fishes and fishing nets (of three types, with square, round or diamond-shaped meshes). In one of the shrines are 29 circles, apparently representing the lunar cycle. Everywhere there are lines symbolising waves.

On the inner surface of the wall round the plaza there are representations of the popular *ansumo*, a marine animal resembling an otter, while the outside of the wall has a handsome decorative scheme made up of *guanays*, waves and fishes. All these figures are shaped without the use of a mould. Here and there can be seen traces of firing in the form of black polished patches, produced by the application of red-hot stones to the wall. In the walls built of adobe brick, and not merely puddled mud, can be seen the remains of carob-wood columns. The shrines were roofed with reeds or bamboos covered with mud.

Beyond the shrines is a *second plaza*, followed by a *water tank* faced with stone, originally some 10 m deep but now partly filled with sand. Each citadel also contains a number of wells, totalling 125 in the city as a whole. After the water tank comes the **burial ground,** surrounded by a wall of black stone and containing some 40 tombs, apparently belonging to nobles. Some of these tombs are of mausoleum type; others show a curious structure, built up in a huge mass of stones and mud which remained in place without support after the mummies were removed, the cavities having been filled with an accumulation of sea sand.

Near the burial ground is an area occupied by *dwellings* of rather primitive type, perhaps for servants. Then, returning towards the plaza, we come to a *military area*, with rooms for storing weapons and barrack rooms for troops. Beyond this are *craftmen's workshops*, mainly metal-workers and particularly goldsmiths, followed by granaries. Near another area occupied by dwellings of rather better quality is an *assembly hall*, containing a number of small separate apartments or boxes with an interesting acoustic system consisting of large bamboo stems which reflect the sound from the roof.

The whole of the citadel is like a labyrinth, with numerous corridors, some of which are blind alleys. The doorways of adjoining rooms are offset so that they are not opposite one another, and the main entrance is offset in relation to the door-way leading into the plaza. There are no staircases, access from one level to another being by ramps.

Another Chimú site, the *Huaca la Esmeralda*, can be seen on the El Cortijo farming cooperative, just outside Trujillo on the Chan-Chan road. 5 km from the town, on the bus route to La Esperanza, is the *Huaca del Dragón*, with anthropomorphic figures and a representation of an animal resembling a gigantic millipede (*cienpiés*); there is an interesting museum.

Trujillo: the Town

The Spanish town of **Trujillo** was first founded by Martín de Estete on 5 December 1534 and re-founded on 5 March 1535 by Pizarro, who named it after his native town in Spain. Like most of the coastal towns, it was founded a short distance (7 km) from the sea, half way between Piura, the first Spanish foundation, and Lima. The establishment of a bishopric here, followed in 1627 by a Jesuit college and later by a university, made Trujillo a centre for the evangelisation of the whole of northern Peru, including Amazonia.

In colonial times the town's prosperity depended on the growing of wheat and sugar-cane, which were exported to Lima in the south and to Colombia, Venezuela and Central America in the north. Large haciendas were now established in the Moche and Chicama valleys. Trujillo attained its highest degree of prosperity in the second half of the 17th and the early 18th century. Like Lima, it was compelled to surround itself with walls in the 17th century as a protection against pirates. Unusually, these were laid out on an octagonal plan, and in consequence the expansion of the town took place on a concentric pattern, unlike other colonial towns with their grid layout. Remains of the walls can be seen in Av. España, four or five blocks from the Piazza de Armas.

Until about 1940 the town grew very slowly. It was mainly an administrative and religious centre and the residence of large landowners, giving it the aristocratic air which it still preserves. Its economy was centred on the large sugar plantations, and it was here that APRA came into being around 1920 — the "American Revolutionary Alliance" which was to play such a considerable part in the trade union activities of the northern coastal region. APRA's struggle against the army led to a confrontation in 1932 during which 5000 people were killed in the town.

After 1940 Trujillo benefited from the development of sugar-cane growing which followed the concentration and modernisation of the plantations and the increase in sugar exports. It also benefited from the construction of a road into the Sierra and the development of the harbour at *Salaverry* (1964), which enabled it to become a very active commercial centre — witness its market and busy streets like Calle Pizarro and Calle Gamarra. Although the industries based on agriculture are still mostly on the haciendas, a number of factories have been established in the town to cater for the increasing urban market (a flour-mill, a plant producing aerated waters, a brewery, fruit and fish canning plants). More recently the metal-working and engineering industries have also come to Trujillo, looking forward to an association with the iron and steel works at Chimbote. In line with the policy of decentralising industry an industrial zone has been established outside the town, with a tractor and car assembly plant. The population of the town, which was only 37,000 in 1940, has now risen to 242,000.

Like all the coastal towns, Trujillo is a city of low buildings, with a few 5- or 6-storey blocks in the centre, many of them modern hotels (the *Opt Gar*, the *San Martín*, the *San Antonio*, the *Premier*).

The **Plaza de Armas** is the largest in Peru. In this square, shaded by a clump of palm-trees, is an imposing *Monument to Liberty and the Heroes of Independence*, the work of a German sculptor, erected in 1929.

Plaques commemorating the various battles in the struggle for independence are surrounded by statues symbolising Art, Science, Commerce and Health (below) and the Depression, Action and Liberation (above), and above this, on a column, is a figure representing Youth perched on a sphere and brandishing a torch.

Unlike the central squares of most colonial towns, Trujillo's Plaza de Armas has no arcades round the sides. The house fronts are painted in bright colours, a mingling of ochre, purplish red, Prussian blue and white.

At the north corner of the square is the **Cathedral,** with white roughcast walls, preceded by a large open space. After suffering damage in earthquakes in 1619 and 1635 it was rebuilt in 1666, once again almost completely destroyed in 1759 and again rebuilt between 1768 and 1781.

The Cathedral is a huge and rather cold three-aisled building. The altar, consisting of a small gilded table, is situated in the centre of the choir of carved wood, with a central pulpit. On either side are imposing **reredoses** of gilded wood dedicated to the Virgin (three), St Peter, St John the Baptist, the Passion and Santa Rosa. Some of them have paintings by Quito artists. The four large *pictures* in the nave are 19th century; the glass is

---

A Piazza de Armas
1 Cathedral
1B Hotel Turistas
2 Casa Bracamonte
3 Casa Urquiaga
4 Municipality
5 Casa del Mayorazgo
6 Casa Orbegoso
7 San Francisco
8 Casa Ganozza
9 Santa Clara
10 Convento del Carmen
11 Casa Iturregui
12 La Merced
13 Santo Domingo

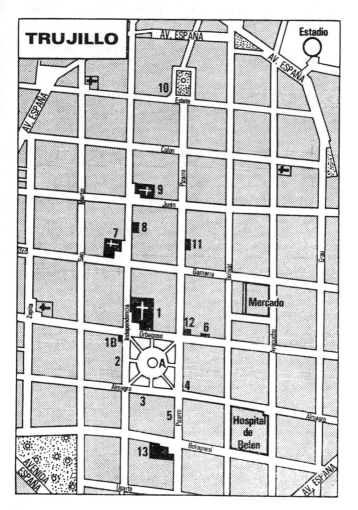

modern. The most interesting chapel is the *Capilla del Sagrario*, to the right of the entrance, with a gilded reredos and a screen of turned wood.

Round the Plaza de Armas are a number of interesting colonial houses. In the **Casa Urquiaga,** now occupied by the Banco Central de Reserva, Bolívar is said to have stayed; his office is shown to visitors. It contains a fine collection of colonial furniture and pre-Columbian pottery. The **Casa Bracamonte** (restored by the Banco Central Hipotecario, which now occupies it) is one of the finest mansions in Trujillo, with a handsome carved wooden door and windows protected by iron grilles. Its patio, of typically Trujillian type, is surrounded by a double gallery topped by the iron railing round the roof terrace. The galleries are high, with fine Greco-Roman columns, coffered ceilings and wide staircases leading up to them. The rooms contain beautiful colonial furniture. To the rear of the house is a garden, in which is a well. The *Archbishop's Palace*, also in the Plaza de Armas, has a patio decorated with blue ceramic tiles; the *Municipality* and *Prefecture* are 19th century buildings.

There are a number of other **colonial houses** worth seeing. The *Casa del Mayorazgo* (between Calle Pizarro and Bolognesi), built by Don Pedro de Tinoco, founder of the *mayorazgo* (entailed estate) of Facalá, at the end of the 16th century, has a main patio with Corinthian columns of wood and an L-shaped gallery; the interior contains a number of large rooms with carved or coffered ceilings. The *Casa Orbegoso* (5th block, Calle Orbegoso: owner's permission required for visit) has a very beautiful patio with wooden lattices and galleries (17th c.). The *Casa Ganozza* (6th block, Calle Independencia), built in the 18th century, has a street front with a portico in the Tuscan order and oriel windows barred with iron grilles. The *Casa de los Condes de Aranda*, in Plaza Iquitos, has a very handsome entrance.

The **Casa Iturregui,** built in 1855, is a fine example of the neo-colonial or neo-classical style. It now houses the Central Club.

The main front has Ionic pilasters on the ground floor, Corinthian pilasters on the first floor and corbelled balconies with wrought-iron grilles. The first patio is surrounded by two tiers of high galleries, offering a striking colour contrast between the white of the Corinthian columns and grilles and the brown hue of the ceilings and walls. The second patio is built of ochre-coloured stone, with a terraced gallery supported on Ionic columns, and Greek statues in the corners. The third patio contains a fountain basin surrounded by flowers. Note the beautiful paving of the patios. The large rooms in the interior contain colonial and Republican furniture.

The two most interesting churches in Trujillo are San Francisco and the Convento del Carmen. The **church of San Francisco** (3rd block, Calle Independencia), built in 1536, was destroyed in 1759 and rebuilt at the end of the 18th century. After suffering severe earthquake damage in 1970 it is now in course of restoration. Huge Baroque *reredoses*, including some of gilded wood; central altar with twisted columns; 18th century *pulpit* of gilded wood.

The **Convento del Carmen** (Calle Pizarro) also suffered severe damage in the 1970 earthquake and is not at present open to visitors. It is the finest example of 18th century architecture in northern Peru. The church has an aisleless nave surmounted by a dome. The central altar is Baroque, the pulpit Churrigueresque. The first cloister is of brick with a timber roof; the second has wooden columns with Corinthian capitals. The monastery contains a *rich collection* of paintings, sculpture, furniture and religious objects.

The **church of La Merced** (5th block, Calle Pizarro) is 17th century, with three doorways in the Renaissance, neo-classical and Baroque styles. The paintings in the dome relate the life of the founder of the Mercedarian order, San Pedro Nolasco. There is a Rococo organ.

Santo Domingo (3rd block, Calle Pizarro), *San Agustín* (5th block, Calle Bolívar), completed 1580–85, *Santa Clara* and the *Compañía* church contain gilded reredoses and interesting pictures. *Santa Ana* and *San Lorenzo* were the parish churches of the Indian population in colonial times; the former is the oldest church in the town. The *Belén* church (Calle Almagro) has a brick front with rather naive statues of the Virgin, St Joseph and the Infant Jesus; it contains interesting paintings of the Presentation in the Temple and the Circumcision.

Trujillo has two **bathing beaches.** The *Buenos Aires* bathing station is nearer the town (4 km: restaurants specialising in seafood), but the one at *Huanchaco* is more picturesque, with its fishing harbour, where the little reed boats ("*caballitos de totora*") used by the Chimú people can still be seen, and its colonial church. The recently developed port of *Salaverry* is devoted almost exclusively to the export of sugar and the import of certain goods for Trujillo.

To the north-east, in the Sierra, are two holiday and recreational resorts: *Coinas* (alt. 1500 m), which offers trout-fishing and shooting, and *Shirán*, 35 km away, the Chosica of Trujillo.

Entertainment facilities in Trujillo include five cinemas, three discotheques, a *coliseo* used for cockfighting and folk dancing displays, a stadium and an excellent swimming pool. The principal fiesta, in honour of the spring, takes place from 22 to 30 September, but this is entirely modern in character and atmosphere, and visitors may prefer the national *marinera* (dance) competition in January, the Huanchaco carnival in February and—rather farther away—the regional fairs at Santiago de Chuco (25 July to 1 August) and Guadalupe (8–9 December).

4. TRUJILLO TO CHICLAYO

On leaving Trujillo the North Panamerican Highway runs along the foot of the famous *Cerro Campana*, the characteristic shape of which is reproduced in Mochica pottery. In Chimú times there was a canal here (*Canal de la Cumbre*) which carried the water of the Chicama to Chan-Chan. The canal, which was 75 km long and went over a pass at a height of 180 m, shows the antiquity of the connection between the Chicama and Moche valleys which was of such significance for the development of Trujillo. The Chicama valley is occupied by sugar-cane plantations with their associated refineries, which can be visited.

To the right of the highway extends the huge estate of *Casa Grande* 28,900 hectares), the largest sugar-cane plantation in South America. On the Pacific side are *Cartavio* (5400 hectares), which formerly belonged to the owners of the Paramonga plantation and is now the most modern, with its own paper-mill; *Chiclín* (5270 hectares); and *Chiquitoy* (27,000 hectares). Small side roads, for the most part asphalted, go off to the villages of *Santiago de Cao* and *Magdalena de Cao*, peasant communities whose lands were steadily whittled away by the *latifundia*. After the Indian community of Paiján another side road goes off on the left to *Puerto Chicama*, at the foot of the Cerro Malabrigo, formerly a private harbour belonging to the Casa Grande estate and now a popular surfing centre.

The road then runs through a further stretch of desert before arriving in the Jequetepeque valley, where rice and cotton are grown as well as sugar-cane. It then passes through a number of townships which owe their origin to the *reducciones* of the colonial period, like *Jequetepeque* and *Chepén*, and "villages of Spaniards" like *San Pedro de Lloc*, with its remains of walls, and **Guadalupe.**

Guadalupe (where the *colectivos* like to stop for lunch) has a beautiful colonial church and old two-storey town houses, and is noted for a fair held on 8 December, the feast of the Virgin of Guadalupe. A country road runs to the remains of *Pacatnamu*, a few kilometres away, which was an important religious centre in Chimú and even in Mochica times. Also in the Jequetepeque valley is the archaeological site of *Cupisnique*, with pottery similar to that of Chavín.

Pacasmayo, on the coast 107 km from Trujillo, is both a fishing port and a commercial port, mainly serving the *departamento* of Cajamarca, with which it is connected by a road up the Jequetepeque valley. Cement factory. There is a comfortable hotel, the *Ferrocarril* (named after the little railway line built by

Henry Meiggs in 1875, leading to Chilete and to the lead and zinc mines in the Jequetepeque valley, 88 km away).

The next oasis is **Saña**, in the *departamento* of Lambayeque. The road runs through *Mocupe*, a large farming township which now overshadows the old colonial settlement of Saña, 14 km upstream near the *Cayalti* cooperative (7585 hectares). Beyond Cayalti, near *Oyotún*, is a huge petroglyph of a bird in flight, 70 m high and with a wing-span of 70 m. In another 27 km the road enters the valley of the Reque, a tributary of the Chancay, and after passing an impressive field of dunes comes to *Reque* and **Chiclayo.**

5. CHICLAYO AND THE LAMBAYEQUE VALLEY

Archaeological Remains

The Lambayeque valley does not show the long continuity of human occupation found in the Trujillo area. Cabello de Balboa tells us in his "History of Peru" that a cacique named Naylamp, coming from the north, built a temple on the banks of the Lambayeque to house an idol of green stone called Ñampallec (from which the name Lambayeque is derived). The temple is believed to be the *Huaca Chotuna*, 11 km from Lambayeque (accessible only on horseback). Visitors spending a few days at Chiclayo with a car at their disposal can see a number of Mochica and Chimú sites in the Chancay and Leche valleys.

Another ancient settlement in the Chancay valley was *Collique*, perhaps to be identified with the *Huaca Collu*, on the territory of the Pomalca cooperative, where there are some very fine petroglyphs. Round the *Cerro Purgatorio*, near *Tucume*, are the remains of a number of temples. At *Batán Grande*, to the east, there are a number of adobe pyramids scattered about among the carob-trees, and fantastic hoards of gold and silver objects have been found here. Near *Motupe*, to the north, is the site of **Apurlé**, which may date back to the 5th century B.C. and was one of the principal Chimú cities. There are remains of a remarkable system of irrigation channels. This fortified town was no doubt a defensive position on the frontier with the turbulent Tallans of the Piura region. Scattered about over the whole area, particularly round Ferreñafé and near the coast at Etén, are numbers of small pyramids. In the Chimú period, and perhaps even as early as the Mochica period, there was a well conceived irrigation system linking the Chancay valley with the Saña valley to the south and the Leche valley to the north (the Raca Rumi and Taymi canals).

The **Brunning Museum** in Lambayeque contains a very fine collection of pre-Columbian material from the area, assembled by a German businessman. (Lambayeque can be reached from Chiclayo in 10 minutes by *colectivo*). The museum, housed in a very modern building, contains examples of Vicus, Chavín and Mochica work, few in number but of very high quality, and much larger quantities of Chimú (red and black pottery) and Inca material. Also of interest are the pre-Chimú pottery and carved wood, labelled "Lambayeque" and regarded as derivative from Tiahuanaco culture. In Chiclayo itself there is a private museum (the *Collección Arellano*) containing both pre-Columbian and colonial material.

Lambayeque and Zaña

The Spaniards founded their first town, **Lambayeque**, near the Huaca Chotuna in 1553, after seven earlier distributions of land (*repartimientos de tierra*) among the Conquistadors from 1532 onwards. The town was soon abandoned, following a native rebellion, and in 1563 the Spaniards founded a new town at **Zaña**, 47 km north-east of Chiclayo (easily accessible by bus or taxi: 1 hour by car). Zaña became exceedingly prosperous through the growing of sugar-cane, for which negroes were brought in to provide additional manpower—a step which had considerable influence on the physical type and the folk traditions of the northern coastal area. In the 17th century the town rivalled Trujillo in importance, but in 1720 it was destroyed by a great flood (which tradition has it was a divine punishment for the licentious behaviour of the inhabitants). The local Spanish dignitaries then returned to Lambayeque, which reached its peak of prosperity in the 18th century. Then it too suffered from floods (1821, 1871), and in the second half of the 19th century was overshadowed by *Chiclayo*, originally a mere village which had grown up round a Franciscan friary on a site previously occupied by the stronghold of an Indian cacique named Cinto. When the *departamento* of Lambayeque was established in 1874 Chiclayo was the obvious choice for its chief town, and thereafter it developed rapidly as a commercial centre.

It is at Lambayeque and Zaña, therefore, that traces of the region's colonial past should be looked for. Lambayeque has a beautiful church and thirty or so colonial houses, and visitors strolling at random through the town will find many an interesting balcony or doorway or patio. Particularly notable are a house in Calle 2 de Mayo (No. 340), the balcony of the *Casa de la Logia* (also known as the *Casa Montjoi*) and the house in the Plaza de Armas which belonged to President Leguía. The Holy Week celebrations in Lambayeque are an important occasion for the whole region. Zaña's four churches (the Cathedral, San Francisco, La Merced and San Agustín) are all in ruins, though there are plans to restore the convent of San Agustín.

Chiclayo

The town of Chiclayo is completely modern, with only one poor reminder of its colonial past—three Gothic arches of the convent of San Francisco which now decorate the front of a garage in a corner of the Plaza de Armas. It has all the characteristics of a busy commercial town, including the heavy traffic.

Chiclayo is now increasingly emerging as the centre of a conurbation, the other parts of which have much of interest to offer the visitor. We have already considered Lambayeque (pop. 18,000), and it would be legitimate also to include *Ferreñafé*,

18 km away, with its beautiful old two-storey houses with over-hanging roofs. 14 km from Chiclayo, towards the coast, is **Monsefú** (pop. 14,000), which, like Etén, is the descendant of one of the "native communities" established by the Spaniards in the north. The inhabitants of this town are mainly engaged in agriculture—largely food crops and, with lucerne as fodder, a certain amount of dairy farming for the Chiclayo market—but also practise a variety of crafts. The numerous small workshops in the town produce straw articles (hats, bags, mats) and shawls and ponchos of white cotton embroidered in bright colours. Confectionery is also made here, in particular the popular sweets known as "King Kongs". The market of Monsefú is very picturesque, with the local women dressed in their traditional black costumes.

Puerto Pimentel, 13 km away, is the port—or at any rate the anchorage—for the conurbation, connected with Chiclayo by a little local railway line. It has a moderately well equipped bathing beach, with many restaurants. *Puerto Etén* is the other local commercial port, while *Santa Rosa* and *Etén* (16.7 km away) are picturesque fishing ports with extensive bathing beaches. The fishermen still use the traditional reed boats (*caballos de totora*), or fish from the shore with a large net (*chinchorro*). The local restaurants serve a variety of fish dishes, in particular *chabela* or *seco de chabela*, a dried fish.

Inland from Chiclayo, the conurbation can be taken as including the townships formed by the sugar-cane growing cooperatives of *Pomalca*, *Tumán* and *Casa Blanca*, with populations of between 5000 and 10,000. On the Chongoyape road, 45 minutes' drive from the town, is the *Tinajones* reservoir, constructed as part of a large-scale irrigation scheme, which may become a holiday and recreation centre for the conurbation. It is planned to use the workers' bungalows here to provide holiday accommodation, and to develop facilities for fishing, sailing and water skiing.

6. CHICLAYO TO PIURA

Distance 272 km.

The sandy desert now gives place to a xerophytic scrub, with carob-trees (*algarrobos*) and *zapote*. In valleys with sufficient water supply sugar-cane is giving place to rice, the regularly planted fields of which round Lambayeque house colonies of graceful white cranes. The Leche valley, round Mochume and Tucume, gives a foretaste of the tropical landscape of the extreme north of Peru, with its mangoes, its flamboyants, its coconuts and other palms.

Near Tucume, at the foot of the *Cerro Purgatorio*, are the remains of a large Chimú town (11th–13th c.). 13 km beyond Jayanca a small country road goes off to the village of *Salas*, famôus throughout Peru for its faith healers and spiritualists. Near *Motupe* (81 km from Chiclayo) is the site of *Apurlé* (see above, p. 167). To the north is the shrine of the *Cross of Chalpón*, which during the first week in August draws large numbers of pilgrims, some of them even coming from Ecuador.

From Motupe the road runs over a narrow pass between mountains covered with arid scrub into the **Olmos** valley. 5 km before the village of Olmos a road goes off to Jaén, Bagua, the Marañón and Chachapoyas over the *Porcullo pass*, the lowest in the Peruvian Andes (2144 m).

Beyond Olmos there are a few plantations of citrus fruits, which grow here with the help of irrigation. Thereafter the road runs along the edge of the vast **Sechura desert** all the way to Piura. There are ambitious plans to irrigate the desert by diverting the Huancabamba, a tributary of the Marañón, towards the Pacific coast, with the help of a tunnel some 20 km long.

The eastern edge of the desert consists of a scrub of carob-trees which, when there is sufficient rain, is covered with a brief growth of grass. The inhabitants of the area rear goats and sheep as well as the traditional mules and donkeys, which were formerly the subject of an active trade. This herding of stock, combined with the burning of wood to produce charcoal, has helped to destroy the vegetation. The peasants' houses straggle along both sides of the Panamerican Highway—mud-walled dwellings, each with one or more enclosures bounded by rough scrub hedges which shelter their livestock, a well and such meagre crops as they can grow.

Rather more than half way between Chiclayo and Piura is *Naupe*, which has a number of restaurants. This is the traditional stopping place for buses and *colectivos* travelling north; south-bound vehicles sometimes prefer to stop at Olmos. A few kilometres beyon the little village of *Casa Blanca*, before reaching the fork where a secondary road goes off via Chulucanas (220 km from Chiclayo) to Sullana, the highway enters the archaeological area associated with the **Vicus culture.**

The most important excavation sites are on the *Hacienda Pabur*, 500 m east of the road. This recently discovered culture, dated to 1250–1000 B.C., is characterised by red pottery specialising in representations of stylised animals in which the eyes and mouth are indicated by long incisions.

7. PIURA

Piura, 272 km from Chiclayo (4 hours by *colectivo*) and 1037 km from Lima, is often given no more than a passing glance by tourists hurrying through it on their way to Tumbes or into Ecuador. It deserves better than this. The first town founded by the Spaniards in April 1532, it occupied four different sites during the colonial period. The first settlement established at *Tangarará* on the right bank of the Chira, downstream from the present-day town of Sullana, and placed under the protection of St Michael, was abandoned on account of its isolated situation, following an Indian rising. The second, which grew up round a Franciscan friary at *Monte de los Padres*, 65 km away on the banks of the Piura, was in turn abandoned in 1574 in favour of

Buenaventura de Paita, on the coast. Following attacks on the town by pirates a compromise between the three sites was reached by moving the town to its present situation.

There are a number of colonial churches in the town — *San Francisco*, the **church of the Carmen** and the **Cathedral.** The two latter churches have very beautiful *altars and reredoses* of carved and gilded wood, among the finest examples of wood-carving in northern Peru. The Cathedral also contains a fine *pulpit* made from a single piece of wood, *Stations of the Cross*, with naive plaster figures, and pictures by the 19th century painter *Ignacio Merino*, including "St Martin Porres and the Thieves". There are also some interesting **colonial houses** which have been declared national monuments (houses of *Enrique López Albújar, Eguigurren* and the *Lama family*). The house in which *Admiral Miguel Graú* was born, dating from the Republican period, now contains a small museum commemorating this hero of the war against Chile.

Material of the pre-Columbian period can be seen in the *private museum of Father Miguel Justino Ramírez* (Calle Tacna) and in the recently opened and very modern **Municipal Museum of Archaeology,** notable in particular for its *Vicus pottery*. There are, however, no ancient city sites in the area, since the people of this region, the Tallans, established no towns or irrigation systems comparable to those of their Mochica rivals to the south.

Unlike the essentially commercial town of Chiclayo, Piura was a town of landowners who grew cotton and practised extensive stock herding. It still has an elegant aristocratic air, with huge houses occupying the whole of a block. To the west and north-east of the town are new residential districts, with sumptuous villas. The *Plaza de Armas* is an oasis of coolness in a town where temperatures are high (annual mean 26.2°C).

The recent development of commerce and the erection of many modern buildings, in particular the new *Civic Centre*, are bringing changes to the centre of the town, which has a promising future ahead of it thanks to the government's new industrial projects. The terminal of a pipeline bringing oil from the Selva (the Tigre valley) is to be at *Bayovar*, just south of Piura, and plans are in hand for developing the large deposits of phosphates located in the desert.

It is perhaps worth mentioning that arrangements can be made for visitors to be admitted to the swimming pools of the Graú Club.

In the **surroundings of Piura** there are a number of places of interest to visitors. **Catacaos** (10 minutes away by *colectivo*) is noted for its handicrafts—articles made of straw (bags, hats, mats, etc.) and silver and gold filigree jewellery. It is famous for its Sunday market and its Holy Week celbrations. *Simbila* is also a village of potters. This area in the lower Piura valley is one of the poorest parts of Peru. Here more than anywhere else there is a dramatic contrast between the great estates which use the best land and the available water resources for the growing of cotton and the small peasant holdings (0.47 hectare per head at Catacaos) on the fringes of the desert. Each year of drought sees more peasants fleeing from the threat of famine to the *barriadas de Castilla*, on the other side of the Piura, and to Lima.

To the west of Piura extends the *sandy desert* of Sechura. Visitors who want to see something of this area can hire a jeep through the Turistas hotel or may be able, with more difficulty, to find a taxi. The route runs through vast expanses of dunes, traversing poor villages which are periodically swept by sandstorms, like *La Arena*, *La Unión* and *Bernal*. **Sechura** has a magnificent *colonial church*, unfortunately much dilapidated, as well as underground structures, apparently of considerable extent, and the remains of an aqueduct. In the Piura delta are numerous small fishing hamlets (*Chulliyachi*, *Matacaballo*, *San Pedro*, etc.) using balsa boats or sailing craft. 5 km north of Sechura, near the *Cerro Chusis*, the remains of a pre-Columbian fishing village were discovered in 1952 by an American archaeologist. The offshore waters here contain an abundance of fish, at the meeting place of the cold Humboldt Current and the warmer equatorial current. Farther north fishing is practised on an industrial scale, particularly at **Paita**, 57 km north-west of Piura, where there are whale-meat canning plants and a large new fishing harbour is nearing completion. There are beautiful bathing beaches at Paita and at *Colán* (73 km), on a secondary road which runs along the coast to Talara parallel to the Panamerican Highway.

In the direction of the Sierra there are a number of places of interest, though these are much less easily accessible. Near

Ayabacá are the Inca ruins of *Aypate*. Near Huancabamba are
the Huaringas, lagoons of mineral water, in a region noted for
its witch doctors. A recent irrigation scheme has created the
large *Lago San Lorenzo* by diverting the water of the Quiroz,
a tributary of the Chira, into the river Piura. This is now developing into a holiday centre, with a modest inn.

Piura's fiestas are at the beginning of January (the Epiphany)
and from 1 to 9 October (the National Festival of the Coast).

8. PIURA TO TUMBES

Distance 276 km.

Between the rivers Piura and Chira the road runs
over a small arid plateau called the *Tablazo*, with which
the green and fertile valley of the Chira forms a vivid
contrast. This oasis is of markedly tropical character,
with bananas, mangoes, date-palms and coconut-
palms framing fields of rice and cotton. At **Sullana**
(pop. 60,000), on the left bank of the river, is the only
ford where it is possible to cross the mighty and
torrential Chira.

During the 19th century, thanks to its busy mule-borne trade
and later to its rail connection with Paita, Sullana was a prosperous commercial town. It has now lost its supremacy to Piura
but is still an important road junction; until the construction of
the new coast road the route through the Andes de Loja was the
only means of access to Ecuador. The town has a number of
modest hotels and some industry. *Mallares*, 59 km from Piura,
has in addition to its rice and citrus fruits a small vineyard — an
unexpected feature in this latitude — which produces wine of high
alcoholic content. Near *Tamarindo* are thermal springs, of which
regrettably little use is made. At *Amotape* we join the road to
Colán, originally a native *reducción*, which is now a bathing
resort for the people of Piura. The road then runs through an
area of mixed woodland and grazing, with small villages like
Miraflores, notable for the windmills which operate water pumps.

There are two routes to Talara — either along the coast or,
more conveniently, by the inland road, passing through the La
Brea and Pariñas oilfields, developed by the International
Petroleum Co. and nationalised in October 1968.

Talara (pop. 30,000), 118 km from Piura, was founded shortly before 1940 and is now Peru's chief oil centre, supplying 70% of the country's energy requirements (refinery, exporting port) and over-shadowing the rival centres at Negritos to the south and Lobitos to the north. It has an airport (daily connections with Lima), a Turistas hotel and beautiful beaches.

At *El Alto*, 148 km from Piura, a minor road goes off to *Cabo Blanco*, under the coastal cliffs, a noted sea-angling centre (particularly swordfish) but now in decline.

After *Los Organos*, another oil town, the road follows the coast. Beyond *Mancora* (175 km from Piura) it leaves the arid zone for good and enters a region with a clearly marked rainy season, though this varies irregularly from year to year. After passing through *Zorritos*, once an oil village but now a pleasant bathing resort with a good hotel, we come to **Tumbes** (pop. 33,000), 276 km from Piura and 1285 km from Lima, near which Francisco Pizarro landed at the end of April 1532 (probably on one of the sandy beaches between the Corrales and the sea, to the west of the town).

The original settlement having been abandoned as too remote, the present town is relatively modern. It has a very hot and humid climate of equatorial type. Its wooden houses with their pillared fronts and their balconies give the town something of an air. It is surrounded by a fertile oasis in which maize, sweet potatoes, rice, manioc and tobacco grow in the shade of coconut palms, bananas and orange-trees.

14 km north, near the Tumbes delta with its mangrove swamps (*manglares*), is the port of **Puerto Pizarro**. The delta, the largest on the west coast of South America (185 sq. km), lies on the southern boundary of the equatorial vegetation zone. Puerto Pizarro's hotel resources are confined to one motel, but

it is planned to establish a modern bathing resort with facilities
for water skiing, sailing, surfing, etc.

Beyond Tumbes the road continues to the frontier post of
Aguas Verdes (26 km) and enters Ecuador.

9. CAJAMARCA

Cajamarca can be reached by air from Lima or Trujillo or by
road. The road leaves the Panamerican Highway soon after the
bridge over the Jequetepeque and the village of *San José* (126 km
from Trujillo, 683 km from Lima). The route (180 km; 6 hours
from Trujillo) presents no difficulties. It runs up the Jequetepeque valley to *Magdalena*, climbs through the very narrow
ravines of Yumagual and Pumamarca to the *Gavilán pass* (3200
m) and then descends rapidly to Cajamarca.

The wide Cajamarca valley, lying at an altitude of
2750 m, runs between low hills. In recent years maize
has increasingly been displaced by lucerne, which
provides fodder for high quality dairy herds whose
produce goes to the condensed milk plants of Cajamarca and Chiclayo. There are fine views of the town
and surrounding countryside from the hill of *Santa
Apolonia*, on which there are a few blocks of dressed
stone known as the "Inca's Chair".

Visitors will at once observe a great difference between
Cajamarca and the coastal towns, both in architecture and in
economic development. It has suffered from the proximity of the
large towns of northern Peru, which have drawn away large
numbers of people from the *departamento* of Cajamarca, giving
it one of the lowest growth rates in Peru. The town itself is of
modest size (pop. 37,000) and has shown little development
since the end of the 19th century, though in recent years the
dairying industry and the tourist trade have brought a certain
amount of activity.

It was at Cajamarca that the Spaniards captured and killed
the ruling Inca, Atahuallpa. After defeating his half-brother
Huáscar at Cuzco the Inca was resting in the town on the way
to Tumibamba, the new town he had founded in Ecuador (near

the present-day town of Cuenca), and while he was here Pizarro sent first Hernando de Soto and then his own brother Hernando to invite him to a meeting. On 16 November 1532 the meeting took place, but Atahuallpa treated the Spaniards with disdain and threw to the ground the breviary offered him by the Dominican priest Vicente Valverde. The Spaniards, who numbered no more than 200, then attacked the Inca's men and took him prisoner. By way of ransom the Inca offered a room filled with gold as high as his raised arm could reach; but although the ransom was duly paid Pizarro kept Atahuallpa in confinement for nine months and then had him garrotted. The death of Atahuallpa is now one of the favourite themes of Peruvian folklore, the subject of dramatic performances as far afield as Bolivia.

Of the Inca town there remain only the "*Ransom Chamber*" (Cuarto del Rescate, Calle Junín), built of undressed stone with trapezoidal niches, and the "*Inca's Baths*", 5 km from the town near the tourist hotel. All the other Inca buildings, including the *Temple of the Sun*, have disappeared, their stones having been used in the building of the Spanish town.

At the time of the Spanish conquest the Incas had been in possession of the town only for some 60 years, having captured it from a cacique of the Casamalca people named Guismancu (or Guzmancu or Chuquimanco) after fierce resistance. The Casamalca culture, discovered by the Peruvian archaeologist J. C. Tello in 1937, is distinguished by its very fine and very hard pottery. Other pottery found at Cajamarca shows the influence of the Chavín, Tiahuanaco and Chimú cultures, and also influences from Colombia and Central America in the 9th or 10th century A.D.

The heyday of the colonial town was at the end of the 17th century, when the Hualgayoc silver mines were in production, but it never attained any great importance. It has three notable churches—the **Cathedral** and *San Francisco* in the Plaza de Armas and the church of *Belén* in the street of the same name.

The **Cathedral** was begun in 1682 but not consecrated until 1762. Unusually, there are no towers on the west front, giving it an unfinished appearance. The façade is decorated with beautiful twisted columns carved with grapes and vine leaves. The interior is austere, with large Churrigueresque altars.

San Francisco was begun in 1699, but has only recently been completed, the two towers having been built only within the last thirty years. The columns on the façade are decorated with cherubs and grapes. The *Dolorosa Chapel*, on the south side of the nave, is notable for the stone tracery of the walls, the vaulting and the windows. The Virgin is clad in a splendid modern velvet cloak and wears a gold crown with a pearl as large as a pigeon's egg. In the floor of the chapel is the tomb of one of the Inca governors (*astopilcas*) of the town. During the 19th century the descendants of these Inca chiefs still led the Corpus Christi procession, Cajamarca's principal religious festival, which is now accompanied by a busy trade fair.

The **church of Belén,** completed in 1743, has a magnificent carved façade with twisted columns and a sumptuously decorated interior. The adjoining *College of Belén* has a carved façade, with an elaborate decorative scheme which includes a sea-shell, grapes, cherubs, many lozenges in relief and two curious caryatids with four breasts.

Surroundings of Cajamarca

7 km from the town is the pre-Inca burial ground of *Otuzco*. At *Cumbemayo*, 9 km away (6 km by road, the rest on foot), is a pre-Inca irrigation canal, the sides of which bear a number of carvings showing Chavín influence. A "pulpit" and two "sacrificial tables" mark the site of a shrine which was built in the shape of a huge human head.

10. CHACHAPOYAS

There is a very difficult road from Cajamarca to *Chachapoyas*, chief town of the *departamento* of Amazonas, 33 km away. The road crosses the canyon of the Marañón (the upper course of the Amazon) on a bridge at *Chacanto* (165 km), at an altitude of 1000 m, and comes to *Balsas*. It then runs through the cordillera at the Barro Negro pass (229 km; alt. 3700 m) and comes to *Tingo* and *Chachapoyas*, on the river Utcubamba. There is also a road (much easier) from Olmos to Chachapoyas, with side roads to Jaén and Bagua. **Chachapoyas** (pop. 10,400) has a Turistas hotel and air connections with Chiclayo and Iquitos.

From *Tingo* there is a track (4 hours' walk) to the site of **Cuelap,** with the ruins of an imposing fortress, now invaded by the vegetation of the *ceja de montaña*, covering an area of 60,000 sq. m. Scattered about in the forest up the Utcubamba valley are numerous remains of a pre-Inca culture about which little is known — *Monte Peruvia*, the "twelve cities of the condors" and **Gran Pajatén.** This last site, situated at an altitude of 2850 m, was discovered by Gene Savoy in 1965. It can be reached from Trujillo by taking the Pataz road as far as Chagual, on the Marañón, and continuing on a mule track (2 days' march). The main features of the site are a series of circular stone buildings laid out on terraces, with carvings of human figures and stylised condors on large blocks of stone, and temples dedicated to the cult of the Sun. The remains still present an enigma to archaeologists, pointing to the antiquity and density of human settlement in this part of the *ceja de montaña* zone in pre-Inca times. They are very difficult of access, and the trip can be undertaken only by a properly equipped party.

3. FROM LIMA
TO THE SOUTHERN FRONTIER

The main place of interest on this route, which covers a total distance of 1340 km, is **Arequipa** (1019 km). The journey can be done in two stages, stopping at Ica or Nazca (or even Chala).

1. LIMA TO ICA

The first valley of any size is that of **San Vicente de Cañete,** 147 km from Lima. Here sugar-cane has given place to cotton, with the highest yields in Peru. The town, founded in 1556 by the Viceroy Andrés Hurtado de Mendoza, Marqués de Cañete, preserves some remains of its earth ramparts towards the sea. The valley was settled at a very early period and has remains of Inca fortresses (e.g. *Huarcu*).

Chincha, 200 km from Lima, was also an important place in Inca times, one of their leading strongholds in the coastal area. There are several pre-Inca *huacas*. Sale of basketwork articles, fruit and wine; good hotel.

At km 230 a country road suitable for motor traffic goes off to **Huancavelica.** Since the cutting of the road between Huancayo and Ayacucho in 1974 this road has been used by buses going to Cuzco. It is a difficult road, with passes of 4500 and 4700 m, but gives access to the Inca site of *Tambo Colorado* (40 km from the junction) and **Castrovirreyna** (160 km), situated at 3900 m, a small and rather austere *puna* town with a beautiful church. After passing the Orqococha and Choclococha lagoons the road bears left for Huancavelica (278 km: see p. 198), while a road to the right continues to Ayacucho.

4 km after the junction with the Huancavelica road another road goes off on the right to the port of *Pisco*

and the *Paracas peninsula* (which can also be reached on another road branching off 14 km farther south).

The development of **Pisco,** which came into existence at the same time as Lima but was not formally founded until 1640, has followed the same pattern as that of other Peruvian ports. In colonial times it exported ore from Huancavelica to Potosí by way of Arica; in the 19th century its prosperity depended on the working of guano on the coastal islands; and in our own time it is involved in the fish-meal boom.

22 km south is **Paracas,** at the base of the Paracas peninsula. Formerly the centre of one of the most important pre-Columbian cultures, it is now an important holiday resort.

The town is easily reached from Lima (c. 3 hours). There are an excellent Turistas hotel, holiday bungalows, a swimming pool and a bathing beach. Small **museum,** displaying specimens of the splendid Paracas fabrics together with the mummies, jewellery and weapons which were wrapped in them. Nearby, at *Cabeza Larga*, is an excavation site which can be visited.

A road runs north along the coast to *Punta Pejerrey*, past beautiful beaches on which seals can be seen basking. From Paracas (or Pisco) visitors can get a boat to the **Ballestas islands,** with huge colonies of seabirds, and on the way back enjoy a view of a huge candelabrum-like figure carved out of the cliffs fringing the peninsula. There is also a road running south from Paracas to *Independence Bay*, with magnificent scenery and an abundance of marine life — unfortunately no longer including the whales which were to be seen here until recent years.

Between Pisco and Ica the road turns inland, and the coastal desert takes on something of the aspect of the Sahara, with beautiful dunes and clumps of date-palms clustering round deep wells. **Ica** (pop. 75,000), 306 km from Lima, is a pleasant town of parks and gardens, with good hotels and restaurants (including a Turistas hotel). The wealth of its landed middle classes was founded on cotton, but also on vines and fruit-trees.

The **Cathedral** (the *Merced*) is worth seeing, and there is a particularly interesting **Museum,** illustrating the history of the southern coastal region since Palaeolithic times, including Chavín and Tiahuanaco material, *Paracas mummies* showing cranial deformations and trepanation, textiles, some very beautiful *Nazca pottery*, wood carving, and wooden yokes and maces.

Near the town is the *Huacachina* lagoon, a popular holiday centre amid sand dunes and palms, with three good hotels and a number of restaurants. It is unfortunately in danger of silting up, as is the *La Huega* lagoon 2 km away. Another interesting excursion from Ica is to the mouths of the Río Ica by way of the *Hacienda Ocucaje* (wine, the local spirit called *pisco*, excavation site).

2. ICA TO AREQUIPA

After passing through the enclosed valley of the Río Grande and the township of *Palpa* (400 km: sale of fruit) the road enters the *Pampa Colorada* (or Pampa de San José), in which are the famous **Nazca figures** and markings on the ground.

The markings, which are barely visible on the ground and must be seen from the air (flights from Lima or Pisco), consist of a series of *gigantic geometric figures and representations of animals* (a monkey, a bird, etc.), some of them several kilometres long, traced on the surface of the stony desert. Various explanations of these markings have been suggested: they have been interpreted as an astronomical calendar, as evidence of a totemic cult, and even as the work of visitors from other planets. The irrigation systems in this area (e.g. at Visambra, near Nazca), based on underground aqueducts, are equally remarkable.

Nazca (450 km from Lima) has a small *Municipal Museum* containing some magnificent pottery. The town, situated at the junction with a road running to Cuzco via Puquío and Chalhuanca, has a number of hotels, including a fine Turistas hotel with a swimming pool.

Beyond Nazca the road returns to the coast at
Puerto Lomas (84 km), with side roads going off to the
recently opened iron mines at *Marcona* and the harbour
town of *San Juan* on the right and to *Acarí* on the left.
In the oasis of **Yauca** (122 km from Nazca) there is a
magnificent olive grove. Thereafter the road runs along
above the sea to **Chala.**

This was the port of Cuzco both under the Incas and in
colonial times. With its Turistas hotel (bathing beach) it makes a
pleasant staging point on the road. At the nearby villages of
Chala Viego and *Atiquipa*, set in the luxuriant vegetation of the
lomas (oases supplied with moisture by the coastal fogs), are
traces of Inca roads and terraces.

Beyond Chala the road runs along the coast, passing
through the oases of *Atico*, *Ocoña* and *Camaná*, with
restaurants where visitors can sample the local crayfish.
Camaná has a Turistas hotel and a small airport. The
road then turns inland and climbs vigorously up
towards Arequipa (2335 m over a distance of 167 km),
passing through vast pampas with crescent-shaped
dunes, with the outlines of the extinct volcanoes of
Ampato and Coropuna on the horizon.

The plateau is slashed by two deep canyons, the Sihuas canyon
at *Tambillo* and the Vitor canyon at *Sotillo*. 25 km before
Tambillo a road goes off to the **canyon of the river Majes** (the
upper course of the Camaná), one of the deepest in America
(amost 3000 m), now being used in a large irrigation scheme.

20 km beyond Sotillo on the Panamerican Highway,
after crossing the railway line to the port of *Mataraní*,
we come to *Partición*, the starting point of the short
stretch of motorway to **Arequipa** (44 km). Arequipa is
1019 km from Lima (18 hours by bus, 15 hours by
colectivo; daily air connections).

3. AREQUIPA

Situation

With its beautiful scenery and climate, Arequipa makes an immediate appeal to visitors. It lies at an altitude of 2335 m in the oasis formed by the river Chili at the foot of three large volcanoes which are frequently snow-capped — Chachani (6075 m) to the left, the regular pyramid of Misti (5835 m) and Picchu Picchu (5674 m), whose indented crest is thought to resemble the recumbent figure of an Indian. The aridity of the desert is intensified by the deposits of ash and lava, in varying shades of light grey and white, laid down by the volcanoes. The Tertiary lava from Chachani, a kind of trachyte known as *sillar*, makes a good building material, both sturdy and light, and its colouring has earned Arequipa the name of the "white city".

The climate is very dry (annual rainfall 106 mm), the air exceptionally clear and the sky intensely blue all year round. The mean annual temperature is 13.8°C; the days are sunny but the nights often cool. In its desert setting the oasis appears all the greener, with its eucalyptuses, willows and poplars lining the roads and irrigation canals. The terraced fields round the outside of the oasis give the landscape something of the air of Tuscany. The agriculture was formerly of Mediterranean type, centred on the growing of wheat, olives, vines, mulberry trees and fruit-trees; more recently there has been an increasing move towards green maize and fodder crops for the dairy cattle which supply a condensed milk factory. The volcanic soil is very fertile, yielding two crops of wheat in the year and several cuttings of lucerne.

History

The name of the town ("behind the pointed mountain" — i.e. Misti, when coming from Puno) points to an Aymará origin, though some authorities believe that it was founded by Mayta Cápac (11th c.) or even by Túpac Yupanqui (15th c.) in which case the name may be derived from the Quechua expression *are qepay* ("yes, let us stop here"). There are numerous **pre-Columbian remains,** but they are some distance away and will be of interest only to visitors spending some time in the town. Among the oldest (6000 B.C.) are the rock paintings at *Sumbay* (beyond

Misti, 113 km by train), with representations of men and animals
(llamas, pumas and even *ñandus*). There are Nazca remains at
Camaná, and nearer the town there are many Huari and Tiahuanaco sites (the impressive terraces of *Paucarpata* and *Churajón*,
the carved stones of *Toro Muerto* in the Majes canyon). There
are also numerous Inca remains (tombs, irrigation works),
particularly in the upper Chili valley. In the town itself there are
the *museums* of the San Agustín University and the Catholic
University of Arequipa.

In 1537 the Spaniards accompanying Diego de Almagro
settled here, in what is now the San Lázaro district, on their
return from Chile, but the town was not formally founded until
15 August 1540, under the sonorous name of Villa Hermosa de
Nuestra Señora de la Asunción de Arequipa. Conveniently
situated on the road into Chile and on one of the roads to
Potosí, linking Lake Titicaca with the now forgotten port of
Quilca, the town became a busy centre of mule-borne trade. By
the middle of the 19th century it had pushed Cuzco, then in a
state of decline, out of its second place among Peruvian towns,
and the coming of the railway, built by British engineers in the
1870s, gave a further stimulus to its development by facilitating
the transport of wool from the *altiplano* to the new port of
Mollendo. British and other European firms settled in the town,
setting up banks and small factories (wool-scouring plants,
tanneries, flour-mills, a brewery) and establishing branches in
other towns which provided Arequipa with markets throughout
the whole of southern Peru. At the present time Arequipa's
importance as a regional centre is steadily increasing, with the
establishment of new industries (cement, condensed milk, nylon,
laboratories, bicycles, radio sets, etc.) and the development of a
modern port at Mataraní (now Peru's second port). Its population has risen from 60,000 in 1940 to over 300,000 today, largely
as a result of an influx of workers from Puno which has led to the
growth of huge *barriadas* round the town.

The Town

Although several times destroyed by earthquakes (particularly in 1600, in 1868 and most recently in 1960), Arequipa has
preserved from the colonial past both its grid plan and its *very
distinctive architecture*. Most of the buildings are of white volcanic
stone (*sillar*); more rarely they are of adobe or brick. They are

single-storied and frequently have vaulted or domed roofs supported by massive piers as a precaution against earthquakes. The doorways are richly carved and the windows, which are narrow and few in number, have beautiful iron grilles. The roof terraces are edged with gargoyles. The general effect is distinctly Andalusian, and the whole town has a very Spanish air, in contrast to the more Indian atmosphere of Cuzco.

The **Cathedral,** with its towers and its esplanade, is of imposing size, but is of little interest, having been rebuilt after the 1868 earthquake. The only 17th century features that have survived are the wooden choir, the pulpit, the sacristy and the organ.

Opposite the Cathedral, near the Municipality, is the **church of the Compañía,** built at the end of the 16th century, which has stood up well to the earthquakes and has recently been restored.

The **side doorway** is the oldest (1654), with a statue of St James (Santiago) as the killer of Moors (here Indians) and beautiful garlands borne by mermaids. The **central doorway** (with an inscription dating it to 1698) is a masterpiece of Plateresque sculpture.

In the interior there are four notable **reredoses** — the one on the central altar and those of the Crucifix, Christ of Nazareth

1 Cathedral
2 La Compañía
3 Santo Domingo
4 Palacio Goyeneche
5 La Merced
6 San Agustín
7 Casa Iriberry
8 Casa del Moral
9 Casa de la Moneda
10 Convent of Santa Catalina
12 San Francisco
13 El Fierro (Museum)
14 San Lázaro
15 Hotel Turistas
16 Santa Teresa
17 Santa Rosa
18 Archaeological Museum; San Agustín University
19 Historical Museum
20 Yanahuara church
21 Cayma church
22 Touring y Automóvil-Club
23 Post Office
24 Banco de la Nación
25 Market
26 Railway station

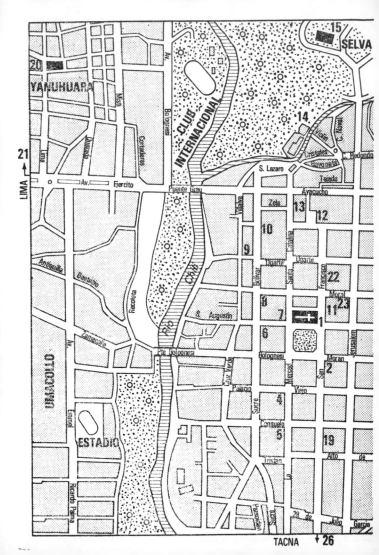

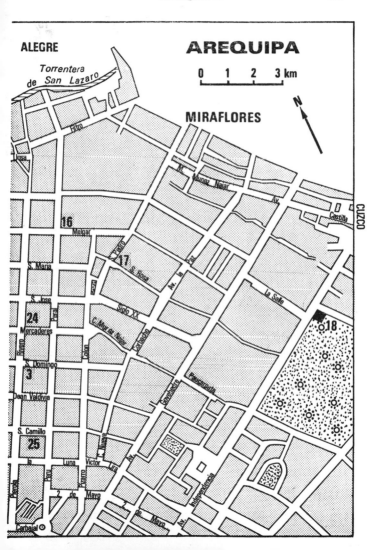

and St Francis Xavier. The carved wood *pulpit* is 17th century. The *sacristy*, restored in 1969, has beautiful frescoes of the colonial period and interesting pictures.

Beside the church are the remains of the **Jesuit Convent,** called the *Pasaje Romana*, with columns and arches carved in similar style to the doorway of the Compañía.

Two blocks east is the **Convent of Santo Domingo,** in the street of the same name, which has recently been restored. It has a magnificent 17th century carved doorway in *sillar* (the church was consecrated in 1680). The brick walls and vaulting in the interior have been stripped of the stucco with which they had been covered and now have a more restrained aspect. The wooden choir dates from 1677.

Three blocks south of the Plaza de Armas is the **church of La Merced,** built in 1607.

The main doorway is distinctly Mudéjar in style; the side door has a beautiful *Virgin of Mercy*. The church contains some interesting paintings. The *cloister* and the beautiful *chapter house* have carving in the same style as the doorway.

In the previous block, on the right when coming from the Plaza de Armas, is the **Palacio Goyeneche,** now occupied by the Banco de Reserva, which has handsome rooms with colonial furniture.

One block west of the Plaza de Armas is the **church of San Agustín,** with a magnificent carved doorway, a sacristy with an octagonal dome and pictures by artists of the Cuzco school.

Opposite San Augustín is the Casa Iriberry (1793), which now houses the law faculty of the San Agustín University (the other faculties are in modern buildings on the south-eastern outskirts of the town).

One block north of San Agustín, in Calle Bolívar, is the **Casa del Moral,** named after the huge mulberry tree in the patio, one of the finest colonial houses in

Peru; it can be seen by arrangement with the British owners. Just before the Convento de Santa Catalina, at the corner of Calle Ugarte and Calle Villalba, is the *Casa de la Moneda* (1798). *Calle Villalba* is one of the most picturesque streets in Arequipa, with many colonial-style houses, balconies of wrought-iron or *sillar*, and windows protected by grilles.

The **Convent of Santa Catalina** (open 9 to 11 and 2 to 4.30), was opened to the public only in 1970, after being closed for some four centuries. It was founded in 1580 for nuns belonging to wealthy families from all over Peru. Its high walls enclose an area of some 2 hectares, containing two groups of buildings, the northern group dating from the 16th century and the southern group from the 17th.

The Convent has stood up well to successive earthquakes and has been skilfully restored. It shows that Spanish architecture in the early years of the Conquest was still strongly influenced by Arab architecture. It consists of a maze of narrow streets named after the Spanish towns from which the nuns' families originally came: Seville under the buttresses of the church; Córdoba, brilliantly white, with a profusion of geraniums; and so on). The houses are low, with or without an upper storey, and the fronts are painted in bright colours (Prussian blue, purplish red, ochre, orange, etc.). Each house usually has a large room for the nun, a smaller one for her servant and an oven. Some still preserve the names and portraits of their owners. Many have a small patio and a roof terrace, reached by an outside staircase.

There are a number of cloisters and squares, for example the *principal* cloister, with huge pillars, and the *Plaza de Zocodover* (as in Granada), with a beautiful fountain. The *church*, built in white *sillar*, has a very large dome. Visitors can see the *convent kitchen* and the curious *laundry* with its huge wide-mouthed jars. There is an excellent **museum** in a vaulted gallery, containing some magnificent paintings by *Zurbarán* and by artists of the Cuzco school, sculpture, liturgical objects, etc.

On leaving Santa Catalina the visitor can either return to the Plaza de Armas by Calle San Francisco, passing the *Casa Ricketts* (No. 108), formerly the Seminary of San Jerónimo (1738), with a beautiful façade bearing the monogram of the Jesuits, or alternatively continue to the **Plaza San Francisco** to see the late 18th century **church of San Francisco,** a massive building in an attractive mingling of *sillar* and brick. In the same square is the *Municipal Museum*, in an old colonial house which has been restored (El Ferro Foundation).

Two blocks north along Calle Santa Catalina is the *church of San Lázaro*, a very sober building in the oldest part of the town, at the foot of the park laid out on the Selva Alegre. The Turistas hotel is on this hill.

To the east of San Francisco, in Calle Melgar, is the enclosed *Convent of Santa Teresa*, founded in 1700, which contains some fine paintings. Nearby are the churches of *Santa Rosa* (18th c.) and *Santa Marta*.

Surroundings of Arequipa

Near the town centre, now swallowed up in the built-up area, are the churches of **Yanahuara** (1571) and **Cayma** (1719), which have magnificent Baroque doorways. From the top of their towers there are fine views, particularly at sunset, of the town and the volcanoes. With their palm-shaded squares, their steep cobbled streets and their Andalusian houses, these old parts of the town are an aspect of Arequipa which no visitor should miss.

Other places of interest in the immediate surroundings of the town are, to the north-east, the thermal springs at *Jesús*; to the east, the villages of *Paucarpata* (Inca terraces), *Sabandía* (fine colonial mill) and *Characato*; to the south, the Palacio Goyeneche at *Huasacache*, *Sachaca* (beautiful colonial church), the village of *Tiabaya* and the recreation centre of *Tingo* (swimming pools, restaurants); to the west, the thermal springs at *Yura*, with a good Touristas hotel; and to the north, the upper valley of the Chili, with the village of *Chilina* and the Charcani gorge. Other possibilities are the *ascent of Misti* (starting from the village of Moyobamba) and a flight in a chartered aircraft over the volcanoes and the Majes canyon.

The little town of Mollendo, 123 km away by road (buses and taxis; also rail services), a bathing resort established at the end of the 19th century, has a certain charm of its own, with its very British air and its beaches. A modern port has been built at *Matarani*.

Arequipa's fiestas are Holy Week and 15 August (international folk festival).

4. SOUTH OF AREQUIPA

It is 321 km from Arequipa to the Chilean frontier. 220 km from Arequipa is **Moquegua,** a charming little colonial town unjustly neglected by tourists, situated at an altitude of 1367 m in an oasis of olive-trees, vines and fruit-trees.

Founded in 1541 and several times destroyed by earthquakes, the town contains a number of imposing **ruined churches** (*Santo Domingo*, 17th c.; the cloister of the *Compañía*; the doorway of the *Cathedral*, built 1792; etc.) and some very fine **colonial houses** with curious steeply pitched roofs and doorways of white *sillar*, like the Casa de Don Ignacio Nieto y Roa, Conde de Alastaya (18th c.). Moquegua gets little benefit from the working of the *Toquepala* copper mines, ore from which is shipped from the port of *Ilo*, connected with Moquegua by rail.

162 km from Moquegua is **Tacna,** a modern town with a cathedral and a fountain in the Plaza de Armas designed by Gustave Eiffel, better known as the builder of the Eiffel Tower. Its agreeable climate, its thermal springs and its bathing beaches make it a popular holiday resort; there is a Turistas hotel. Industry is developing. There is a road from Tacna to *Ilave* on Lake Titicaca.

Arica, 20 km south of the frontier, is a free port in Chilean territory.

4.   LIMA TO HUANCAYO, AYACUCHO AND CUZCO

This route, the "Highway of the Incas", was cut between Huancayo and Ayacucho in 1974, and to reach Ayacucho it was necessary to make a detour by Pisco, Castrovirreyna and Huancavelica (see p. 198).

1. LIMA TO HUANCAYO

Huancayo can be reached either by train (332 km: dep. 7 a.m., arr. 4.20 p.m., except Sundays) or by road (319 km: 6 hours by *colectivo*, or by bus).

The **railway,** built by Henry Meiggs in the 1870s, is the highest line in the world, crossing the Andes at an altitude of 4781 m (Ticlío Pass, Galera Tunnel). Its construction was a great technical achievement, involving the building of 61 bridges and the boring of 65 tunnels; though it contributed to the foreign economic domination of Peru by permitting the export of Peruvian minerals to Europe and the United States. The line follows the narrow valleys of the Rímac and some of its tributaries.

Beyond San Bartolomé the train goes over the impressive *Verrugas bridge* (70 km), named after the wart disease which was formerly endemic in the valley; it is also a monument to the Peruvian doctor Daniel Carrión who inoculated himself with the condition in order to study its effects. After passing through Surco, Matucana and San Mateo it enters the *El Infiernillo gorges* (several tunnels). After Chicla (alt. 3780 m) the vegetation becomes extremely sparse, and it disappears altogether after Casapalca (4150 m), 139 km from Lima. The *Ticlío pass* (157 km) and the tunnel which follows it are not far short of 5000 m high, in the immediate vicinity of the glaciers. Km 208: *La Oroya* (alt. 3726 m. pop. 26,000), with the Centromin plants for concentrating lead and zinc ore, formerly owned by the Cerro de Pasco Corporation. At *Jauja* (287 km) the train enters the Mantaro valley and continues to Huancayo (332 km).

The **road** (tarred) follows much the same route as the railway, going through the mountains at a rather higher altitude (*Anticona* *pass*, 4843 m). At La Oroya a road goes off on the left and runs via Cerro de Pasco, Huánuco and Tingo María to Pucallpa in the Amazonian forest (see chapter 8). Another side road leads to *Tarma* (pop. 28,100; Turistas hotel), *San Ramón* (airport, hotels), *La Merced*, *Oxapampa* and *Pozuzo*. This is the valley in the *ceja de montaña* which is most easily accessible from Lima. Its development was promoted by the building of the railway line through central Peru, combined with the foundation of La Merced in 1870 and the arrival of large numbers of German settlers.

The Mantaro Valley

The Mantaro depression, between Jauja and Huancayo, has a landscape pattern of Mediterranean aspect, with a sharp contrast between the arid slopes on the right bank of the river and the greener and more fertile land on the left bank. On the right bank there are much gullied surface limestones and areas of red clay soil, producing a landscape of open fields and large villages with tiled or thatched roofs. The left bank is watered by the small mountain streams which rise in the Eastern Cordillera and have laid down small alluvial fans on the valley terraces; the landscape on this side is mixed woodland and grazing with hedges of eucalyptus, agave and broom, and the houses are dispersed in small hamlets. Cereals (wheat, barley, maize) now alternate with lucerne. The recent development in the use of fertilisers has made it possible, on these tiny plots of land, to do without fallows and produce relatively good yields. Stock-herding is closely associated with crop growing, and is mainly confined to the *puna* zone, where this has not been monopolised by the large estates.

Here more than anywhere else in Peru there was a conflict between the peasant communities in the valley, where the land was grossly over-populated (up to 500 inhabitants to the sq. km in the plain), and the stock-farming haciendas on the higher ground, which developed steadily as communications improved from the end of the 19th century onwards. The road and railway run through numbers of large villages (some with populations of over 4000), originally established under Viceroy Francisco de Toledo's programme of *reducciones*. These communities of practically independent small peasant farmers have now been formed into socialised farming units (SAIS), whose very energetic members, often organised trade unionists, enter into contracts with mines, towns (Huancayo, Lima) and plantations in the hot lands. Many of these peasants go in for craft production, which is particularly active at *Sapallanga* and *Hualhuas*. The weaving of ponchoes in this area continues a tradition established when the Spaniards set up the first *obrajes* (textile workshops) in the valley, particularly at Sapallanga. At *San Jerónimo de Tunán* silver filigree articles are made. Other places make hats, brightly coloured blankets, etc. All these articles are now sold in Huancayo's Sunday fair and in the shops of Lima.

Features of Interest

The Mantaro valley was settled in very early times and was the heart of the territory occupied by the Huancas, who were defeated by Pachacuti shortly before the Spanish conquest. There are numerous **Inca remains,** but most of them are some distance from the main road and difficult to access. Among sites of interest are *Huarihualca* (5 km south of Huancayo), *Tunanmarca* and *Waturi*.

It was in this valley that the Spaniards decided to found their first, very ephemeral, capital of **Jauja** in 1534.

Jauja is now a quiet little town (pop. 14,000) which has lost its administrative and commercial importance to Huancayo, with two beautiful churches (the *Cathedral* and the *Capilla del Carmen*) and a few colonial houses. Near the town is the Paca lagoon, with a Turistas hotel. According to tradition—like many other lagoons—it contains a treasure collected for Atahuallpa's ransom which the local natives threw away when they heard of his death.

Although it was founded in the 16th century **Huancayo** has the appearance of a modern town, with many corrugated iron roofs. It has few buildings of the colonial period apart from the *Cathedral* (restored) and the *Capilla de la Merced*.

The town's prosperity in modern times has resulted from the coming of the railway in 1908 and the building of roads connecting it with the hot lands. It is an important staging point on the road to Cuzco and a busy commercial town, with numbers of shops, banks and transport agencies lining both sides of its main street, the *Calle Real*. Its Sunday market, mainly for the sale of manufactured goods, has associated with it a craft fair which is a great attraction to tourists. The population has risen from 26,730 in 1940 to 120,000 today. A University was established in 1960. The construction of the Mantaro hydroelectric station is likely to promote the town's industrial development still further.

Huancayo's fiesta is on 25 July (Santiago). There are also various fiestas in the neighbouring villages, often with interesting folk dancing displays and bullfights: 4 August at *Sicaya*, 16 August (St Roch) at *San Jerónimo de Tunán* and *Sincos*, 23 August at *Hualhuas*, 30 August at *Santa Rosa de Ocopa*, 8 September at *Sapallanga* (the Virgin of Cocharcas), etc.

28 km before Huancayo (5 km from the village and railway station of Concepción, on the road to Satipo; 1 hour by bus) is the **monastery of Santa Rosa de Ocopa** (open 9 to 12 and 3 to 6). Founded in 1724 by the Franciscans (Father Francisco de San José), it was a base from which missionaries were sent out into the Amazonian forest. It was closed by Bolívar but reopened in 1836. The *church* contains some interesting paintings and bas-reliefs in Huamanga stone (alabaster). There are several very silent *cloisters*, a magnificent *library* with very ancient books and a small *museum of ethnology and natural history* devoted to the Selva. Visitors can be accommodated in the monastery, which will appeal to anyone seeking peace and tranquillity.

2. HUANCAYO TO AYACUCHO

The road from Huancayo to Ayacucho (250 km) was blocked in 1974 by flows of mud (narrow passage; one-way traffic on alternate days; several dangerous bends).

At *Izcuchaka* (72 km) a road goes off on the right to **Huancavelica** (145 km), which can also be reached by train (127 km, 4 hours; daily service).

Huancavelica (pop. 16,000), situated at an altitude of 3660 m, is a very isolated town, retaining the austere atmosphere of an old colonial and mining town such as it was in the 16th and 17th centuries. It was founded in 1572 at the behest of Viceroy Francisco de Toledo under the name of the "Villa Rica de Oropesa", and prospered on the working of the mercury mines, the output from which was used in the production of silver amalgam at Potosí. It has a fine arcaded Plaza de Armas, a 17th century *Municipality* and several 16th and 17th century **churches,** to which the mine managers made valuable gifts (pictures, altars and pulpits of carved and gilded wood, liturgical objects, etc.). The most interesting churches are *San Antonio* and *Santo Domingo*, with Baroque doorways. In the vicinity visitors can see the old mine workings and the "petrified forest" of *Sachapite*.

Ayacucho

Ayacucho (569 km from Lima, 631 km from Cuzco), situated at an altitude of 2760 m, has remained relatively small (pop. 28,500) and has preserved its colonial character thanks to its isolation in the remoteness of the Sierra and to the poverty of the *departamento*, one of the aridest in the Andes, with a high rate of emigration to Lima.

The town was founded by the Spaniards, principally for strategic reasons, on 9 January 1639, half way between Cuzco, recently threatened by Manco Inca's rising, and Lima. It was given the name of *San Juan de la Frontera de Huamanga*, and was known in practice during colonial times as *Huamanga* ("Cliff of the Falcon"), being renamed *Ayacucho* on 15 February 1825 in honour of the victorious battle fought nearby which won Peru its independence. In colonial times it was a small Sierra town of landowners, monks and officials, with a certain amount of commercial activity in virtue of its situation on the Cuzco–Lima road and its proximity to the Huancavelica mines. It acquired a university in 1677. Decline set in after Independence, when the wealthier families moved to Lima and the economic development of the Coast reduced the Sierra to marginal status. Ayacucho is now a quiet little town of very Spanish aspect, which will appeal to visitors with its multitude of churches — there are said to be 37 in all — its old colonial houses and its numerous craftsmen.

As at Arequipa, the beauty of the town arises from the local building materials — a mixture of ochre-coloured stone and brick which gives the town a golden colouring well matched to the arid landscape of burnt earth which surrounds it. Most of the churches are massively built, with rather austere exteriors, and have suffered little damage from earthquakes. They were mostly founded in the latter part of the 16th century, and show a variety of styles, reflecting the alterations and additions made in later centuries.

The very large **Plaza de Armas** is one of the most harmonious in Peru with its whitewashed stone arcades. Its few trees are insufficient to bring much shade or coolness into this town without vegetation. In the centre of the square is a *monument to Antonio José de Sucre*, the victor of Ayacucho.

On the east side of the square is the **Cathedral,** one of Ayacucho's youngest churches (1632–77). The façade, flanked by two square towers topped by small pinnacled domes, is in the classical style, much restored. In the interior are magnificent 18th century wooden *reredoses* and a number of fine paintings ("El Señor de Burgos", "El Niño Llorón", "Immaculate Conception", etc.). Beside the Cathedral is the *Town Hall*, and opposite it, in a 17th century palace, the *Prefecture*, with a vaulted entrance and a beautiful pillared patio.

---

1 Cathedral
2 Town Hall
3 Prefecture
4 University
5 San Agustín
6 Santo Domingo
7 Hotel Turistas
8 La Compañía
9 Regional Museum
10 San Francisco de Paula
11 La Merced

12 Santa Clara
13 San Francisco de Asís
14 Hospital of San Juan de Dios
15 San Cristóbal
16 Santa Teresa
17 Casa Orcasitas
18 Santa Ana
19 San Juan Bautista
20 San Sebastián

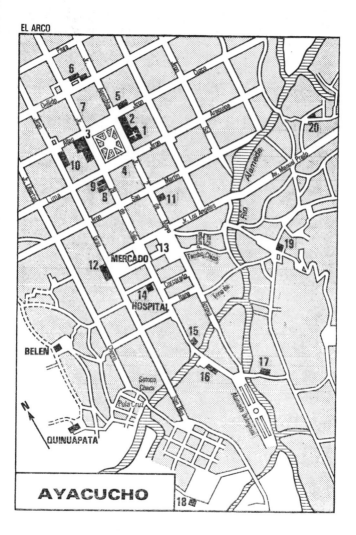

To the south, in the 17th century house of Bishop Cristóbal de Castilla y Zamora, which has beautiful patios and arcades, is the **University,** reopened in 1959 after being closed for nearly a century, which has provided a considerable stimulus to the town's cultural life.

At the north-east corner of the square, on the corner of Calle Asamblea and Calle Cuzco, are the *church of San Agustín* and the *Archbishop's Palace*, an attractive colonial house. One block north, adjoining the Turistas hotel, is the **church of Santo Domingo.**

This is a massive 16th century building (1548–61) which would have a rather austere aspect but for the two-storey portico which has been added to the façade and the indented roof gables between the two small square towers. To the left is the base of a tower destroyed by lightning in 1640, on which a pinnacled turret with three arched openings has been erected. To the right is a Corinthian column bearing a stone cross. In the interior is a beautiful carved wooden figure of the *Virgin Dolorosa*.

On the south side of the square, near the corner of Calle 28 de Julio, is the Baroque **church of the Compañía** (1605), a single-aisled church which contains a fine Churrigueresque altar and the image of Christ in Agony which is carried in procession on Good Friday. The *cloister* and *sacristy* are also worth seeing. To the right of the church is the *Regional Museum*.

Behind the Prefecture is the church of *San Francisco de Paula*, with an elegant Renaissance façade.

In Calle 2 de Mayo is the *church of the Merced*, one of the oldest in the town (late 16th and 17th c.), with three wide aisles and beautiful chapels containing pictures of the colonial period.

In the picturesque market square (market on Sunday morning) are two churches facing one another, Santa

Clara on the west side and San Francisco de Asís on the east side.

Santa Clara, founded in 1568 through the munificence of the owner of a silver-mine, has a very plain and rather severe façade with a lantern tower. In the interior, which has a ceiling showing Mudéjar influence, are an 18th century pulpit and a number of interesting pictures (including one of "Jesus of Nazareth", patron of the town).

San Francisco, founded in 1552, is rather neglected. It has a fine Renaissance doorway with figures of saints and angels.

Continuing along Calle 28 de Julio, we pass on the right the *chapel of San Juan de Dios* and the *hospital* attached to it and come to the **church of San Cristóbal,** on the banks of the river Alameda. This little chapel, unfortunately now abandoned and neglected, is the oldest church in the town (1542).

It has a very simple but elegant *Renaissance doorway* of white stone, contrasting with the fairly crude workmanship of the walls. To the left is a massive square tower. In this church are buried members of the Pizarrist force which defeated Almagro's supporters at the battle of Chupas in 1542.

In a square beyond the river is the *church of Santa Teresa,* with beautiful pictures in the choir. Near this church is a shady promenade, the *Alameda Bolognesi.* Returning across the river, we can see the *Casa Orcasitas,* with a chapel from which came the pictures of the Passion now in the church of the Pilar in San Isidro, Lima.

Each of the outer districts of the town has a little chapel, often very old, standing in its small square. The most interesting of these are *Santa Ana,* in the south, and *El Arco,* to the north.

The town contains numerous **colonial houses** with patios surrounded by galleries, old staircases and balconies with wooden screens or wrought-iron grilles. Some are in course of restoration.

The finest of these houses are the **Casa Jáureguy;** the **Casa Vivanco,** now occupied by the Banco Industrial; the **Casa Chacón,** occupied by the Banco de la Vivienda; and above all the

Palacio de los Marqueses de Mozobamba (near the Town Hall), which ranks as one of the oldest houses in America (mid 16th c.). The patio of the Mozobamba Palace has a fountain with the figure of a monkey and columns whose capitals are decorated with snakes carved by native stone-masons.

Handicrafts and Folk Traditions

Ayacucho is famous for its **craftsmen,** whose workshops will be found all over the town. They work in Huamanga stone (alabaster), leather (caskets, chairs and tables in colonial style), wood (furniture, carved frames), silver (filigree silver peacocks) and now tinplate (used to make crosses bearing the instruments of the Passion which the peasants set up on the roofs of their houses, or more modern articles for tourists, like light-shades, candlesticks and masks). Other local specialties are gourds decorated with pokerwork (*mates*), Quinua pottery and the very striking reredoses (*retablos*) of wood and alabaster, painted in bright colours and incorporating a Nativity scene or a scene of country life (particularly the gathering of prickly pears).

The **folk traditions** of Ayacucho are among the richest in Peru. Particularly notable is the "Scissors Dance", the music for which is provided by a group of Indians blowing curved cows' horns (*huacrapucus*).

Ayacucho's **Holy Week** celebrations are the most famous in Peru. The old colonial tradition of the *Reseña* is still preserved. This is a ceremony lasting five days in which penitents clad in black or purple robes are tapped with a black flag bearing a red cross (an allusion to the old tradition that after a battle in which their leader was killed the surviving soldiers should be struck with his standard in token of mourning).

Every day during Holy Week there are **processions** from the town's churches. The most important of these are: Palm Sunday, the Chamiza (in which mules carry branches of broom which are later burned on Easter Day), the procession of the Palms and the procession of the Señor de Ramos, celebrating Christ's entry into Jerusalem; Wednesday, procession of Jesus of Nazareth and the Virgin Dolorosa; Good Friday, procession of the Holy Sepulchre; Easter Day, procession of the Risen Christ (starting at 5.30 in the morning, to the light of candles, burning broom branches and fireworks). There are fairs on Good Friday at Chupas and on Easter Saturday on the Cerro de Acuchimay. Folk dancing and singing, particularly on Easter Day.

Surroundings of Ayacucho

1. *Quinua*, near which the famous **battle of Ayacucho** was fought, can be reached by a minor road which runs direct to the village or by taking the Huancayo road and turning off into a country road on the right leading to the lower Apurímac valley (the *Valle de San Miguel*). A monument marks the spot where the troops commanded by the Venezuelan General Sucre defeated the Spanish loyalist army on 9 December 1824. The village of **Quinua** (alt. 3400) is very picturesque, with a church which is frequently represented in the local pottery; other popular subjects are bulls, llamas, etc. Near Quinua, in the direction of Chacco, is the site of **Huari,** the centre of an empire contemporary with that of Tiahuanaco (8th–12th c.), with imposing circular buildings.

2. The road through the Valle de San Miguel gives access to the *ceja de montaña*, with the settlers' villages of *San Francisco* and, on the other side of the Apurímac, *Luisiana* and *Pichari*. In this are some impressive Inca remains contemporary with Machu Picchu which have recently been excavated, and there is another site similar to Machu Picchu at *Vilcashuamán* (accessible only on foot: one hour's walk from the town).

3. 68 km from Ayacucho, on a road which branches off the Cuzco road soon after the Tocto pass, is **Cangallo,** where the last supporters of Diego de Almagro the younger took refuge after their defeat by the Pizarrists in the battle of Chupas (16 September 1542) The road runs over the battlefield shortly after leaving the town. The peasants in this area, known as *morochucos*, show a smaller admixture of Indian blood than in other parts of Peru, having lighter coloured hair, complexion and eyes; they are of relatively tall stature and often grow beards. They are excellent horsemen, which gives a distinctive character to the fiestas and bullfights in the village and in Ayacucho.

3. AYACUCHO TO CUZCO

Distance 631 km.

This is the loneliest and ruggedest section of the route, running through arid valleys at an altitude of 2000 m and over *punas* at more than 4000 m (Huamina pass, 4420 m).

After leaving the Pampas the road comes to *Chincheros* and *Andahuaylas* (260 km), situated in fertile and densely populated valleys (modest restaurants and hotels). **Abancay** (396 km), at an altitude of 2400 m, is the chief town of one of the poorest and most isolated *departamentos* in the Sierra. Its sugar plantations are declining, and the economy of the town depends mainly on its rôle as an administrative centre and a road junction (the Chalhuanca–Puquío–Nazca road goes off here). There is a Turistas hotel.

Just before *Curahuasi* (441 km) a side road goes off to the interesting site of **Saywite,** a short distance away, with a carved stone which is thought to be a map of the Inca empire. After crossing the Apurímac at *Cunyar* on a modern bridge which has replaced an Inca suspension bridge, the road comes to *Limatambo* (515 km), with the Inca ruins of *Tarahuasi*. Thereafter it runs over the *Anta* plain to **Cuzco** (see next chapter).

5. CUZCO

Cuzco can be reached by road from Ayacucho or Arequipa;
by air (three flights daily from Lima, two flights weekly from
Arequipa on Fridays and Sundays, one flight weekly from
Ayacucho); and by rail (services from Puno and Arequipa: see
Practical Information).

Situation and History

The best view of the town can be had from the fortress of
Sacsayhuamán, to the north, or from the neighbouring "White
Christ". Cuzco lies at an altitude of almost 3400 m in an amphitheatre of mountains with its open end to the east at the head
of the valley of the Huatanay, a short tributary of the Vilcanota–
Urubamba. The depression was formerly occupied by a lake
which has left high terraces round the sides (clearly visible near
the airport), the memory of which is preserved in the legends
about the Inca foundation of the town. According to one of these
legends, Manco Cápac and his sister and wife Mama Ocllo, having
emerged from Lake Titicaca, set out towards the north-west to
bring men the arts of civilisation. Travelling up the Vilcanota
valley, they came to Huanacauri (the mountain facing Sacsayhuamán) and threw a gold baton into the air, resolving to
establish a city on the spot where it landed. Another legend has
it that the founder was Ayar Manco, one of the four sons of
Ayar who came out of the Tampu Ttocco caves (near Pacarrec-
tambo-Paruro, south-west of the town), accompanied by their
wives. Both of these supposed founders were of Aymará origin
and conquered Quechua tribes. The actual establishment of the
first settlement here is thought to have taken place not earlier
than the 11th century, in a depression where remains of a culture
dating back 1000 years before the Christian era (Chanapata-
Marcavalle) and also Huari material have been found. The name
"Cuzco" is believed to mean "the navel": i.e. the centre of the
Inca empire and indeed of the world.

The Plaza de Armas occupies the position of the Huacaypata,
the esplanade which lay in the centre of the Inca city (although
this was in fact larger, taking in also Plaza Regocijo, in which
are the Town Hall and the square white structure of the Turistas
hotel). It is still possible to trace the course of the three rivers,

now flowing underground, which bounded the original town-
the Saphy, represented by the south-west side of the Plaza de
Armas and the Av. del Sol; the Tullumayo, under the avenue of
that name; and, to the south, the Chunchulmayo, under the Av.
del Ejército. The three streams join opposite Plaza Orellana
(facing the Savoy Hotel) to make the Huatanay, which has been
diverted to flow along the foot of the hills to the south. The Inca
city lay round the present Plaza de Armas within the triangle
between the Saphy and the Tullumayo. It had the form of a
puma, with the tail at the junction of the rivers and the head on
the Sacsayhuamán hill. As rebuilt by Pachacuti in the 15th
century it was an imposing assemblage of temples and palaces
(of which each successive Emperor built his own), huge buildings
of carefully dressed stone separated by narrow lanes, comprising
not only halls designed for cult purposes and residences for the
Emperor and the priests but also craftsmen's workshops.

The town's functions were essentially political and religious,
and it was relatively small (area 70 hectares, population probably
50,000). It was divided into two parts on the line of the street
between the Plaza de Armas and the Compañía church, with the
older part, Hanan-Cuzco (Upper Cuzco) to the north-west and
Urin-Cuzco (Lower Cuzco) to the south-east. There was also a
division of the city into four parts oriented on the cardinal
points, reflecting the quadripartite structure of the Inca empire,
the Tahuantinsuyu ("empire of the four furrows"). Each of these
four parts, from which the four principal roads set out for the
four parts of the empire, had three outer districts (i.e. a total of
twelve), containing adobe buildings occupied by craftsmen,
soldiers, compulsory settlers from all over the empire (mitimaes)
and farmers. In these districts there were also round buildings
which served as granaries (colqas).

After the Spanish conquest, and particularly after Manco
Cápac's rising, Cuzco and its fortress were dismantled and a new
Spanish town was built, using the stones and sometimes even the
foundations of the Inca buildings. The outer districts of the Inca
city were re-formed into parishes in 1559 — San Cristóbal, on the
slopes of Sacsayhuamán, near the old Inca palace, the Colcampata; San Blas to the north-east; Santiago and Belén to the south
of the Chunchulmayo; Santa Ana to the west; and San Sebastián,
5 km away in the valley. In the 17th century La Recoleta to the
east and La Almudena to the south-west were added.

The colonial town developed within the triangle formed by
the three rivers, at the foot of the northern hills, although the two

southern parishes of Belén and Santiago remained until the beginning of this century isolated beyond the deep ravine of the Chunchulmayo. In the east the town ended on the line of Plaza Limacpampa, the church of Santo Domingo and Av. Grau, the rest of the valley being given up to cultivation. The real growth of the town began only after an earthquake in 1950, bringing the population from 40,600 in 1940 (scarcely more than at the end of the 18th century) to its present 125,000. Visitors will notice the difference between the old town, with its closely packed grid of streets and its colonial houses—which, seen from the hill above the town, look like so many little boxes laid out round a central patio—and the modern town. This extends along the valley on both sides of the Av. de la Cultura (the Puno road) and the old Velazco Astete airport in smart new blocks and on to the neighbouring hills in the working class quarters (Pueblos Jovenes) of little adobe houses. In clear weather Mt Ausangate (6384 m), the tutelary "Apu" (Lord) of Cuzco in Quechua mythology, can be seen on the horizon.

Character of the Town

Because of the terraces and the Inca buildings the Spaniards were unable to lay out their town on an exactly regular grid in accordance with their usual practice. The Plaza de Armas itself is irregular in shape and not quite level. It is surrounded by arcades of the traditional kind, and is full of charm in spite of the incessant restoration to which it has been subjected. Thus of the four arches over the corners of the square, with their accompanying fountains, there remains only the one in the north corner, recently rebuilt. Most of the balconies have also been rebuilt, most recently after the 1950 earthquake. In the centre of the square is a fountain with white cranes, presented to the town at the beginning of this century, which until 1969 also bore a figure of a redskin, complete with feathers and arrows. There are plans to replace it by a monument to Túpac Amaru, leader of the Indian rising in the 18th century, who was executed and quartered in the square. Under the arcades are remains of Inca palaces, including in particular the **Palace of Pachacuti** (Caxana), which was presented to Francisco Pizarro (Portal de Panes on north-west side).

Most of the buildings in Cuzco, including the religious houses founded shortly after the Conquest, were rebuilt after an earthquake in 1650 under the direction of Bishop Manuel de Molli-

nedo y Angulo, and were faithfully restored after the 1950 earthquake. They are built of pink or grey stone, volcanic or granitic,
often using stones from Inca buildings. The doorways are
Plateresque or Baroque, usually with two or three registers
decorated with Corinthian columns. The towers are low and
massive, as a precaution against earthquakes, and are topped by
graceful domes, as are most of the roofs. Every church is a real
museum of colonial art, with numerous pictures, gilded reredoses, statues and choirs and pulpits of carved wood (choirs of
the Cathedral, the Merced and San Francisco; pulpits in the
Cathedral, the Compañía and San Blas).

Far from being a dead town, however, the former Inca capital
will surprise the visitor by its animation, particularly by the
bustle of activity in the squares and round the market. Situated
in the heart of a region which has remained strongly Indian, it is
the least Western of Peruvian towns. It has a varied range of
handicrafts, notable among which are the beautiful textiles
(red ponchos from Qeros, white ones from Canchis), naive
statuettes on Christian themes or realistic treatments of everyday
life (notably by Mendívil and E. Mérida) and delicately worked
objects in wood or silver. There are frequent exhibitions of local
handicrafts, particularly at Christmas (Santoranticuy).

Festivals. Cuzco is famous for its Holy Week celebrations;
but even greater occations are the Cruz Velakuy festival in each
parish (May) and *Corpus Christi* (beginning of June), when the
patron saints of each church are carried in procession on silver
litters. 24 June is *Inti Raymi*, the festival of the Sun, modelled on
the Inca ceremonies performed at Sacsayhuamán, with folk
dancing contests, etc. Folk dancing displays every evening in the
Centro Qosqo (Av. del Sol).

Cuzco has 27 hotels in the first and second categories, including three in the luxury class, with a total of 613 rooms, plus 19
more modest hotels. There are numerous restaurants of all types;
visitors are recommended to go out to the *quintas* and sample
local dishes in the open air.

1. Centre of the Town

On the site formerly occupied by the Temple of
Viracocha (Quishuarcancha) stands the **Cathedral,**
imposing in its size and in its situation on a spacious
esplanade. It was begun in 1559 but not consecrated

until 1668. The *doorway* is Baroque (1658), with a heavy wooden door studded with bronze nails (*Puerta del Perdón*). Along the edge of the roof is a row of pinnacled turrets, with statues of St Peter and St Paul on either side of a cross in the centre. In the left-hand tower is a heavy bell (bronze, with an admixture of gold) popularly known as "María Angola".

The spacious nave has a vaulted stone roof. In the choir, which is surrounded by an ambulatory, is an imposing silver **altar,** with a late 17th century mensa and Doric columns added in 1803. Behind it is the original wooden **reredos** (1637), with beautiful and sometimes rather naive carving. Nearby is a fine gilded Plateresque reredos. At the west end of the church is a 17th century **wooden choir,** carved with curious figures — half angels, half bare-breasted mermaids — whose faces show Indian characteristics (the work of Diego Arias de la Cerda, who was also responsible for the doorway). There is a very beautiful Plateresque pulpit.

Among the **chapels** in the aisles are the Chapel of the Nativity (or *La Antigua*), facing the central doorway, with a marvellous Virgin presented by Charles V; the chapel of the *Virgen de los Remedios* (first on right); the chapel of the *Señor de los Temblores* (fourth on right), with a figure of Christ presented by Charles V, blackened by soot from candles, which is carried in procession on Good Friday; the Chapel of the Immaculate Conception or *La Linda* (third on left after the altar); the chapel of *Santiago* (fifth on left); and the chapel of the *Virgen del Carmen*, with pictures by A. Sinchi Roca.

On the walls are a profusion of **pictures,** including a "Circumcision" (to right on entering); the *Virgin of Belén* (beyond the choir, right-hand aisle); the fifty pictures of the *Letanía Lauretana* of *Marcos Zapata* (1655); four pictures by *Basilio Santa Cruz* in the transept; a "Last Supper" (showing strong Indian influence) at the far end of the choir, with a scene from the Apocalypse opposite it; the "Good Shepherd" in the north aisle; the *Virgin of La Almudena*, opposite the chapel of Santiago; "Jesus among the Doctors"; and pictures by *Diego Quispe Tito* on the parables, the twelve months and the four seasons.

The sacristy has beautiful doors and contains a reredos with a Christ attributed to *van Dyck* and a collection of colonial furniture, jewellery and liturgical objects (monstrance).

To the right of the Cathedral is the **church of the Triunfo,** the oldest in the town (1536) but rebuilt in the early 18th century, with fine stone vaulting and five Plateresque reredoses. Above the stone central altar is a cross, believed to be the Cross of the Conquest presented to Atahuallpa at Cajamarca. In the sacristy is a picture of Cuzco at the time of the 1650 earthquake.

To the left of the Cathedral is the *Chapel of Jesus, Mary and Joseph* (early 18th c.), with a magnificent Plateresque central altar. Beside it is the *Court of the Inquisition*, with a charming arcaded gallery.

Also in the Plaza de Armas is the **church of the Compañía,** built on the site of Huayna Cápac's palace, the Amarucancha. It was originally founded in 1571 but the present church dates from the second half of the 17th century (consecrated 1668). The *doorway* is Baroque, with three registers divided by slender Corinthian columns and a series of niches, some of them blind, framed in arches. Above all this is a larger cusped arch surmounted by a cornice decorated with rosettes, which in turn bears a cross and two pinnacled turrets. The towers which flank the doorway have *oeil-de-boeuf* windows and are topped by pinnacles and graceful ribbed domes. The whole effect is of great elegance, in a conscious attempt to rival the nearby Cathedral.

The nave is aisleless, with a huge dome borne on a drum over the crossing. All the **altars** are of notable quality. The central altar is of gilded wood (Baroque); the second on the right (Churrigueresque) is of wood, painted in a pastel shade, with naive caryatids which already show Indian influence. The balconies for monks have beautiful wooden screens. The pulpit is Plateresque.

There are a number of **paintings** of some value, in particular those under the wooden choir depicting the marriages of two nephews of St Ignatius Loyola, one of them with an Inca princess, Colla Beatriz. Near these is a "Life of St Ignatius" by *Marcos Zapata* (18th c.). On the central altar are fine paintings of the Ascension and the Archangels Michael and Raphael. Above the doors leading into the side chapels are two copies of Rubens by *Basilio Santa Cruz.*

To the south of the Plaza de Armas, in Calle Mantas, is the **church of the Merced,** founded in 1534 but rebuilt in the second half of the 17th century. The main front has a classical *doorway,* and above this is an oval recess communicating with the choir which until 1950 contained an altar to the Virgin of Mercy used in the celebration of mass for the crowds of Indians who gathered in the square. To the left is a square Baroque tower with clusters of Corinthian columns and an octagonal dome lit by *oeil-de-boeuf* windows.

CUZCO

P Palace of Pachacuti
1 Cathedral
2 Church of Triunfo
3 Church of Jesus, Mary and Joseph
4 Court of the Inquisition
5 La Compañia
6 La Merced
7 Hotel Turistas
8 House of Inca Garcilaso de la Vega
9 Town Hall (Cabildo)
10 Santa Teresa
11 Archaeological Museum
12 Casa de Jara
13 College of San Bernardo
14 Casa Marqués de Valleumbroso
15 San Francisco
16 Santa Clara
17 San Pedro
18 Santa Ana station (Machu Picchu)
19 Santiago
20 La Almudena
21 Church of Belén
22 Palacio del Almirante
23 Las Nazarenas
24 San Antonio Abad
25 Museum of Art (Palace of Inca Roca)
26 House of the Four Busts
27 Santo Domingo (Temple of Sun)
28 Casa Concha (Prefecture)
29 Santa Catalina
30 San Cristóbal
31 San Blas
32 La Recoleta
33 Santa Ana
34 Puno-Arequipa station
35 Museum of Folk Art (Touring y Automóvil-Club)

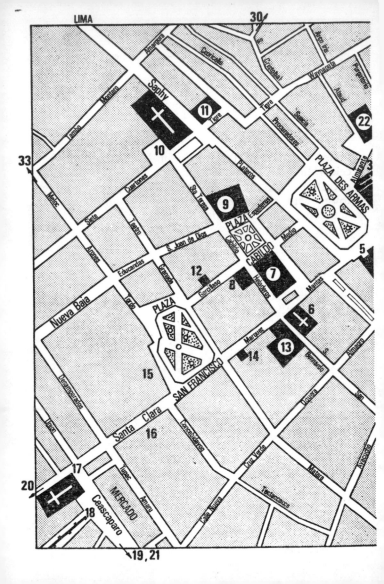

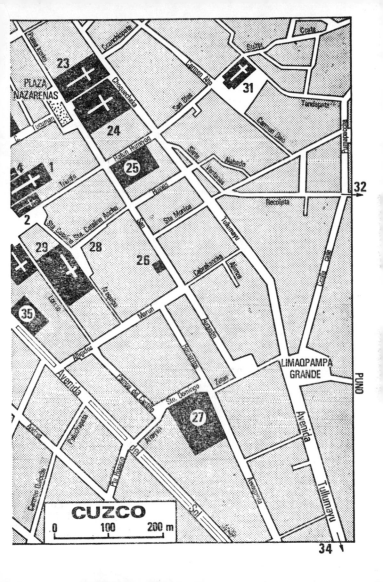

The nave is three-aisled, with vaulted stone roofs. On the high altar is a *reredos* of gilded stucco with a beautiful image of the Virgin of Mercy. Of the lateral chapels the most interesting are the chapel of the *Señor de Huanca* (to the right on entering), with a magnificent Plateresque reredos and a fine carved figure of Christ; the chapel of *San Pedro Nolasco*, patron of the Mercedarian order (fourth on right), with a fine reredos; the reredoses of the Virgin of Mercy (Renaissance), with a splendid Virgin, the **Virgen de la Soledad,** one of the finest pieces of sculpture in Cuzco (to the left of the altar); and (to the left of the choir) the reredos of Jesus of Nazareth, surrounded by ex-votos. In the undercroft of the church are buried Diego de Almagro and his son, and Gonzalo Pizarro. The choir is Plateresque (early 17th c.), with beautiful carved wooden figures of the Virgin, Evangelists and saints, and an elegant balustrade.

The *first cloister*, in pink stone, has massive pillars flanked with graceful carved Corinthian columns. There are fine cornices round the base of the upper storey and the roof. The fountain is 17th century. The galleries and the imposing staircases leading up to them (late 17th c.) have splendid coffered ceilings and paintings. The picture of the saints of the Mercedarian order is by Basilio Pacheco. The *second cloister*, more sober in style, is in course of restoration. On the left-hand staircase is *Father Salamanca's cell*, with fine frescoes (late 17th c.) and a small Baroque organ. To the south is the *chapter house* and above it the *library*, both containing fine colonial paintings.

The *sacristy* contains a wooden reredos (Plateresque) with a copy of Velázquez's "Christ", embroidered chasubles, liturgical objects, including in particular the first bell cast in Peru (1534) and a celebrated gold monstrance made in 1806, with 168 valuable pearls and 687 diamonds (displayed daily at 5 p.m.).

Near the Merced, in Calle San Bernardo, is the **College of San Bernardo,** founded by the Jesuits in 1619 and now in course of restoration (late 17th c. doorway). Beyond the Turistas hotel is Plaza Regocijo, connected with the Plaza de Armas by a number of short streets. It is bounded on the west side by the **Town Hall,** a 17th century building on Inca foundations, with two pillared galleries and a beautiful patio with a fountain.

In *Calle Santa Teresa*, which runs west to the church of Santa Teresa, are houses with Inca carvings (in particular pumas). At the far end is a colonial mansion, the *Casa de los Condes de Peralta*. The church and convent beside it (not yet open to the public) are also built on Inca foundations. Built at the end of the 17th century, they contain some magnificent pictures and an altar covered with silver.

Facing the entrance to the Turistas hotel, on the other side of the Plaza de Armas, is the *House of the Inca Garcilaso de la Vega*, son of a Spanish official and an Inca princess, who was Peru's first mestizo writer. It has been restored in the style of the late 17th century and now houses the National Institute of Culture and an important **Museum of Colonial Art.**

We can return to Plaza San Francisco by Calle Marqués, the busiest street in the town, passing on the left the mansion of the Marqués de Valleumbroso, with a handsome classical doorway of grey stone surmounted by a balcony (destroyed by fire in 1971), or by Calle Garcilaso (formerly Calle Coca). In this street are a number of colonial houses recently converted into hotels, in particular the late 17th or early 18th century *Casa de Jara* (No. 256), with a stone doorway and an attractive patio with brick arches decorated with curious terracotta medallions.

The *Plaza San Francisco*, now laid out as a botanic garden, is dominated by the bulk of the *College of Science*, founded by Bolívar in 1825, and by the **Convent of San Francisco.** The convent was founded in 1534, but did not come to this site until 1549; it was completed after 1650. It is of massive and sober effect, with *two doorways*, the one on the left being in Renaissance style and the other, the principal doorway, Plateresque, with a niche in the upper part framed between two pilasters decorated with chimaeras. Between the two doorways is a tower with a flattened dome, which gives the building a rather fortress-like air.

The magnificent original wooden reredoses were replaced at the beginning of this century by new ones in neo-classical or neo-Gothic style, made of brick or adobe covered with plaster; some of them still retain interesting pictures or carving. The wooden *pulpit* is inlaid with ivory and has a fine figure of St Francis. At the far end of the church is the Plateresque oak choir (by Father Luis Montes), one of the finest in Cuzco. The arms of the stalls have carvings of mermaids and eagles, and the high backs of the upper range of stalls have figures of saints. The cornices are decorated with chimaeras and geometric patterns. On the left-hand side is a mid 17th century *organ*, and in the centre a carved *lectern* inlaid with mother-of-pearl (1678).

The cloister is reached through the *reception room*, which contains some excellent pictures, in particular a Virgin Dolorosa. The **cloister,** like the church, is sober in style, with two arcaded galleries. It contains some fine *pictures* by Basilio Santa Cruz, Juan Inca Raurahua, Juan Sinchi Roca and others. The second cloister is more rustic in style.

One block away from San Francisco, to the right are the, remains of the entrance to the Hospital of *San Juan de Dios*, built for the benefit of both Spaniards and mestizos (between Calle Nueva Baja and Calle Arones).

To the left of the College of Science is a 19th century arch marking the entrance to Calle Santa Clara, which leads to the market, passing on the right the Inca substructures of the College. On the left is the church of **Santa Clara,** founded in 1549, built on this site in 1558–60 and rebuilt after the 1650 earthquake.

The exterior is sober, with two low and massive doorways framed by pilasters and a square tower topped by a ribbed dome. In the nave are magnificent altars resplendent with mirrors. The **central altar** (1685) has a beautiful silver tabernacle. There is a curious picture relating the Virgin's descent on Mt Sunturhuasi. The cloisters are still closed to the public.

Near the market and Santa Ana railway station is the church of **San Pedro,** built in 1668 on the site of a hospital for the Indians (founded 1556) which was destroyed in the 1650 earthquake. It has a fine Renaissance façade.

· The church contains interesting **paintings and sculpture:** the *Virgin of Candlemas*, *St Peter* and the *Apostles* on the Baroque central reredos; *St Anthony*, *St Francis* and *Jesus of Nazareth* (fourth chapel on the right); *St Peter* (right arm of transept); the *Virgin Dolorosa* (second chapel on the left); the *Virgen del Carmen* (third on left); and the *Immaculate Conception* (fourth on left). There are also portraits of the celebrated Bishop Don Manuel de Mollinedo y Angulo and his nephew, who was responsible for building the church. Fine wooden pulpit (Plateresque); stone-built choir.

2. North-East of the Plaza de Armas

Between the Court of the Inquisition and the remains of Sinchi Roca's palace is the *Cuesta del Almirante*, which leads to the *Plaza Nazarenas*.

On the left of this street is the early 17th century **Palacio del Almirante** (in course of restoration), named after Admiral Francisco de Alderete. As rebuilt after the 1650 earthquake it has a beautiful Plateresque window and doorway. The entrance corridor and some of the rooms have coffered ceilings. There is a very elegant patio.

The church of **Las Nazarenas** was built from 1715 onwards in an Inca building called the *Yachayhausi* (House of Learning). The left-hand doorway is in classical style; the one on the right, surmounted by a companile, is typically mestizo, with a lintel decorated with two mermaids and Inca carvings of snakes. The pre-Columbian wall continues along the narrow little "Street of the Seven Snakes" between the Nazarenas and San Antonio.

The **Seminary of San Antonio Abad,** founded in 1598, was rebuilt in 1678 and completed about 1740 (the date of construction of the beautiful façade with a statue of St Anthony and the arms of Spain and Bishop Mollinedo y Angulo). In 1592 it became the *University of*

San Antonio Abad, which was later amalgamated with
the Jesuit University. It contains two large cloisters
built on Inca terraces. The church (entered from the
cloister) has a number of *magnificent reredoses,*
including one with mirrors, which illustrate the diversity of the religious art of Cuzco.

Continuing to the right along Calle del Palacio, we
come to the former **Archbishop's Palace,** which has
been a **Museum of Art** since 1968. Built on the *Palace
of Inca Roca,* it is one of the finest achievements of
Cuzco architecture, with the Spanish superstructure of
light adobe bricks, whitewashed and decorated with
beautiful wooden balconies, resting on the Inca foundations. These are built of huge dressed stones, one of
which has twelve angles (Calle Hatun Rumiyoc).

From here we can continue towards the San Blas district (see
below) or alternatively turn round the corner of the Palace into
Calle Herrajes, continuing along the beautiful Calle San Agustín,
lined with Spanish buildings on *Inca foundations.* The finest of
these (at the foot of the street, on right) is the *House of the Four
Busts* (probably late 16th c.), with a lintel bearing four medallions
and a twin-bayed window. The street runs into the *Plaza de
Limacpampa Chico,* from which we can either go right along
Calle Zetas to **Santo Domingo** (see below) or turn right to reach
the busy **Limacpampa Grande,** which until very recently was the
eastern entrance to the town, and the new districts round the
Avenida de la Cultura (large schools, University, old airport,
Hospital, Seminary). The *Convent of the Recoleta,* to the east
(until recently outside the town), was founded in 1599.

3. East of the Plaza de Armas

To the left of the Compañía is the narrow *Calle
Loreto,* which runs past (on left) the former **Palace of
the Virgins of the Sun** (Acllahuasi), now occupied by
the church and convent of **Santa Catalina.**

The church, founded in 1601, has two doorways in classical style in Calle Santa Catalina Angosta. It contains *interesting paintings* of the mid 17th century (by Albano and Juan Espinoza de los Monteros among others), two choirs with wood and wrought-iron screens, and Moorish balconies.

Opposite the church is the **Casa Concha** (now the Prefecture), in the *Palace of Túpac Yupanqui*, with fine Inca walls (particularly in Calle Maruri) and an elegant colonial balcony.

Continuing along Calle Arequipa and Calle Pampa del Castillo, we come to the **Convent of Santo Domingo,** founded in 1534 on the site of the *Temple of the Sun* and completed in 1681. The sobriety of the *south doorway*, framed in Doric columns, contrasts with the Churrigueresque style of the *tower*, with its clusters of twisted Corinthian columns and its octagonal dome surrounded by pinnacles.

As in San Francisco, the old reredoses of gilded wood have been replaced by modern brick and plaster altars. Only the *pulpit* is Baroque. The choir is simpler than in the other Cuzco churches. There are a number of interesting *pictures*, including "El Señor de la Caña" (Christ of the Reed), and a figure of *Santo Domingo* by a mestizo sculptor (1670). The Renaissance-style *cloister*, of notable sobriety, is under restoration; the pictures in the galleries include a "Vision of the Cross" by Diego Quispe Tito.

The 1950 earthquake, by bringing down the plaster and paintings of the colonial period, revealed the old Inca walls of the **Temple of the Sun** (Inticancha). To the right are the rooms dedicated to the cult of the Sun, the Moon, the stars and Venus, with handsome trapezoidal niches for idols or offerings. A stone with a number of holes in the surface is thought to have supported the gold disc representing the Sun. In one of the rooms the mummies of dead Emperors were deposited. To the left are smaller rooms dedicated to the cult of thunder, lightning and the rainbow. In one of them are three openings running down to the street below. The apse of the church, with its elegant bays framed between twisted columns supporting a small balcony with a lattice screen, rests on a magnificent *Inca wall* of elliptical form. On the terrace below this was a garden which contained gold offerings in the shape of animals and plants.

According to some authorities the two Incas of Vilcabamba (Sairi Túpac and Túpac Amaru) and Juan Pizarro are buried in the convent. As in the Cathedral and the Compañía, there are large vaulted undercrofts.

4. The Outer Parishes

1. Close to the town centre are the two northerly parishes of *San Cristóbal* and *San Blas*. **San Cristóbal,** on the slopes of Sacsayhuamán (late 17th c. tower), was built on the remains of the *Colcampata Palace*, which is attributed to the founder of the Inca empire, Manco Cápac, on account of the relatively crude construction of its terraces, which have handsome trapezoidal niches with double jambs.

The church of **San Blas,** built of adobe with a white-washed roughcast facing, has a stone basement storey and a tower surmounted by a three-storey campanile.

The aisleless nave is very dark, with magnificent Plateresque gilded **reredoses** (central altar with a silver mensa; reredos of the Virgen del Buen Suceso to the right; huge pictures relating the life of San Blas, painted in 1671). The **pulpit** is the finest piece of wood-carving in Peru, and no doubt in the whole of America. It was made about 1670–80 by an unknown sculptor (Luis Montes? Diego Arias de la Cerda, who built the Cathedral? Juan Tomás Tuyru Tupa?). At the base are the figures of eight heretics (including a woman and an Arab), bare to the waist, who appear to be supporting the whole weight of the pulpit, with seven chimaeras from whose mouths emerge festoons of grapes and vine leaves. The main structure of the pulpit is decorated with Baroque columns carved with grapes, birds, mitres, etc., and rests on a cornice borne by angels. Between the columns are figures of the Evangelists and the Immaculate Conception. The back, against the wall, has a figure of San Blas. The sounding board is decorated with a profusion of foliage, angels, garlands, pinnacles and keys, with figures of the Doctors of the Church, and on the summit of the whole structure a figure of the Redeemer holding a cross. Between the leaves is a death's head of the sculptor. Near the pulpit is a very beautiful balcony. The sacristy contains magnificent carved furniture.

2. To the south, rather farther from the centre, are the parishes of **Belén, Santiago** and **La Almudena**.

The church of **Belén,** founded in 1550, became a parish church in 1559, and was rebuilt in the second half of the 17th century. The façade is Plateresque, with a carved representation in the tympanum of the Adoration of the Kings (the original dedication of the church). The central altar has a silver mensa and a reredos of gilded wood containing a beautiful figure of the *Virgin of Belén,* decked with magnificent jewels, and a fine Crucifixion. The other reredoses are Plateresque. Most of the pictures are fine examples of colonial religious art.

The church of *Santiago,* founded in 1571, is of more rustic type. The cross outside the church dates from 1606. The reredoses and pictures in the interior are in rather poor condition (fine statue of the Apostle St James).

To the west of the town, near the cemetery, is the church of **La Almudena,** founded in 1683, which in 1698 rehoused the hospital for the Indians formerly at San Pedro. Of the huge colonial building (which had seven courtyards and three wards for patients) there remain only the chapel, badly damaged by the 1950 earthquake, and some accommodation which is now occupied by Cuzco prison. The church contains a beautiful reredos on the central altar, a Baroque pulpit and a splendid statue of the *Virgen de la Almudena* (1686).

On a promontory just outside the town, on the old road to Lima, is the little country church of **Santa Ana,** with eight very fine pieces of sculpture by the late 17th century sculptor Juan Tomás Tuyru Topa (recumbent Christ, Virgin Dolorosa, St Anne, St Jerome, etc.), a series of twelve pictures vividly depicting the Corpus Christi procession in colonial times and the miraculous effigy of the "*Señor del Cabildo*", painted on adobe bricks in the old town prison.

3. At the opposite end of the town is the church of **San Sebastián,** founded in 1559 and rebuilt after the 1650 earthquake, with a *Baroque doorway* (1678) which is one of the finest in Cuzco. It contains some excellent paintings by Diego Quispe Tito (who was born in the village) and a carved figure of San Sebastián.

5. Museums

The **Archaeological Museum** at Calle Tigre 15 (near
Calle Saphy) is mainly devoted to Inca art (pottery,
carved stones, weapons, mummies). Notable items are
a number of beautiful *qeros* (painted wooden goblets)
and small turquoise idols found at Pikillacta.

There are two museums devoted to colonial art, one
in the *House of the Inca Garcilaso de la Vega* (which
contains pictures and furniture from the old Viceregal
museum) and the recently opened **Museum of Art** (Calle
Hatun Rumiyoc), containing the Orihuela Collection.
There are also a number of private collections. In the
Tourist Galleries in the Avenida del Sol there is a
museum of handicrafts and anthropology; and there
are frequent exhibitions of work by artists and craftsmen of both the present and the past.

6. SURROUNDINGS OF CUZCO

1. INCA REMAINS NEAR THE TOWN

The **fortress of Sacsayhuamán,** 3 km north of the town, built according to some authorities in the reign of Túpac Yupanqui but according to others at a much earlier date, has three huge and impressive zigzag walls on the north side and on the other side a series of terraces and platforms overlooking Cuzco. The *outermost wall* is built of huge blocks of stone up to 9 m high, one of which has an estimated weight of 361 tons: it is difficult to conceive how a people ignorant of the use of the wheel contrived to transport the stones to the site and lay them so accurately.

The other walls, which are lower, are laid out on terraces above the outer rampart. To the north-west are the bases of three towers (*Muyocmarka, Sallaqmarka, Paucarmarka*). One of them is round, with an elaborate system of channels bringing water from a nearby spring (perhaps serving a calendric function?). On the other side of the huge esplanade (on which the *Inti Raymi* festival is celebrated every year) excavation is continuing to reveal further extensive remains, including the "Inca's Throne". There are also underground passages ("Chincanas") which are said to communicate with the town and with the Temple of the Sun in particular.

4 km east of Sacsayhuamán are the **ruins of Qengo,** which consist of two parts, a limestone crag carved into a multitude of steps, water channels, basins and animal figures (particularly snakes) and an elliptical amphitheatre bounded by a stone wall, with 19 seats set around a monolithic slab of stone almost 6 m high. Underneath all this are a number of underground chambers, one of which had platforms and trapezoidal niches carved from the rock. The site has been inter-

preted as a cult site dedicated to the Sun or the Moon or alternatively (on account of the amphitheatre) as some kind of court or tribunal.

A short distance beyond Sacsayhuamán on the Pisaq road are the fortress of *Pukapucará* (the Red Fortress), on the right, and 500 m farther on **Tambomachay,** on the left.

This consists of a series of four terraces, with a water channel running down the hill to a stone basin. In the carefully dressed uppermost wall are four trapezoidal niches, and there are other higher niches on the right-hand side of the second and third walls. This site has been interpreted as a bath (with hot and cold water) or alternatively a small shrine dedicated to the cult of water.

2. MACHU PICCHU

Machu Picchu can be reached by rail-car (dep. Santa Ana station 7 a.m., arr. 10.30; return journey dep. 3.30 p.m., arr. Cuzco 6.20) or by the ordinary train, which is slower. From the Machu Picchu station (alt. 1900 m) there is a bus service (20 minutes) to the site (alt. 2300 m), where there is a small Turistas hotel (advance booking necessary). Nowadays many people also reach the site on foot from Ollantaytambo on the "Inca Trail" (3–4 days), arriving at the upper end of the site, which was the original entrance. It must be remembered that the Incas rarely travelled in the valleys, which in this region are particularly deep (up to 400 m) and were until recent times unhealthy, but laid out their roads half-way up the mountainside or along the relatively level surface of the *puna*. The Spaniards concentrated on developing the valleys, and accordingly did not discover Machu Picchu, which was quickly swallowed up by the dense forest of the *ceja de montaña*. The "lost city" was not re-discovered until 1911, when it was found by an expedition from Yale University led by Hiram Bingham.

Machu Picchu was not a fortress but a *tambo* (posting station) on one of the principal routes into the Selva, two days' march from Cuzco and one day's march from Vilcabamba, where Inca Manco Cápac II took refuge in 1539. It had certainly also a considerable magico-religious importance, in virtue of the splendour of the surrounding landscape. Some archaeologists have suggested in addition that some of the terraces may have been experimental fields in which the plants of the forest were acclimatised to this high altitude.

Starting from the south entrance, near the hotel (the north entrance being on the peak of Huayna Picchu), we come at once into an area of terraced fields, after passing through a small *group of houses*. One of the houses has been reconstructed, with a steeply pitched thatched roof secured by leather thongs. From here we can either make for the "aristocratic quarter" or head straight for the **upper town** in order to get a general view of the site. The main entrance to the town, which was enclosed within a massive crenellated wall 5 m high, was at the top end, to the south-west. Underneath the wall there was probably the cemetery, with the house of its keeper (*acamayoc wasi*), and a stone on which the bodies of the dead were laid out. From here there is a fine view of the ruins. Slightly lower down is the *main gateway*, which is trapezoidal in shape, with double jambs and a curious arrangement for hanging the door, probably based on the use of leather hinges (with a pair of holes half-way up each jamb and a ring in the middle of the lintel). From here we continue on to the agricultural terraces, passing through a group of crudely made low houses with external courtyards, probably occupied by workers. In passing we can see the system for irrigating the terraces and the channels bringing water from a spring higher up.

The **"aristocratic quarter"** is so called because of the high standard of construction of the white granite houses. These are rectangular in plan and may have had a patio and an upper storey, as is suggested by the house known as the "Dwelling of the Ñusta" (princess). They are laid out in terraces, in lines of houses separated by narrow passages, and have windows on the east side and trapezoidal niches in the walls.

Continuing north, we come to the **Torreón** (Tower), a well built structure, unique of its kind, which is rectangular at one end and semicircular at the other and is familiarly known as the Caracol (Snail). Below this, hewn out of the rock, is a complex known as the *Tomb*—a series of niches of different sizes, with a block of stone cut in a series of steps in a fashion similar to the Intihuatana (see below).

Beyond the tower is a rectangular courtyard with nine niches separated by projecting studs of rock, and beyond this again is a system of water channels and small square basins on different levels. Opposite the main basin is a house consisting of four rooms and three patios, all with trapezoidal niches (ten of them in the largest room). Its size and beautiful masonry have earned this building the name of the **Inca's Palace.**

From here we pass by way of various terraces and staircases to the **Plaza Sagrada,** roughly square in plan, in the middle of the western part of the site. On three sides of this are large chambers open on one side. The one on the east side has three handsome windows; the others have seven, eight or nine trapezoidal niches separated by studs of rock. These are apparently shrines, containing flat slabs of rock which may have served as altars. In the chamber on the north side the stones are laid in courses of decreasing size towards the top.

Finally a further series of steep staircases and terraces brings us to the group of structures known as the **Intihuatana** (note in passing the retaining terraces on the west side of the town).

On a small esplanade of roughly oval plan, dominating the rest of the complex, is a block of greenish-grey granite (height

1 South entrance	9 Intihuatana
2 Terraced fields	10 Esplanade
3 Aristocratic quarter	11 Temple of Moon and
4 Torreón and Tomb	Acllahuasi
5 Workers' quarter	12 Workers' houses
6 Main entrance and	13 Houses of *amautas* and
cemetery	craftsmen
7 Inca's Palace	14 Prison and tribunal
8 Temples	

HUAYNA PICCHU

HOTEL

1.80 m, circumference 8.60 m) carefully hewn into a series of horizontal planes, with a prism-shaped vertical projection in the centre. This has been interpreted as an altar used for ritual sacrifices or, more probably, as a sundial. The prism is inclined at an angle of 12° to the plane below it (i.e. roughly the latitude of the site), so that at midday on the summer solstice, when the sun is directly overhead, it will cast no shadow. It could thus readily serve as a solar clock.

A spacious esplanade on two levels, which may have served as a place of assembly, lies between these various features in the western half of the site and the **eastern part** of the site. The structures here are rather simpler. The upper section consists of a *Temple of the Moon* (situated at a lower level than the Temple of the Sun) and the *Acllahuasi* (women's quarters). To the north is a complex group of houses, apparently intended for the lower classes of the population. To the south, at the foot of a large staircase, is a district of houses occupied by *amautas* (the educated class) and craftsmen, with handsome rooms containing niches. On the floors of some of the rooms are mortars (for use in dyeing or metal-working). Lower down are prisons, with rooms used for judgment and for punishment.

Dominating the whole site is **Huayna Picchu** (the "young peak", Machu Picchu being the "old peak"), from which there is a splendid view. On this too there are remains of terraces, platforms, buildings and subterranean structures similar to those in the lower town. It is climbed by a difficult path; the ascent takes about half an hour.

Round Machu Picchu there are numerous sites with remains of similar type, in particular *Intipata*, *Wiñay Huayna*, *Phuyupata-marca* and *Sayaqmarca* (these last two having high towers). Visitors to Machu Picchu should take the opportunity of continuing by train to *Chaullay-Quillabamba* (pop. 10,000: modest hotels) and beyond this (by lorry) to the mission station of *Coribeni*, in the beautiful tropical valley of La Convención.

3. PISAQ, URUBAMBA AND OLLANTAYTAMBO

This is one of the most popular excursions run by the Cuzco travel agencies; the trip, which takes a full day, can be done by bus, taxi or lorry. From the final bends on the road from Cuzco (which has been widened and resurfaced with asphalt) there are magnificent panoramic views of Pisaq (30 km from Cuzco) and the *Vilcanota valley*. (Lower down this river is known as the Urubamba. It joins the Apurímac in the Amazonian forest to form the Ucayali, a tributary of the Amazon).

The Vilcanota flows through a wide glacial valley, dominated on the right bank by the glaciers of the Eastern Cordillera. Here it is easy to observe the contrast between the Inca settlements on the high ground, with their formidable systems of terraces (ruins of Pisaq), and the villages established by the Spaniards in the valley (Pisaq, with Taray to the left), laid out on a regular plan round the Plaza de Armas. Here too can be seen the contrast between the haciendas, whose large regular fields occupy the fertile terraces, and the little plots of the settlers or the Indian communities on the steeper slopes.

The charming village of **Pisaq** has in recent years attracted increasing numbers of tourists to its Sunday market, held under the shade of the flamboyants in the Plaza de Armas, which is attended by the handicraft dealers of Cuzco. Here, after the service, can be seen the chiefs of the Indian communities (*varayocs*), with their chased silver canes and their high hats. The **Inca remains** are reached by taking the track along the imposing wall of terraces above the village or, more easily, by way of Cuyo Chico (to the right). They consist of an elaborate complex of temples with trapezoidal windows, towers, military quarters and a temple of the Sun (*Intihuatana*).

Between Pisar and Ollantaytambo the road runs through a number of sizeable townships and passes some old colonial landowners' houses (e.g. shortly before Calca). *Calca* commands a road to the *ceja de montaña* valley of Lares and, beyond this, to Quillabamba. **Yucay** has some remains of Inca terraces, and in one of its squares are the foundations of the *Palace of Sayri Túpac*. **Urubamba** (25 km from Pisaq, 55 km from Cuzco) has a Turistas hotel (swimming pool), restaurants and petrol stations, and is now an important holiday centre. 12 km west is **Ollantay-tambo,** a village built on the remains of an Inca *tambo* (posting station), with a *fortress* consisting of a series of impressive terraces, crowned by a temple with six carefully dressed mono-liths (one of them carved with a device in the form of a flight of steps, pointing to Tiahuanaco influence). Associated remains are the "Bath of the Ñusta" and the *chullpas* (round burial towers) of Cachiqhata.

4. CHINCHERO, MARAS AND URUBAMBA
OR THE ANTA PLAIN

Some visitors may prefer to the Pisaq market the even more typical one at **Chinchero** (25 km from Cuzco on the Lima road, turning right at Cachimayo; lorries on Sundays, or taxis). This market still preserves its old peasant character, with the trade taking the form of barter between the women of the local communities and those who have come from the Urubamba valley or from Cuzco. The local women, dressed in their ample black skirts and red *mantas* and wearing *monteras* on their intricately plaited hair, exchange potatoes or *ollucos* for the maize, fruit and herbs brought by the incomers, who wear brighter and richer garments, aprons and high white hats.

The square is dominated by the bulk of the church, built on the considerable remains of an *Inca palace*, the *ornacinas* of which serve to mark out the pitches of the market women. The adobe *church* (with a free-standing tower) contains magnifi-cent frescoes in vivid colours (recently restored), a beautiful altar and various pictures. To the right of the square is an arcaded house in which Mateo Pumacahua, one of the heroes of Peruvian independence, was born.

From Chinchero a country road suitable for cars links up with the Anta–Urubamba road, which leads to the village of **Maras,** on a bluff overlooking a

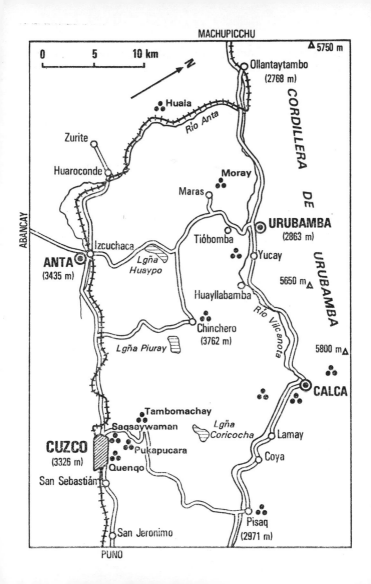

limestone plateau in the grandiose setting of the glaciers of the Eastern Cordillera (Verónica, Chicón), at altitudes of 5000 m.

The village has a fine church and some colonial houses with carved slabs serving as the lintel of the entrance doorway. Nearby are curious salt-pans on a multitude of small terraces, which have been worked since Inca times, and the site of *Moray*, with tiers of concentric terraces forming a kind of amphitheatre (reached from Maras on a road passable by cars in 15 minutes).

From Maras there is a road descending in hairpin bends to Urubamba (about half an hour's drive), passing on the right the colonial church of *Tiobamba* (interesting fair on 15 August). Alternatively it is possible to return to Cuzco via **Anta** (25 km from Cuzco), skirting the *Huaypo lagoon* (magnificent sunsets). In the Anta plain there are a large agricultural cooperative, formed by the amalgamation of the old haciendas and native communities, and the charming villages of *Huarocondo* and *Zurite*.

For excursions which can be done in a half-day trip from Cuzco (Oropesa, Pikillacta, Andahuaylillas, Huaro), see the next chapter.

7. CUZCO TO PUNO AND LAKE TITICACA

From Cuzco to Puno the road and railway run up the Vilcanota valley to the pass where the river Raya rises. This sub-
tributary of the Amazon forms the boundary between the two
departamentos. Beyond this is the *altiplano*, the high grassy
plateau round Lake Titicaca which extends as far as La Paz in
Bolivia. This is the meeting point between two different landscapes,
the fertile valley shut in between its high banks and the vast
horizons of the *icchu* steppe; between two types of economy, one
agricultural and the other mainly pastoral; between two different
pre-Columbian heritages, one Quechua-speaking and dominated
by the Inca civilisation and the other Aymará-speaking and under
Tiahuanaco influence. There is, however, one feature which the
departamentos of Puno and Cuzco have in common: they are the
most Indian, economically the most marginal and the poorest
parts of Peru.

1. THE VILCANOTA VALLEY
(FROM CUZCO TO THE LA RAYA PASS)

The **Vilcanota valley** is one of the most beautiful and most
populous in Peru. The traveller going down the valley from Puno
to Cuzco will be surprised by its green and fertile landscape after
the arid and treeless horizons of the *altiplano*. Its terraces and
alluvial fans produce crops of maize, potatoes (irrigated) and
beans as far upstream as Sicuani; and on the mountainsides
there are barley, wheat and, higher up on the borders of the
puna, potatoes. The Spaniards established a succession of townships on the right bank of the river, along the main road from
Lima via Cuzco to Potosí and so to north-eastern Argentina and
Buenos Aires.

The prosperity of Cuzco was closely bound up with the prosperity of this valley and its associated territories in both the hot
lands and the cold (particularly Paucartambo), whose economy
was founded on agriculture, trade and craft industries, with
numerous mills and large textile *obrajes*. At the end of the 18th
century the establishment of the independent Viceroyalty of

Buenos Aires, the closing down of the Potosí mines and Túpac Amaru's rebellion led to the decline of the area, and this was aggravated after Independence, though a certain economic revival was brought about by the building of the railway at the end of the 19th century and, more recently, by the construction of roads.

The road first runs up the wide and gently sloping valley of the Huatanay to the Huarcarpay lagoon; the train accompanies it to the junction with the Vilcanota and after passing through a narrow gorge rejoins it in the Andahuaylillas basin. After *San Sebastián* it comes to **San Jerónimo** (12 km), still within the suburban area of Cuzco, with which it is connected by an asphalt road (extending to about Urcos). The church was built built in 1622; there is a busy Sunday market.

At **Oropesa** (to the left) the road enters the province of Quispicanchis. The village, which is noted for its numerous bakers, has a beautiful church with a fine pulpit and some interesting pictures (including in particular a "Holy Family"). Shortly before Oropesa, to the left of the road, some old landowners' houses with whitewashed arcaded fronts are passed. Near the village are the fine Inca ruins of *Tipón*. The **Huarcarpay lagoon,** the level of which varies according to the rainfall, is in process of developing into a small holiday centre, with facilities for picnicking (and even camping) and boating.

At the foot of a steep uphill gradient, before Pikillacta, a road goes off on the left to **Paucartambo** and the *ceja de montaña* valley of Cosñipata. (Soon afterwards, at Huambutío, a road goes off on the left to Pisaq via San Salvador. The road to Paucartambo is narrow, with one-way traffic on alternate days). Paucartambo (100 km from Cuzco; 3 hours' drive) was a place of great importance in colonial times through the trade in coca, which was grown in the neighbouring hot lands, and it has preserves the appearance and characteristics of a small colonial town, with attractive old houses. On 16 July the festival of the

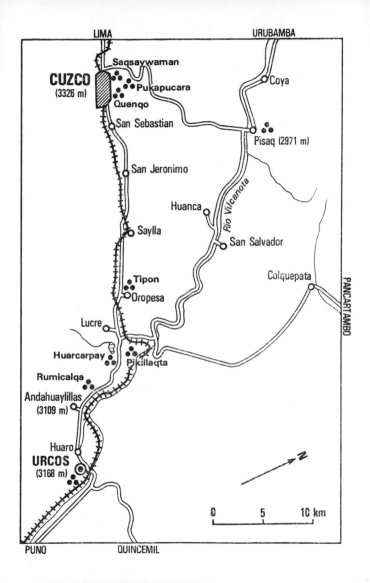

LIMA   URUBAMBA

Saqsaywaman

CUZCO
(3326 m)

Pukapucara

Qenqo

San Sebastian

Coya

Pisaq (2971 m)

San Jeronimo

Huanca

Rio Vilcanota

Saylla

San Salvador

Colquepata

Tipon

Oropesa

PANCARTAMBO

Lucre

Huarcarpay

Pikillaqta

Rumicalqa

Andahuaylillas
(3109 m)

N

Huaro

URCOS
(3168 m)

0   5   10 km

PUNO   QUINCEMIL

Virgen del Carmen is celebrated; it lasts two or three days, with folk dancing and other displays of exceptional interest. It is a journey of only some 4 hours from here to the forest. From the viewpoint of Tres Cruces near the pass the sunrise over the Selva is a magnificent sight in June.

Above Huarcarpay a country road goes off on the left to the ruins of **Pikillacta** (literally the "city of fleas"—a term which is unexplained): the remains of a large pre-Inca city (some 60 hectares), probably of the Huari culture (8th–9th c.), with a very regular grid layout surrounded by walls, narrow streets and the ruins of *colqas* (round granaries).

On the right-hand side of the road is the site of *Rumicolqa*, with terraces and a well-made wall and the remains of an Inca fortress (and perhaps also of a *tambo* or posting station) guarding the eastern approaches to Cuzco.

The road then runs down into the fertile **Andahuay-lillas** basin. The village has a charming square planted with *pisonays* (flamboyants), a few old houses and a splendid *church* with frescoes which have earned it the name of the American Sistine Chapel; the church also contains an old colonial organ worked by a bellows. 4 km farther on is *Huaro*, with an almost equally beautiful church, and at the top of the little pass is the picturesque chapel of *Canicunca*, with interesting pictures. The road then descends to **Urcos** (45 km from Cuzco), under a lagoon into which the golden chain of Inca Huáscar is said to have been thrown after his defeat by the Spaniards. This village also has a beautiful church (modest inn and restaurants).

From Urcos a road goes off to another valley in the *ceja de montaña*, the Marcapata-Quince Mil valley. It begins by running through the *puna* round **Ocongate** (3900 m), situated at the foot of the glacier on Mt Ausangate (6384 m). Near this village the

Indian festival of *Coyllur Riti*, in honour of the Sun and the snow, is celebrated at the beginning of June. From Ocongate or Paucartambo it is possible to reach, in 3 days' difficult walking, the Indian community of *Qeros*, one of the purest blooded in Peru. **Quince Mil,** situated in the forest, has had periods of prosperity in the past, associated with the quest for gold. The road continues to **Puerto Maldonado,** chief town of the *departamento* of Madre de Dios, one day's journey from Quince Mil (Turistas hotel; air connections to both places from Cuzco three times weekly).

After Urcos the main road continues to the villages of *Quiquijana* (colonial bridge; beautiful church), *Cusipata* and **Checacupe** (103 km), in the province of Canchis. At the Chuquicahuana bridge shortly before this last village a road goes off on the right and climbs to the Pomacanchis lagoon and the *Acomayo valley*, with some picturesque villages (Accos; Pillpinto, with a bridge over the Apurímac). The *church* at Checacupe has a magnificent *pulpit* similar to that of San Blas and some interesting pictures. At **Combapata** (113 km from Cuzco) there is a fine colonial bridge.

From Combapata a road goes off on the right to the **punas south of Cuzco**. It runs through a ravine with a succession of mills on different levels to the village of *Tungasuca* on the Pampamarca lagoon, from which Túpac Amaru's native rebellion started in 1780. The road then continues to **Yauri** (country roads to Arequipa via Imata or Cailloma) and **Santo Tomás,** the chief towns of two very picturesque provinces which are still little known to tourists.

Beyond Combapata the Puno road passes on the right *Tinta*, an old colonial capital with a beautiful church (potters). At *San Pedro*, another potters' village with a charming chapel, is the important site of **Raqchi**, a pre-Inca city with a regular grid layout, fine rectangular houses and a group of *colqas*. Adjoining it is an Inca temple dedicated to Viracocha, with a high façade of stone and adobe. In June an interesting traditional festival is celebrated here.

After passing through *San Pablo*, a village of silversmiths, the road comes to **Sicuani** (147 km from Cuzco), a town of 13,000 inhabitants situated at an altitude of 3600 m, with modest hotels and retaurants. It is an important commercial centre with a busy market and many craftsmen, specialising mainly in the working of furs. Near the town is the beautiful Langui-Layo lagoon; road to Yauri.

Between Sicuani and La Raya (42 km) the valley becomes narrower and vegetation sparser. Before the pass are the curious mud volcanoes and fumaroles of *Aguas Calientes*, where Bolívar stayed. *La Raya* (4313 m) lies under the glaciers of the Eastern Cordillera (to left). Nearby is an experimental farm devoted to the rearing of vicuñas.

2. LA RAYA TO PUNO

The road and railway run over the *altiplano*, with large stock-farming haciendas on both sides, many of them now cooperatives (mainly sheep but also cattle; llamas, etc., on the high ground in the Eastern Cordillera).

At *Santa Rosa* (30 km from the pass) a road passable for cars goes off to the *ceja de montaña*, passing through Nuñoa and Macusani. 74 km from La Raya (263 km from Cuzco) is **Ayaviri,** with a beautiful church which already shows some of the characteristics of the churches of the Collao district (modest hotels). **Pucará** (108 km) is famous for its pre-Inca remains and also for its potters, who are known particularly for their figurines of dancers, animals, grotesques to meet present-day tastes and above all their bulls.

Pucará is also an important road junction: to the left are country roads to *Asillo* and *Azángaro* and the *ceja de montaña* valleys of Carabaya and Sandia respectively; to the right is *Lampa* (20 km), with a beautiful colonial church.

In another 67 km the road comes to **Juliaca** (pop. 38,400), a busy modern town which has grown up at a road and rail junction (364 km from Cuzco, 46 km from Puno, 273 km from Arequipa by road). It has good hotels and restaurants (including a recently built Turistas hotel), an airport (connections with Arequipa and sometimes Cuzco) and a fair (Sundays and Mondays) which offers a rich display of craft goods (mainly skins and furs, woven articles and woollen goods).

3. LAKE TITICACA AND PUNO

On the islands in Lake Titicaca live the descendants of what may have been the earliest inhabitants of South America, the Urus. On its banks, in Bolivian territory, are the remains of *Tiahuanaco*, capital of an empire which dominated southern and central Peru from the 9th to the 12th century. And it was from an island in the lake (or from its foam) that the founders of the Inca dynasty, Manco Cápac and his wife, were supposed to have come. This area, therefore, known as the **Collao** district, is one of outstanding archaeological importance. After the Spanish conquest it retained considerable importance through its situation at the meeting place of the roads from Cuzco and Arequipa to Potosí and into north-eastern Argentina. At the end of the 19th century the construction of the railway (1876) promoted trade with Bolivia and led to the modernisation of stock-farming for the production of wool. In our own day, apart from its importance as an intermediate point on the route between Cuzco and Bolivia, it will appeal to the tourist through its rugged beauty and its rich fund of folk traditions.

Lake Titicaca

Lake Titicaca is the highest navigable lake in the world (3812 m). Most of it is in Peru; Bolivia has the "Little Lake", or Lake Guaqui (with the famous Islands of the Sun and the Moon), which is separated from the main part of the lake by the Copacabana peninsula and the Tiquina strait. With a maximum depth of 230 m, the lake is subject to considerable storms from time to time. Round its much indented shoreline extends a peaceful landscape, with striking colour contrasts between the deep blue of the water, the lighter blue of the sky, the ochre or tawny hues of the hills, the brown earth of the fields and the intense green of the expanses of reeds (*totorales*) and the young cereals. It is well stocked with fish—*suche* (a kind of catfish), porgy and, since 1941, trout, which are contributing to the disappearance of the indigenous species.

The moderating influence of the lake on the climate makes agriculture possible, and the economy of the regions round its shores is very different from the essentially pastoral economy of the *altiplano*. Nevertheless conditions round Lake Titicaca are difficult: the mean annual temperature at Puno is 9°C (January maximum 10°, July minimum 6.5°), with sharp daily variations, and the rainfall ranges between 500 and 800 mm. Crops are often endangered by night frosts and showers of hail. The soil is thin, low in nitrogen and slow to regenerate, and the plains round the lake are liable to frequent flooding.

In spite of these difficulties the density of population is as high as 100 inhabitants to the sq. km, and the land is fragmented into tiny plots. The population is scattered about in a multitude of little hamlets of a few adobe houses, each with its own small enclosure; the traditional reed or tile roofs are now frequently replaced by corrugated iron. Barley, wheat, oats, *quinoa* and small quantities of beans are grown under a system of collective rotation known as *aynoqa*. The land left fallow, often for long periods, provides pasture for sheep. The cattle (which are taken to market young) wander into the reeds to eat a water weed called *llacho*. The average income is one of the lowest in Peru (around 100 U.S. dollars per head), and the daily consumption of calories is under 2000 per head; in years of drought the people are soon on the verge of famine. The peasants eke out their limited resources by fishing, small-scale trade (many of them being pedlars) and the sale of craft products (the sandals made

243

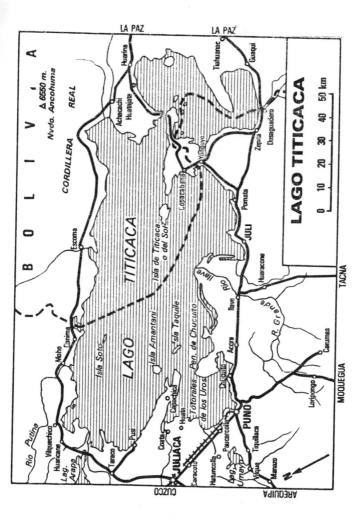

from old tyres known as *ojotas*, and various woollen goods for
tourists—carpets, blankets, ponchos, hats and various items of
knitwear).

Puno

The late foundation of this town (1668, under the name of
Villa Rica de San Carlos de Puno) demonstrates the Spaniards'
lack of interest in living on the high plateaux and the *puna*.
This minor staging post on the road to Potosí began to grow
after the discovery of a rich silver mine at Laicacota which was
worked by the Salcedo brothers from 1657 onwards. It became
a town of adventurers, noted for its violence, leading the Viceroy,
the Conde de Lemos, to raze it to the ground in 1668, execute
José Salcedo and found a regular town in the vicinity. Puno
now has 41,000 inhabitants (compared with 3000 in 1876, before
the coming of the railway) and is mainly of importance as an
administrative centre, being the headquarters of the departmental
authorities and of various Peruvian and international development bodies. Its commercial importance, however, has been
reduced by competition from Juliaca, the decline in ship-borne
trade with Bolivia and the tendency of the local *hacendados* to
look to Arequipa rather than Puno as their centre. Like all the
puna towns, it appears a little austere, though it is a clean and
busy town. It has good hotels (in particular a Turistas hotel) and
restaurants.

The **Cathedral,** dedicated to St John the Baptist, has
a splendid *Baroque façade* with columns carved with
intricate patterns of flowers, fruit and birds. Other
buildings of the colonial period are the *Hospital of
San Juan de Dios*, the *College of San Carlos* and the
Arco de Duestua (completed in 1847). Some houses
have preserved their old cobbled patios. There are
three museums: the *Municipal Museum*, the *Museum of
Folk Art* and the *Carlos Dryer Museum* (a private
archaeological museum with a fine collection of
Tiahuanaco material). From the Cerro Huajsapata
there is a fine view of the town and the lake. There is a
very picturesque market, with a whole section devoted
to a variety of local handicrafts.

Puno's **fiestas** are the occasion for some extremely interesting displays of local folk traditions. The best known are the *Candlemas* festival in February, which marks the beginning of the Carnival; the *Festival of the Cross* on 3 May; the feast of *St Peter*, patron of fishermen, on 29 June; and "Puno Week" at the beginning of November, commemorating Manco Cápac's emergence from Lake Titicaca. The most notable local dances are the Diablada, performed by a troupe of 80 dancers with striking devils' costumes and masks; the Wifala, danced by young people; the Pandilla, in which the women dancers wear beautiful Manila shawls; the Morenada; the Machu Tusuc or old people's dance; the "Ichu Carnival"; the Llamerada, the dance of the llama herdsmen; and the dance of the muleteers of Tucumán. The music of Puno is also very unusual, with groups of *zampoyas* (or *sicus*, Pan pipes made of reeds) and gay "carnivals".

Excursions from Puno

The chullpas of Sillustani (42 km from Puno: leave on the Juliaca road and turn off into a side road to Atuncolla).

The *chullpas* (an Aymará word) are tall burial towers, usually round but occasionally square or rectangular. They are built of dressed stones, the upper part being sometimes of adobe brick. They contained mummies and grave goods (pottery, weapons, etc.), and are mostly earlier than the occupation of the Collao area by the Incas (15th c.). The finest of the *chullpas* are to be seen at *Sillustani*, overlooking the beautiful Umayo lagoon, but there are other examples at various places in the *departamento* of Puno and even in the *departamento* of Cuzco (e.g. at *Arku Punku*, near Chucuito, and Pucarà).

The floating islands of the Urus (a morning excursion by motorboat from Puno to a group of islands off the Capachica peninsula). The islands are occupied by the descendants of the Urus or Kot-Suns (in Aymará, "people of the lake"), who formerly lived on the shores of the lake but are now dying out.

They live in close symbiosis with the lake, which provides them with the fish on which they subsist and the reeds (*totoras*) which they use to make houses, boats and "floating islands" made of layers of reeds 30 to 50 cm thick, constantly renewed. The boats are made of four banana-shaped bundles of reeds, two on top and two below, and are longer and lower than the "*caballos de totora*" used by the Chimús of the northern coastal region. The motive force is provided by a long-handled paddle; but many of the boats also have a sail made of dried reeds. The Urus are darker-skinned than the other Indians and are usually dressed in black. They are very poor, and have always been treated as inferiors by the Aymarás. According to Jehan Vellard, they themselves, in their mythology, do not regard themselves as men.

Other possible excursions are to the Amantani and Soto islands, occupied by communities of Aymará fishermen and craftsmen making objects from stone (mortars and pestles, and also small statuettes of magical significance).

The northern shores of the lake. The large village of *Huancané* (58 km from Juliaca), famous for the Indian rebellion of 1920, has curious conical houses of puddled mud. From *Moho* (40 km) there is a difficult and little used track into Bolivia.

4. PUNO TO THE BOLIVIAN FRONTIER

During the colonial period the largest settlements were on the south side of the lake — *Chucuito*, chief town of a province which was so populous and so rich that it was directly subordinate to the King of Spain, and *Juli*, where as early as 1579 the Jesuits had established a training centre for missionaries to be sent into Paraguay and the territory of the Mojos. The churches in all the little townships on this route preserve the memory of this period: usually built of adobe, their rather rustic and massive architecture contrasts with the riot of decoration on their stone-built Baroque doorways, in which the local flowers and birds are mingled with those brought by the Spaniards. All the churches had in front of them a large open square surrounded by arcades with over-hanging roofs. The churches themselves are of very simple plan (in the form of a Latin cross, usually without aisles) but are richly decorated with Baroque altars, paintings and statues.

Chucuito (21 km) has a *church of the Assumption* built in the early 17th century. In the square is a column (the *picota* or pillory) on which the heads of executed crminals were displayed. 15 km beyond this is *Acora*, with a beautiful church dedicated to St Peter. Near the village are *chullpas*. At *Ilave* (58 km from Puno), which has modest hotels and restaurants, a road goes off to Tacna, on the coast. **Juli** was the centre of the Jesuit missions to the hot lands and has *four beautiful churches*.

In the square is *San Pedro*, with fine Baroque altars and bronze Stations of the Cross. Opposite the church is a fine 17th century house, the *Casa de la Inquisición* or *de Zavala*. The *Church of the Assumption* stands above the village in a large square with an arch, from which there is a fine view of the lake. The interior is much dilapidated but has some fine frescoes in the transept crossing. *San Juan de Latrán*, the oldest of the churches (1590), has a magnificent carved doorway, a fine sacristy and interesting pictures. *Santa Cruz*, standing a little apart, is much damaged but has a fine doorway. Beside it is the old Jesuit cemetery. There is an excellent Turistas hotel in the village.

Pomata (108 km) has one of the finest churches in Peru, completed in the late 18th century. Dedicated to St James (Santiago), it is built of pink granite and has a fine carved doorway; the interior has a stone vaulted roof and contains some fine paintings (in particular the Virgin of Pomata).

From here the road continues to the Bolivian frontier at *Yunguyo* (26 km) and beyond this to *Copacabana* (with a well known church and pilgrimage), crossing the Tiquina strait on a ferry.

There is also a road to **Desaguadero** (44 km from Pomata, 154 km from Puno, 116 km from La Paz), passing through *Zepita*, which has a beautiful church dedicated to St Peter.

From Puno it is possible to sail to *Guaqui* and continue by train to **La Paz.** The boat, the "Ollanta", leaves on Wednesdays at 8 p.m., arriving at Guaqui at 6 a.m.; the train leaves at 8 a.m. and arrives at La Paz at 12.30 p.m. The return service from Guaqui to Puno is on Fridays.

8.   PERUVIAN AMAZONIA

Peruvian Amazonia is the third region of Peru, no less fascinating than the other two—the Coast and the Sierra—but much more mysterious and difficult of access. It has always exerted its fascination on men. The Incas valued its gold, the plumes of its birds, various plants which provided dyes and the coca from the *ceja de selva*. Along the roads leading into the hot lands they laid out a series of towns—partly posting stations (*tambos*) and partly also fortresses to provide protection from the Indians of the forest—of which the remains are found from Machu Picchu in the south to Chachapoyas in the north. For the Spaniards the exploration of the Amazonian forest was associated with the quest of El Dorado, the legendary territory with an untold wealth of gold. The Amazon was discovered by Don Francisco de Orellana in 1541, but the Spaniards had already sailed down the Marañón, its upper course, in 1536 and 1538. Mission stations were established in the *ceja de selva* round Chachapoyas and Moyobamba and in the valleys of the large right-bank tributaries, the Huallaga (round Huánuco), Apurímac, Urubamba (La Convención valley) and Tambopata. They were manned by Franciscans from 1580 onwards, with their bases at Huánuco and, in the 18th century, at Ocopa, and by Jesuits based at Maynas (now Iquitos) or Cuzco. The missionaries founded small settlements which grew sugar-cane for the production of spirits, cocoa and above all coca, which was exported to the Sierra and particularly to Potosí. After a sharp decline in the pace of settlement in the early years of independence there was a resumption of the movement at the end of the 19th century, associated with the search for wild rubber in the Selva and the introduction in the *ceja de montaña* of coffee, tea, rice, and—in a few areas—oil palms and rubber plantations. At the present time the Peruvian government is looking to the settlement of the Amazonian valleys to make good the shortage of farming land in the Sierra, and hopes to find in oil—now beginning to be worked in the upper valley of the Río Tigre—a major source of revenue.

The *ceja de montaña* and even more the Selva will appeal to all visitors with the luxuriant beauty of their forests—tall trees of many different species, evergreen, often with slender trunks and branches extending horizontally like a parasol. There is a dense undergrowth of lianas, tree ferns and epiphytic plants, with impenetrable thickets of bamboos (*pacales*) at intervals. The soil is often damp, with areas of swamp in the principal beds of the rivers; for in this relatively flat terrain the rivers spread over considerable areas in time of spate and meander about the valley in wide bends, which are frequently cut off when the river changes course. These "ox-bow lakes" (*aguajales*) provide fertile soil for the growth of handsome palm-trees. The climate, warm and humid throughout the year, is another attraction. It is relatively healthy, with only the occasional case of malaria or yellow fever, which is quickly dealt with by the medical services. More dangerous are the various parasites, to be found particularly in water. Wild animals are fairly rare in the more easily accessible parts of the area: those found include tapirs, peccaries, *tigrillos* and a great variety of birds, monkeys, snakes (particularly anacondas) and insects. The scenery of the *ceja de montaña* is often more beautiful, and is certainly more varied, than that of the relatively featureless forest, with more variety of ups and downs, rivers which sometimes flow through deep gorges and sometimes follow a gentler course in wide valleys where human settlement is possible, beautiful clearings where fields and plantations have been established, and small towns in areas of very agreeable climate.

The Indian tribes which visitors will see in their travels are adapted to western culture, the others having retreated to less accessible areas. There are thought to be between 60,000 and 100,000 of these *selvaticos*, whose numbers are falling rapidly. There are some fifty tribes speaking thirty or so dialects belonging to the large Arawak and Tupí-Guaraní language families, radically different from Quechua and Aymará. The main tribes are the Aguaranas and Achuals of the Marañón valley, who speak a Jivaro dialect; the Capanahuas, the Shipibos, the Conibos and the Cashibos of the Ucayali valley, who belong to the Pano language group; the Campas of the central valleys (Oxapampa and Apurímac); the Machigengas of the Urubamba valley; the Mashgos, Huachipaires, Amaracaires and Piros in the *departamento* of Madre de Dios, belonging to the Tupí-Guaraní language family; and the Yaguas and Omaguas round Iquitos. The Indians usually live in groups consisting of a small number of families which lead a nomadic life, establishing temporary dwellings near the rivers. Their huts are made of interwoven bamboo stems with roofs of palm-leaves, perched on piles of a height which varies according to the season. They are of considerable size, often housing an extended family.

The Indians live by fishing, hunting and food-gathering, using bows and arrows, blowpipes, harpoons and more rarely nets. Many practise slash-and-burn agriculture, growing *yuca* (sweet manioc), beans, plantains, sweet potatoes (*camote*) and sometimes cotton. From the *yuca* they make a fermented drink called *masato*. Some of them, in the upper Urubamba valley, also grow a little coffee and cocoa, which they sell at low prices to mestizo collectors. Some tribes make cotton cloths, which they colour with vegetable dyes. They also make white pottery with geometric patterns in black. Their social and magico-religious practices call for the making of various plumed headdresses, ornaments and jewellery. Many paint their faces and bodies, and some practise physical deformation (e.g. of the ears or lips). Some are said to be still cannibals, and the Jivaros are famous for their "shrunken heads".

When these Indians come into contact with the modern world they very rapidly lose their native culture; and interference with their traditional hunting grounds and the disturbance of their health and physiological equilibrium are leading to their progressive disappearance. Their numbers were decimated by the activities of the 19th century *caucheros* (rubber workers) who sought to use them as slaves: it is to be hoped that the firms and organisations who in our own day are developing the resources of the forest by building roads and bringing out oil and timber will have more regard for their interests.

The *ceja de montaña* and the Selva can be reached by way of the various valleys on the western side of the Andes which have featured in the preceding itineraries. From Cuzco there are three main routes to the hot lands: to Quillabamba by train, and from there by lorry to Coribení; to Cosñipata or Quince Mil by lorry; and to Puerto Maldonado by lorry (2 or 3 days) or by air. The most important centre in Peruvian Amazonia, however, is **Iquitos.**

1. Lima to Iquitos

The first part of the journey is done by road, the second part by boat. The road from *Lima to Pucallpa* (875 km) can be covered in 24 hours if atmospheric conditions permit, but it is preferable to take two days, stopping at Huánuco (10–12 hours from Lima, 10 hours from Pucallpa), or even three days, stopping also at Tingo María. From *Pucallpa to Iquitos* is 4 to 6 days' journey by boat. There are daily *air services* between Lima and Iquitos (1 hour 40 minutes to 2 hours 30 minutes), Lima and Pucallpa (1 hour 5 minutes) and Pucallpa and Iquitos (1 hour).

The road to Tingo María and Pucallpa starts from La Oroya. (For the route from Lima to La Oroya by road or rail, see the itinerary from Lima to Huancayo, p. 195). The road (accompanied by the railway as far as Cerro de Pasco) runs across the *puna*, skirting the beautiful Junín lagoon (4015 m), through a fairly densely settled area (50 inhabitants to the sq. km), with large native communities (Ondores, Carhuamayo) engaged in sheep-farming and the growing of potatoes in very difficult conditions. **Cerro de Pasco** (135 km from La Oroya, 324 km from Lima) is the chief town of Peru's principal mining region, with a population of 47,000. Altitude 4388 m; mean annual temperature 4°C. The town, founded in 1771, has a beautiful colonial church. In view of the danger to the town from mine workings a new town was founded in 1965 2 km from the old one. (Cerro de Pasco can also be reached from Lima by way of the Canta road and the La Viuda pass).

From Cerro de Pasco the road descends rapidly into the hot lands, Huánuco (111 km away) lying at an altitude of only 1900 m. **Huánuco** (pop. 41,000) is situated on the river Huallaga in the high *ceja de montaña* (Turistas hotel). Tea and coca are grown in the area, which is a pleasant one with a good climate.

In the vicinity are two important archaeological sites, the old Inca city of *Huánuco Viejo* and (4 km away) the ruined temples of *Kotosh*, noted for their mysterious representation of two crossed hands, which are thought to be earlier than the Chavín culture.

Farther away and more difficult of access is the Inca site of *Tantamayo*, with buildings of more than one storey.

Beyond Huánuco the road runs through the little cordillera of Carpish at an altitude of 2750 m (55 km) and then down to **Tingo María** (144 km from Huánuco, 579 km from Lima), situated at an altitude of 670 m in the *selva alta*.

The town, founded in 1830, has developed in recent years, and had a population of just over 20,000 in 1972. It is typical of the towns established to promote settlement in the forest, with a spacious grid plan and wide streets lined by houses with galleries on the front and small gardens to the rear. The traditional type of construction (timber walls and roof of palm-leaves) is, however, increasingly giving place to the use of concrete for the walls and asbestos cement for the roofs.

There is an airport with two connections weekly with Lima, Tarapoto, Pucallpa, Iquitos and Yurimaguas. Turistas hotel.

In the neighbourhood are picturesque caves (Cueva de las Lechuzas, gorges of El Afilador). Tingo María lies in the centre of one of the largest forest settlement areas in Peru, with plantations of coffee, tea, coca, cocoa, bananas and oil palms.

Visitors with sufficient time at their disposal can reach the forest region by going down the Huallaga valley. The journey begins with 3 hours' drive to *Tocache*, followed by a day's journey by boat (dangerous between January and June) to *Juanjuí*. From here it is another 5 hours by road to *Tarapoto*, a pleasant town of 27,000 inhabitants (Turistas hotel), and another 5 hours, passing in a tunnel through the last ranges of the Andes, to *Yurimaguas* (pop. 21,000). From Tarapoto there is a road to **Lamas** (20 km), the centre of an old established and picturesque Quechua community, continuing to **Moyobamba** (pop. 10,000: 2 hours' drive), chief town of the *departamento* of San Martín, and *Rioja* (3 hours' drive), both of which have preserved a colonial aspect reflecting their early foundation. The completion of the road to Olmos and the northern coastal region can be expected to give them a fresh lease of life. From Juanjuí it is possible (one day's journey by boat, followed by a two-day walk through the forest) to reach the site of *Gran Pajatén* (p. 179).

Soon after Tingo María the road leaves the Huallaga valley and follows the valley of the Aguaytía and the Alejandro (tributaries of the Ucayali) through the Cordillera Azul or Blue Cordillera (1600 m). In this very humid area there are plantations of tea and rubber. The road runs through the narrow and very picturesque canyon known as the *Boquerón del Padre Abad* on the river Yuracyacu, which was first discovered in 1757 and re-discovered in 1937 when the road was built. It then reaches the Amazonian plain and after running for almost 200 km across the Pampa de Sacramento comes to **Pucallpa,** a town established when the road was built (1937 onwards). It grew very rapidly, reaching a population of 60,000 by 1972 (compared with 21,000 in 1961).

The town is like one huge *barriada*, disorganised and often squalid, but, situated as it is as the point of transhipment between road and river transport, is a busy commercial town (6 or 7 1st category hotels). It has numerous sawmills, and handles almost half Peru's output of tropical woods.

14 km away is the magnificent *Yarinacocha lagoon*, where until 1974 the University of Oklahoma ran a summer language school for missionaries working with the Indians. From Pucallpa it is possible to take motorboat trips to the little forest villages.

From Pucallpa **Iquitos** can be reached either by air (daily flights by the Faucett or Aeroperú lines and the Cívico service) or by boat. There are regular services by small steamers two or three times a week, but it is also possible to travel on one of the smaller vessels which carry goods. The journey downstream lasts a minimum of 4 days and may take anything up to 8;

the return journey takes a minimum of 5 or 6 days. Traffic on the Ucayali is slower during the period of spate (January–March). The boat trip through the forest (which as a result of the many meanders of the river covers a distance of almost 1000 km) gives visitors an opportunity of seeing little towns like *Contamana* (pop. 5000) and *Requena* (pop. 7000). At Nauta the Ucayali flows into the Amazon, which has already received the waters of the Huallaga.

2. Iquitos

Iquitos (pop. 111,000) was founded in 1864 on the site of a Jesuit mission station on the left bank of the river which had been established in 1739 as a base for the evangelisation of the Yagua Indians. It benefited from the feverish economic activity stimulated by the harvesting of wild rubber between 1883 and 1912, but thereafter was gravely affected by the development of rubber plantations in the Far East. The recent establishment of a free port here, at the highest point on the Amazon which can be reached by cargo ships, 4000 km from the Brazilian coast, was designed to give the town a fresh lease of life. The port exports a certain amount of timber, *barbasco* (a poison used in the manufacture of insecticides), *leches sapi* (an ingredient of chewing gum), Brazil nuts (*castañas*) and some rubber. The town is also a centre for the hunting of wild animals, for sale either live or as dried meat (caymans, *tigrillos*, peccaries, etc.). It has attracted an influx of people from the small surrounding villages, who make a living from the tourists and live in the expectation of the future income from oil. There is little industry (a few sawmills and a small refinery). Rice plantations and market gardens have been established to meet the town's needs. Two recent and apparently promising developments have been the growing of jute and the rearing of zebus.

The centre of the town has retained something of the style and the charm of the little trading towns of the beginning of this century, with stone-built houses of European type decorated with ceramic tiles from

Portugal. The most celebrated building is the *Iquitos Club*, originally a pavilion built by Gustave Eiffel for the Paris Exhibition of 1889. In the shady **Plaza de Armas** are a statue by Rodin and a church in modern style, *Santa Ana*. There is a Turistas hotel in the Malecón.

The outer districts of the town, near the market, consist of *barriadas* of wood and corrugated iron, occupied by the poorest of the poor. At the mouth of the Río Itaya is the *Belén* district, with picturesque houses built on piles, also occupied by poor families.

Features of interest in the town are the **Amazon Museum** (Calle Lima), with fine collections of ethnology, natural history and handicrafts; the *Aquarium* run by the Ministry of Agriculture (Calle Ramírez Hurtado); and the *Vidal Zoo* (Calle Ricardo Palma).

Excursions on the river and its tributaries to see Indian tribes are run by the travel agencies (motorboats, with guides). The main trips are to the Río Momón, the inn at *Yanamono* (2 hours), Nañay, Pucayacu, Quisto Cocha, *Indiana* (handicraft school) and, farther away, the lake and natural park of *Rimachi*.

Visitors can buy in Iquitos various Indian handicrafts, sample local dishes, eat some of the tropical fruit which grows here (*cocona, maracuya, tumbo, caimito*) and try the local drinks, some of them reckoned to have aphrodisiac qualities (*chuchuhuasi, morure, masato*).

Iquitos has air connections with Chiclayo (Mondays and Fridays), Rioja, Yurimaguas, Tarapoto (Mondays) and Puerto Maldonado (first and third Wednesdays in the month). It also has connections with Colombia, via the port of *Leticia* (air service on Wednesdays; boats) and Brazil (by cargo ship).

Practical
Information

PERU

CONTENTS

WHERE TO OBTAIN INFORMATION ABOUT PERU

Peruvian Embassy, 52 Sloane Street, *London* SW1 (tel. 235 1917).

Anglo-Peruvian Society, 52 Sloane Street, *London* SW1 (tel. 235 3601).

Peruvian Embassy, 1320 16th Street NW, *Washington* (tel. DU 7 5150).

Peruvian Embassy, 539 Island Park Drive, *Ottawa* 3, Ont. (tel. 722 7186).

Enturperú, Conde Superunda 298, *Lima* (tel. 288 225 and 281 608).

Dirección General de Turismo, Ministry of Industry and Commerce (10th floor), Urbanización Corpac, San Isidro, *Lima* (tel. 407 120 ext. 176–177).

Touring y Automóvil-Club, Av. César Vallejo 699, *Lima* (tel. 403 270); letters to Casilla 2219, Lima.

Tourist Office, *Lima* Airport (tel. 529 570, ext. 216).

Arequipa: Merced 117 (tel. 20 630).

Cuzco: Capilla de Loreto, Plaza de Armas (tel. 3962).

Puno: Hotel Turistas, A. Ugarte 255 (tel. 244).

I. HOW TO SEE PERU

There are two main ways of seeing Peru. The commonest way nowadays is a package tour arranged by one of the travel companies: a method which has obvious advantages (an all-in price, and usually a very reasonable one; all bookings looked after; the services of a guide and interpreter) but also certain disadvantages. It means travelling in a group, with a fixed timetable which leaves no room for personal preferences or sudden changes of plan; and of course it provides no guarantee against such hazards as mistakes in booking or the last-minute cancellation of a flight. Above all it does not allow visitors to come into close contact with the country and absorb its atmosphere freely, since they are caught up within their group, speaking their own language, and are unable to discover the civilisation of Peru for themselves. It is of course possible to book an individual tour through an agency in accordance with the visitor's own requirements: this is perhaps the ideal method, but it is, inevitably, expensive.

Those who prefer to make their own arrangements will find it difficult to make the necessary bookings (hotels, trains, aircraft) from Europe or the United States. The best plan is to apply to a Peruvian travel agency (or to an international agency with a branch in Peru) well in advance of the proposed date of travel. To leave these arrangements until you arrive in the country is asking for trouble.

Not all visitors like to be constantly on the move, and there is much to be said for selecting a town with good hotel resources and staying there for some days to explore the surrounding area before moving on to the next stopping place. An interesting tour of Peru could be built round a number of central points like Lima, Arequipa, Cuzco, Puno and Iquitos. It is worth remembering, in this connection, that except in the area round Lima there are no bathing resorts with facilities for visitors of the kind found in other holiday areas, since the cold Humboldt Current flows along most of the coast, leaving only limited scope for sea bathing.

In any case Peru is not a country which lends itself to sedentary holidays. Tourists do not travel so far merely to sit in an armchair: they come to Peru to discover the country and its civilisation. It is necessary, therefore, to plan your visit and prepare for it with some care—always remembering that Peru is four times the size of Great Britain and Ireland together and two and a half times as big as France. For those who want to plan their own trip the following programmes are put forward merely as suggestions:

One week: Lima (one day); fly to Cuzco (the town and Machu Picchu, 3 days); to Arequipa by air or night train (one day); then return to Lima by air. Alternatively replace Arequipa by Puno and Lake Titicaca.

Two weeks: Lima and Pachacámac (2 days); fly to Arequipa (one day); to Puno by air or train (3 days, including excursions); by train to Cuzco (3 days, including Machu Picchu); then return to Lima by air (1 hours) or bus (32 to 36 hours). Excursion to Iquitos by air (2 or 3 days).

Three or four weeks: add a tour of northern Peru, taking in Trujillo, the Callejón de Huaylas, Cajamarca and Tumbes.

Much time can of course be saved by using the domestic airlines, the fares on which are very reasonable. Travel by rail (where services exist) or by road (buses or *colectivos:* see p. 269) is even cheaper, but is only for those with plenty of time; thus the journey from Lima to Iquitos takes something like 10 days if you travel by bus (to Pucallpa) and boat.

II. WHEN TO GO

Although situated in tropical latitudes, Peru is not really a hot country in the generally accepted sense of the term, except in Amazonia, in the far north (beyond Chiclayo) and on the Coast from December to March. In the Sierra the nights are cold in consequence of the altitude, and it is necessary to have warm clothing with you. (It is worth remembering that excellent woollen garments, either knitted or woven — pullovers, jackets, caps, ponchos, etc. — can be bought in Lima and elsewhere in the country).

Most foreign visitors come to Peru between June and September, during the southern hemisphere's winter. Lima has a mean temperature of 16°C, with relatively little variation over the 24 hours (of the order of 6 to 8°). It does not rain (Lima has one of the driest climates in the world, with an annual rainfall of some 50 mm), but the relative humidity of the atmosphere is very high (around 90%) as a result of the *garúa*, a kind of thin fog or Scotch mist which is all-pervasive, under dull and cloudy skies. If you climb up on to the slopes of the Sierra you emerge from the clouds at a height of between 700 and 800 metres, and mild and sunny weather predominates to an altitude of some 3500 m: Arequipa, for example, is renowned for its perpetual spring. Still higher (Cuzco, 3400 m) the air becomes cool and indeed cold at night, when frost is by no means rare (at Puno, situated just below 4000 m, temperatures as low as $-12°$C have been recorded). At Cuzco the mean daily temperature ranges between $8°$ and $10°$ from June to September, and the sky remains clear most of the time (4 mm of rain in July, 11 mm in August).

The summer of the southern hemisphere, which corresponds to our winter, brings Lima a warm and humid climate and skies which are usually clear, in contrast to the winter months. The temperature remains around 23-25°C, rising on occasion to $30°$. The climate becomes steadily hotter towards the northern regions of the Coast. In the Andes it is a little milder than in winter (around $12°$ at Cuzco), but October to March are the rainy months: during this period the rain, falling mainly in the afternoon, reaches a total of 700 mm (out of the annual figure of 800 mm). Gullies and landslides, sometimes of catastrophic proportions, can occur, cutting the roads and interrupting traffic.

The Amazonian Selva has a climate of equatorial type, hot and humid throughout the year. At Iquitos the temperature fluctuates according to the time of year between $24°$ and $29°$, with a very narrow range over the 24 hours, and the rainfall is fairly evenly spread over the year, reaching its maximum between December and April.

In these latitudes day and night are of about equal length. The dawn comes at about 6 a.m. and night falls about 6 p.m. It is advisable, therefore, to begin your day early (as do railway and air services).

III. PASSPORTS AND CUSTOMS

Passports

Nationals of most countries (in particular the countries of Western Europe and America) need only a valid passport without visa to enter Peru. The length of stay must not exceed 90 days without special authorisation (for which application must be made to the Immigration Service, Huallaga 400, Lima).

Visitors must possess a return ticket. They must complete (usually on the aircraft before arrival) a Tourist Card (Cédula C). This is in duplicate, one copy being given to the police on arrival, the other returned when leaving Peru. The intended period of stay will be entered on the card by the Peruvian authorities.

Vaccinations

An international smallpox vaccination certificate more than 6 days and less than 3 years old is compulsory. Yellow fever vaccination is optional, but is recommended for visitors intending to go into Amazonia.

Customs

The customs examination usually gives the bona fide tourist no difficulty. No duty is payable on personal belongings or on one camera and one ciné-camera with a reasonable quantity of films (in theory five for each camera), a typewriter, a tape-recorder, 400 cigarettes and two bottles of spirits. It is forbidden to take out of the country any pre-Columbian antiquities or objects of colonial art of significant cultural value.

Animals

An international health certificate is necessary, and there is an entry tax of 40 soles on each animal. It is not advisable to try to take out of Peru—as visitors to Amazonia, for example, may be tempted to do—animals like parrots and monkeys: the health regulations are very complicated indeed.

Cars

In addition to the port of Callao, through which cars may be brought in by sea, there are three points of entry into Peru by road: from Chile by the Concordia–Tacna road; from Bolivia by the Desaguadero–Puno road; and from Ecuador by the Aguas Verdes–Zarumilla–Tumbes road. It is necessary to produce a *carnet de passages en douane* issued by the Alliance Internationale de Tourisme or the Fédération Internationale Automobile. Since a national driving licence is valid for only 30 days (after which it is necessary to obtain an extension from the Automóvil-Club) it is advisable to have an international driving licence, valid for a year.

When applying for a carnet it is necessary to specify that you intend to visit Peru, for carnets issued in Europe, for example, are not automatically valid for South America. The carnet is valid for 12 months from date of issue; an extension of three months can be obtained in Peru if required.

IV. CURRENCY

The unit of currency is the *sol* (*de oro*), which is divided into 100 *centavos*. A unit frequently employed, but without any official status, is the *libra* (10 soles). There are banknotes for 1000, 500, 200, 100, 50, 10 and 5 soles and coins with the value of 10 and 5 soles (nickel), 1 sol and 50, 25, 20, 10 and 5 centavos (bronze alloy).

Visitors cannot bring in or take out more than 1000 soles in Peruvian currency. Foreign currency and travellers' cheques can be brought in without limit of quantity, provided that they are declared on entry. On leaving the country visitors can exchange any surplus of Peruvian currency on presentation of their entry declaration and receipts for money changed. It is advisable to carry U.S. dollars rather than European currencies, which are not always known outside Lima; they can be changed at the Banco de Lima (address below).

Money can be changed only in approved banks on presentation of passport and entry declaration. There are branches of the Banco de la Nación all over Peru, open in the morning and sometimes also in the afternoon on weekdays (Monday to Friday). Other banks are usually open only in the morning. The exchange office at Lima airport is open 24 hours a day. Some of the larger hotels also have an exchange office.

The main credit cards (particularly American Express) are accepted in Peru.

Addresses of the principal banks in Lima:

Banco Central de Reserva del Perú, Ucayali 271 (tel. 283 000).
Banco de la Nación, Abancay (tel. 286 070).
Banco de Lima, Carabaya 698 (tel. 275 860).
Banco de Londres y América del Sur, Carabaya 442 (tel. 275 850).
First National City Bank, N. de Piérola 1062 (tel. 283 200).
Swiss Bank Corporation, Camaná 370 (tel. 288 141).
Banco de Tokyo, Cuzco 582 (tel. 289 450).
Banco Español de Crédito, Miró Quesada 247 (tel. 280 214).

V. GETTING TO PERU

By air

This is the means of transport used by almost all visitors to Peru. The only international airport in the country is the Jorge Chávez Airport at Lima, named after the Franco-Peruvian aviator who was the first to fly over the Alps at the Simplon pass in 1910. The airport is 15 km from the city centre (taxi fare 250 to 300 soles).

Many European (Air France, British Airways, Iberia, Lufthansa, KLM, etc.), North American (Braniff) and South American airlines (the Brazilian Varig, the Venezuelan Viasa, the Colombian Avianca) operate services to Lima. The flight from Europe takes between 14 and 19 hours, depending on the route. Air France has opened a service from Tokyo to Lima via Tahiti.

Aerolíneas Argentinas, Av. N. de Piérola 634, Lima (tel. 318 522).

Air France, 119 Champs-Elysées, Paris (tel. 225 7050); Av. N. de Piérola 699, Lima (tel. 275 010).

Air Panama, Av. N. de Piérola 780, Lima (tel. 239 967).

Alitalia, via Bissolati 13, Rome (tel. 4688).

Avianca, Av. N. de Piérola 964, Lima (tel. 289 760).

Braniff International, Plaza San Martín 921, Lima (tel. 283 848).

British Airways, West London Terminal, Cromwell Road, London SW7 (tel. 370 5411); Dorland Hall, Lower Regent Street, London SW1; Av. N. de Piérola 1001, Lima (tel. 283 253).

CP Air (Canadian Pacific), Centro Cívico, Paseo República (tel. 249 262).

Cruzeiro do Sul, Carabaya 927, Lima (tel. 279 467).

Cubana de Aviación, Paseo República 126, Lima (tel. 316 324).

Ecuatoriana de Aviación, Av. N. de Piérola 632, Lima (tel. 324 559).

Iberia, Av. N. de Piérola 765, Lima (tel. 283 833).

JAL, Av. N. de Piérola 882, Lima (tel. 324 069).

KLM, Leidseplein 1–3, Amsterdam (tel. 73 12 12); Av. N. de Piérola 750, Lima (tel. 230 315).

LAN Chile, Av. N. de Piérola 826, Lima (tel. 316 324).

Lloyd Aéreo Boliviano, Av. N. de Piérola 757, Lima (tel. 285 033).

Lufthansa, Hauptbahnhof 2, Frankfurt/Main (tel. 33 05 21); Av. N. de Piérola 603, Lima (tel. 289 630).

Olympic Airways, Miró Quesada 247, of. 604, Lima (tel. 275 490).

Panam, Panam Building, Manhattan (tel. 973 4000); World Center Building, 16th and K Streets, Washington D.C. (tel. 833 1000); 30 S. Michigan Avenue, Chicago (tel. 326 4494); Rufino Torrico 837, 3° Piso, Lima (tel. 289 999).

SAS, Unión 926, Lima (tel. 282 930).

Swissair, Aéroport de Genève, Cointrin (tel. 92 21 21); Av. N. de Piérola 742, of. 704–705, Lima (tel. 318 694).

TWA, East Side Terminal, New York (tel. OX 56700); Carabaya 837, of. 219, Lima (tel. 271 796).

Varig, Av. N. de Piérola 616, Lima (tel. 247 900).

Viasa, Av. N. de Piérola 608, Lima (tel. 311 759).

By sea

A number of shipping lines run services to Peru (Callao, the port of Lima) from Europe and the United States. The ships are usually cargo vessels carrying a limited number of passengers. The main companies concerned are:

Pacific Steam Navigation Company of Liverpool, Plaza San Martín (Av. N. de Piérola 1006), Lima.

Knutsen Line (Norwegian), Lloyds Building, Leadenhall Street, London EC3.

Johnson Line (Swedish), Camaná 780, Lima.

Compagnie Générale Transatlantique, Paseo República 3587, San Isidro, Lima.

Compañía Italiana de Vapores, Junín 330, Lima.

Compañía Real Holandesa de Vapores, Miró Quesada 247, Lima.

Grace Line (U.S.), Lampa 594, Lima.

Hamburg-Amerika, *Norddeutscher Lloyd*, Miró Quesada 260, Lima.

There are also services between Peru and Japan (Nippon Yusen Kaisha), Australia (Kawasaki Kisen Kaisha) and India (Bank Line). The Booth Line has a service from Iquitos to Liverpool and New York via the Amazon, with fortnightly sailings (Booth Line, F. Tudela y Varela 100, San Isidro, tel. 222 029).

VI. TRAVEL WITHIN PERU

By air

Apart from a few small companies serving the remoter parts of the country, particularly the Amazonian Selva (e.g. the *Loretana de Aviación*, D. Cueto 541, Lima, tel. 710 164), domestic air services in Peru are provided by two main airlines, *Faucett* and *AeroPerú*.

The *Compañía de Aviación Faucett*, a private airline established in 1928, has a network of services covering the whole of Peru, with over 130 flights weekly. Lima is connected with all the principal towns, and there are also services between these other towns, e.g. Arequipa–Juliaca–Cuzco, Cuzco–Pucallpa, Chiclayo–Moyobamba–Tarapoto and Trujillo–Juanjuí.

AeroPerú, the national airline, absorbed in 1973 the Satco line, which was under the control of the Peruvian air force. In addition to its domestic services, it is constantly expanding its activities in the international field.

Fares, which are very reasonable, are the same on AeroPerú and Faucett. It is advisable to make bookings (including return bookings) well in advance. The busiest route is the Lima–Cuzco line.

Addresses of airline offices:

(A = Aeroperú, F = Faucett)

Lima:	(A)	Av. N. de Piérola 910–914 (Plaza San Martín) (tel. 317 626).
	(F)	Unión 926 (Plaza San Martín, Hotel Bolívar) (tel. 273 987 and 276 120).
Arequipa:	(A)	Merced 106 (tel. 23 080).
	(F)	San Agustín 151 (tel. 22 740).
Ayacucho:	(A)	Portal Constitución 3 (tel. 253).
	(F)	Portal Independencia 66 (tel. 269).
Cajamarca:	(F)	Lima (tel. 2100).
Chiclayo:	(A)	Av. Balta 995 (tel. 2387).
	(F)	Av. Bolognesi (tel. 2046).
Cuzco:	(A)	Heladeros (tel. 4419).
	(F)	Av. Sol 393 (tel. 3666).
Huánuco:	(A)	2 de Mayo 1071 (tel. 2077).
	(F)	2 de Mayo 1243 (tel. 2110).
Huaraz:	(A)	Los Lirios 161 (tel. 2832).
Iquitos:	(A)	Malecón Tarapaca 262 (tel. 2254).
	(F)	Arica 130 (tel. 4560).
		(Loretana) Sargento Lores 170 (tel. 2699).
		(Transperuana) Lima 219 (tel. 2037).
Piura:	(A)	Callao 494 (tel. 3420).
	(F)	Tacna 308 (tel. 2323).

Pucallpa:	(A) Tarapaca 856 (tel. 326).
	(F) 7 de Junio 883 (tel. 271).
	(Loretana) Raimondi 552 (tel. 536).
Puno:	(A) A. Ugarte, Hotel Turistas (tel. 24).
Talara:	(A) Principal (tel. 683).
	(F) Centro Cívico 273 (tel. 694).
Tinge María:	(A) J. Prieto 213 (tel. 2250).
	(F) Raimondi 133 (tel. 2234).
Trujillo:	(A) Junín 537 (tel. 4960).
	(F) F. Pizarro 532 (tel. 2219).
Tumbes:	(A) Teniente Vásquez 309 (tel. 2402).
	(F) Bolívar 137 (tel. 2042).

By rail

There are only a few railway lines in Peru. This method of transport is slow, but cheap even in first class, and it gives the traveller an opportunity of coming into close contact with the realities of Peruvian life. The climb through the Andes is a thrilling experience, and visitors will do well, for the sake of the experience, to include at least one rail trip in their programme (e.g. Lima–Huancayo or Cuzco–Puno). Seats should be booked in advance through an agency or at the Desamparados station in Lima (tel. 276 620 and 278 482).

Lima to Huancayo via La Oroya (350 km), with a branch line to Cerro de Pasco. The journey takes 9 hours, leaving Lima daily except Sundays at 7 a.m. The line, built in 1870 by a British company, has innumerable bridges and tunnels, and crosses the Andes at an altitude of 4781 m, making it the *highest railway line in the world*. Medical help is available for passengers who suffer from altitude sickness (see p. 281).

Arequipa to Puno and Cuzco, via the Crucero Alto pass (4490 m). This is a relatively comfortable service, with a restaurant car and couchettes on the night train, running through magnificent scenery. The journey from Arequipa to Puno by the "Andino" takes about 10¼ hours; in the other direction it takes an hour less, having the advantage of a considerable descent (from 4000 m to 2350 m). There are departures from Arequipa on Monday, Wednesday and Friday mornings and from Puno on Tuesday, Thursday and Saturday mornings. The Arequipa to Cuzco service (the "Chasqui") follows the same route for part of the way, with departures from Arequipa on Wednesday and Sunday evenings and from Cuzco on Tuesday and Friday evenings; the journey takes 17 hours (860 km).

Cuzco to Puno, via the La Raya pass (4313 m). The journey takes about 10 hours, with departures from Cuzco on Monday, Wednesday and Friday mornings and from Puno on Tuesday, Thursday and Saturday mornings.

Cuzco to Machu Picchu. Departures from the San Pedro station in Cuzco. The return trip, which can be done on the same day when travelling by rail-car, should be booked at the same time as the outward journey. See p. 226.

By bus or communal taxi

There is an extensive network of bus services covering every corner of the country. On the Coast, along the Panamerican Highway, there are comfortable modern buses, but elsewhere, particularly in the mountains, the buses are picturesque and jolting old vehicles, always crowded. The fares, however, are very low. The following are the main bus companies with offices in Lima:

Ancash, Leticia 655 (tel. 288 657); Expreso Victoria, N. de Piérola 1219 (tel. 274 140); Roggero, N. de Piérola 1324 (tel. 274 093); Los Andes, 28 de Julio 2405 (tel. 230 660); Panamericano, N. de Piérola 1136 (tel. 289 756); TEPSA (Turismo Express Pullman), Paseo República 129 (tel. 289 995); Huancayo Express, Bolívar 1323; Hidalgo, Bolívar 1541; La Perla, 28 de Julio 1515.

The *colectivos* are communal taxis which leave for a particular destination when all five seats have been taken. They are a little dearer than the buses but are faster and more comfortable, though some passengers may feel some alarm at the drivers' virtuosity on mountain roads. The *colectivos* stop only for a quick lunch. There are services between the various coastal towns along the Panamerican Highway, so that it is possible to work out an itinerary for seeing this part of the country by moving from place to place by *colectivo*.

In towns the local *colectivos* and ordinary taxis provide a convenient alternative to the crowded buses. The town *colectivos*, often minibuses, run on the same routes as the buses: passengers can hail them at street corners and can get out wherever they want. The ordinary taxis have no meters, and the fare (whether for a short trip or for a tour of the town) should therefore be agreed in advance. Fares are reasonable, and in some cases are officially regulated (from Lima airport to the city centre 250–300 soles; Cuzco airport to the city centre 100 soles). Drivers need not be tipped.

By private car

In the coastal region, and particularly on the Panamerican Highway, the roads are asphalted and well marked and signposted, but in other parts of the country conditions are very different. In particular the roads in the Sierra are often difficult and sometimes dangerous. Even in the towns driving is not without its hazards, since Peruvian drivers tend on occasion to treat the traffic lights with some nonchalance. It is not really advisable, therefore—except for excursions north and south of Lima—for visitors to drive themselves, more particularly since hire charges are fairly high. The main car hire firms in Lima are *Hertz*, Ocoña 262 (tel. 288 477); *Avis*, Av. Dupetit-Thouars 901 (tel. 321 990 and 323 023); and *Turamérica*, Ocona 164 (tel. 276 415). "Self-drive" cars can also be hired at Arequipa, Cuzco, Trujillo and Chiclayo.

A visitor's national driving licence is valid for 30 days. For an extension apply to the Automóvil-Club de Perú, Av. César Vallejo 699, San Isidro, Lima (tel. 403 270).

It should be remembered that the distances between towns are considerable, and that there are more lorries than private cars on the roads. In the Sierra the roads are unsurfaced (with some exceptions like the Lima–Huancayo and Cuzco–Urcos roads) and difficult, so that average speeds cannot be expected to exceed 30 or 40 km p.h. During the rainy season the roads may be blocked by landslides (*huaycos*), and in the dry season the dust can be troublesome. Petrol stations are often far apart (sometimes 100 km or more), and it is therefore advisable to carry a spare can, as well as tools, food, a thermos flask, warm clothing and rugs. Night driving should be avoided.

Petrol is sold by the gallon (3.8 litres). There are three grades— *corriente* (70 octane), which is not to be recommended; *extra* (84 octane); and *importada* (94 octane), which is difficult to find outside Lima.

The best road maps are those produced by the Automóvil-Club de Perú (address as above); London agency Renis Commodities Ltd, 15–17 Eldon Street EC2 (tel. 628 7407). Simpler maps are issued free by Petroperú, Av. Central 717, San Isidro.

Hitch-hiking

Hitch-hiking as it is understood in Europe is not much practised in Peru. There are relatively few private cars outside Lima, and the traffic consists mainly of lorries. Lifts can be obtained on lorries, the degree of comfort varying according to the load carried (connoisseurs maintain that the ideal is a lorry carrying a heavy cargo of sugar). It is usual to pay the driver a small sum at the end of the journey (ranging between 5 and 20 soles according to distance).

On horseback

To reach some of the remoter places, particularly in the Sierra, which are far from any road the only means of transport is a horse or a mule. A guide should be taken and the price agreed in advance.

By river boat

In Amazonia places without an air service can be reached only by boat—though the timetables are very irregular, it is difficult to make bookings from Lima, and the comfort and the food provided on the boats are usually of a low standard. By way of example, the journey from Pucallpa (which can be reached from Lima by bus, *colectivo* or air) to Iquitos, a distance of 530 nautical miles, takes 6 or 7 days (8–10 days for the return journey). Departures depend on the goods carried. Apply to Teixeira, Huáscar 117, Pucallpa (tel. 422). From Iquitos boats sail down the Amazon to the Colombian–Brazilian frontier (calling in at Leticia, in Colombia, from which there is an air service to Bogotá), and to the mouth of the river (Booth Line and Enapa: apply to a travel agency in Iquitos or Lima).

VII. DIPLOMATIC MISSIONS IN LIMA

Argentina: Pablo Bermúdez 143, 2° Piso (tel. 245 989).

Australia: Av. Arequipa 330, of. 101 (tel. 288 315).

Austria: Av. Wilson 1494, 7° Piso (tel. 276 032).

Belgium: Av. Angamos 380, Miraflores (tel. 463 335).

Bolivia: Av. Orrantia 145, San Isidro (tel. 228 231).

Brazil: Comandante Espinar 181, Miraflores (tel. 462 635).

Canada: Edificio Pacífico, 7° Piso, Plaza Washington (tel. 287 420).

Chile: Av. Javier Prado 790, San Isidro (tel. 407 965).

China: Av. Javier Prado 1415, San Isidro (tel. 400 782).

Colombia: Av. Arequipa 2685, Lince (tel. 407 662).

Costa Rica: Camino Real 159, of. 400 (tel. 409 982).

Cuba: Centro Cívico, of. 5 (tel. 327 219).

Czechoslovakia: Av. Salaverry 3119, San Isidro (tel. 225 339).

Denmark: Camino Real 479, 8° Piso, San Isidro (tel. 407 512).

Dominican Republic: Coronel Portillo 558, San Isidro (tel. 223 998).

Ecuador: Las Palmeras 356, San Isidro (tel. 221 062).

Egypt: José Pardo 273, Miraflores (tel. 459 597).

Finland: Eucaliptos 291, 7° Piso, San Isidro (tel. 406 660).

France: Plaza Francia (Recoleta) 232 (tel. 238 618).

Germany (*Federal Republic*): Av. Arequipa 4240, Miraflores (tel. 459 997).

Greece: G. Marconi 340, San Isidro (tel. 403 064).

Guatemala: N. de Rivera 495, San Isidro (tel. 403 249).

Haiti: Javier Prado Oeste 1480, 3° Piso (tel. 238 812).

Honduras: Junín 434–443, Miraflores (tel. 256 730).

Hungary: Eucaliptos 395, San Isidro (tel. 222 648).

Iceland: Roma 366 (tel. 222 906).

India: Edificio Anglo-Peruano, Paseo República 219, of. 1201 (tel. 277 498).

Israel: Natalio Sánchez 125, 6° Piso, Edificio Pacífico, Plaza Washington (tel. 318 860).

Italy: Av. Dupetit-Thouars 369 (tel. 233 477).

Japan: Av. San Felipe 356, Pueblo Libre (tel. 614 041).

Jordan: Los Castaños 205, San Isidro (tel. 223 750).

Lebanon: Lampa 247 (tel. 273 325).

Mexico: Av. Javier Prado Oeste 270, San Isidro (tel. 405 465).

Netherlands: Las Camelias 780, 10° Piso, San Isidro (tel. 228 302).

New Zealand: Av. Salaverry 3006, San Isidro (tel. 621 890).

Nicaragua: Camino Real 479, 7° Piso, San Isidro (tel. 220 392).

Norway: Rufino Torrico 977 (tel. 311 546).

Panama: Orrantia 350, San Isidro (tel. 406 592).

Paraguay: Mariano José de Arce 190, San Isidro (tel. 228 544).

Poland: Av. Salaverry 1978, Jesús María (tel. 713 920).

Portugal: Orrantia 718, San Isidro (tel. 409 905).

Romania: Orrantia 690, San Isidro (tel. 409 396).

El Salvador: Av. S. Cruz 488, San Isidro (tel. 221 320).

Spain: Av. República de Chile 148 (tel. 310 496).

Sweden: Las Agatas 189, Balconcillo (tel. 722 425).

Switzerland: Las Camelias 780, San Isidro (tel. 227 706).

Thailand: Puno 573 (tel. 288 320).

United Kingdom: Natalio Sánchez 125, Edificio Washington, 12° Piso (tel. 283 830).

USA: Esq. España y Garcilaso de la Vega 1400 (tel. 286 000).

USSR: Av. Salaverry 3424, San Isidro (tel. 616 473).

Uruguay: Junín 165, Miraflores (tel. 461 119).

Venezuela: Av. Arequipa 298 (tel. 249 120).

Yugoslavia: Av. Santa Cruz 330, San Isidro (tel. 221 014).

VIII. ENTERTAINMENTS

Theatres

The principal theatres in Lima have very varied programmes. Productions by foreign companies are put on at the Municipal Theatre, Jirón Ica, which is also used for concerts. Modern and avant-garde plays are performed in the Club de Teatro, Colmena 757, and the Corral de Comedias in Miraflores. The Teatro Segura, Jirón Huancavelica, specialises in operettas and variety.

Cinemas

Peruvian cinemas show American and European films and also Mexican and Argentinian productions. Performances are not continuous, and there are usually three showings—a matinee at 3 p.m., the so-called "vermouth" show at 7 and the evening (*noche*) show at 10. The usherettes do not expect tips. Some film clubs put on weekend shows of foreign films (Ministry of Labour, Av. Salaverry; Museum of Art, Av. Colón).

Horse-racing

There is racing on Tuesday, Thursday, Saturday and Sunday afternoons at the Monterrico racecourse near Lima (tel. 403 500).

Bullfights

Bullfighting—which was introduced by Pizarro himself—is a favourite sport in Lima and many other towns. Every festival or other celebration in a place of any size is accompanied by bullfights. The biggest events are those held in the Arenas de Acho in Lima (north of the river Rímac), on Sundays and public holidays from October to December, and also in March. The high point of the season is at the end of October, during the festival of Christ of the Miracles, when the toreros compete for the famous "Gold Scapular". As in Spain, there is a distinction between the better seats in the shade (*Sombre*) and the cheaper seats in the sun (*Sol*).

Cockfighting

This is a popular sport in Lima and on the Coast. Like bullfighting, it was introduced by the Conquistadors. In Lima cockfights take place in the Coliseo de Gallos, Sandia 150 (tel. 281 204), usually at the weekend: times are advertised in the newspapers.

Sport

There are a number of *golf* courses (9 and 18 holes) round Lima. Information from the Sudex travel agency, Plaza San Martín (tel. 286 054).

Riding can be enjoyed at very moderate cost in Lima and in the Sierra.

For *shooting* (e.g. duck on Lake Junín) it is necessary to have a permit from the Dirección de Parques Nacionales y Vida Silvestre, Av. Salaverry 982, Lima. A permit will be issued only on production of a firearm licence on stamped paper (*papel sellado*) granted by the Ministry of the Interior, Av. Corpac.

Sea-fishing is practised mainly round Ancón (north of Lima) and Cabo Blanco (north of Talara). It is forbidden to hunt seals or to land on the guano islands. There is also *river fishing*, mainly for trout (La Oroya area and the region round Juliaca and Lake Titicaca).

Swimming. Conditions are not favourable in Peruvian coastal waters on account of the cold Humboldt Current, except in the extreme north. There are of course swimming pools in many of the larger hotels and in clubs.

Folk traditions

Apart from the picturesque and colourful Carnival most Peruvian festivals are of religious origin (Holy Week and various other Catholic festivals and processions). Details are given below. But visitors to Lima at any time of year can gain some idea of the rich folk heritage of the different parts of the country by going to the performances of folk singing and dancing in traditional costume which are given every Sunday (4 p.m.) in the Coliseo Nacional, Av. Bolívar. (On the folk arts generally, see p. 77 above).

Calendar of Festivals

January	1	Religious and folk festival at *Ayacucho*.
	6	Epiphany (Festival of the Kings) at *Lima* ("Ciudad de los Reyes").
	1–12	International fair (Feria de los Reyes) at *Piura* (Sullana), with dealers from Ecuador and Colombia (duty-free sale of craft products). Cockfighting, folk dancing.
	(mid)	*Lima Week*, commemorating the foundation of the town on 18 January 1535.
	20	Jala Pato festival at *Jauja*, with local dances (the Tunandada, the Muliza, the Chonguinada).
	20	At *Huancavelica*, battle between Moors and Christians.
	20	At *Caraz*, pilgrimage of the Virgin of Chiquinquirá, with bullfights and cockfighting.
	(end)	At *Cuzco*, procession of "Mamacha Belén", Queen of Cuzco.
February		The month of the Carnival, with fiestas on the four Sundays.
	2	(until the following Sunday). At *Puno*, procession of the Virgin of Candlemas, with typical local dances (Diablada, Llamerada, Pandilla).
		At *Jauja*, fiesta of Tumba Monte. At *Iquitos*, parade of floats and fiesta of the Humishas.
March (beginning)		At *Catacaos* (Piura), traditional fiesta.
	8–15	At *Ica*, Vintage Festival, with cockfighting and a horse fair.

March–April		Holy Week. The main celebrations are at *Ayacucho* and *Porcón*, near Cajamarca (Palm Sunday procession), *Cuzco* (on Monday, procession of the Señor de los Temblores, patron of the town), *Lima* and *Ica* (Thursday) and *Catacaos* (procession every day). On Good Friday there are processions at *Arequipa* and *Tarma* and the Reseña ceremony in the Cathedral at *Ayacucho*. On Easter Day the Mass of the Resurrection is celebrated at 4 a.m. in *Ayacucho* Cathedral, followed by a procession with thousands of Indians who have gathered for the fair on the Cerro de Acuchimay.
April	23–30	*Ayacucho Week* (Semana de Huamanga), commemorating the foundation of the town, with displays of handicrafts and processions in traditional costume.
May	1	At *Arequipa*, pilgrimage to Chapí.
	2–3	Throughout Peru (particularly at *Huaraz* and *Cuzco*) Fiesta de la Cruz.
June		Corpus Christi celebrations at *Cuzco* and *Cajamarca*. At Cajamarca the procession is accompanied by fanfares of *clarineres* (trumpets 4 m long which are used on this occasion only).
	23–25	At *Iquitos*, Midsummer Festival (St John's Day).
	24–30	*Cuzco Week*. On 24 June, Inti Raymi, an Inca festival celebrated on the esplanade at Sacsayhuamán.
	29	Festival of St Peter, patron of fishermen, particularly at *Ichu* (Puno) and *Chorrillos* (Lima).
July	8	Festival of St Isabel at *Huaylas* (Ancash).
	12–22	Pilgrimage of *Puerto Etén* (Lambayeque), commemorating an apparition of the Infant Jesus at the beginning of the 19th century.
	16	Festival of the Virgin of Carmel at *Paucartambo* (100 km from Cuzco) and *Pomata* (Puno).

	22–29	At *Tingo María*, a large agricultural show and Coffee Festival.
	23	(to 1 August) Festival of St James at *Santiago de Cucho*.
	28	Peruvian National Day, with parades of troops and school children and displays of folk dancing, etc.
August	1–3	Santa Cruz de *Motupe* (Lambayeque).
	5	Festival of the Virgin of the Snows at *Ayacucho*.
	(3rd week)	*Huánuco Week* (14 August onwards).
	15–22	*Arequipa Week*, commemorating the foundation of the town on 15 August 1541, with folk festival.
	21–31	At *Cañete* (south of Lima), fiesta mainly devoted to negro art.
	26–29	At *Tacna*, fiesta commemorating the town's return to Peru.
	29–30	Festival of St Rose of Lima, patroness of the Americas, the Philippines, policemen and nurses, with a pilgrimage to *Santa Rosa de Quives* (64 km from Lima), where the saint lived.
	30	Festival of St Anne at *Ayacucho*.
September	8	Religious festival at *Cocharcas* and *Sapallanga* (Huancayo) and *Huamantanga* (Lima).
	14–18	Fiesta of Monsefú, *Chiclayo*.
	23–30	At *Trujillo*, International Spring Festival (Creole music and singing, election of a beauty queen, parade of flowers, etc.).
	24	Festival of the Virgin of Mercy, patron of the armed forces (procession in *Lima*).
(during the month)		Inkari folk festival.
October	1	At *Arequipa*, procession of the Paso.
	1–6	At *Cajabamba* (2 hours' drive from Lima), festival of the Virgin of the Rosary, with the "Devils of Cajabamba", a unique folk group.
	7	At *Yauyos* (Lima), festival of the Virgin of the Rosary, with the sowing of potatoes, accompanied by folk music and songs.

	5–12	At *Pucallpa*, regional fair.
	8–14	*Piura Week*.
	12	Commemoration of Columbus's discovery of America in 1492. At *Moquegua*, festival of St Fortunata.
	18–28	Festival of the Señor de los Milagros at *Lima*, with splendid processions on 18, 19 and 28 October. Bullfights.
November	1	All Saints Day, celebrated all over Peru.
	1–7	*Puno Week*, with a representation of the emergence from Lake Titicaca of Manco Cápac and Mama Occlo, founders of the Inca empire.
	4–10	*Sullana Week*.
	12–28	International Pacific Fair at *Lima* (alternate years).
	10–18	Festival of St Martin Porres, protector of the poor, who was canonised by Pope John XXIII.
December	6–8	Festival of the Virgin of Guadalupe.
	8	Immaculate Conception, particularly at *Tumbes*.
	9	At Quinua (Ayacucho) re-enactment by school children and troops of the battle of Ayacucho (1824).
	8–15	At *Cuzco*, festival of the Virgen de la Puerta.
	24	Santoranticuy fair at *Cuzco*.
	25	Christmas, celebrated all over Peru, but with particular fervour at *Ayacucho* and *Cuzco*.

IX. MISCELLANEOUS

Electricity

220 volts (occasionally 110).

Weights and measures

Peru uses the metric system. Petrol is, however, still sold by the gallon (3.8 litres).

Tipping

In a restaurant add 5% to the bill. Porters at airports and hotels should get 10 soles for each item of luggage. Taxi drivers and usherettes in theatres and cinemas are not tipped.

It is advisable to have plenty of small change, for any minor services received (e.g. a lift in a lorry for a hitch hiker) tends to call for a tip.

Time

Peruvian time is 5 hours behind GMT and 6 hours behind British summer time and European time.

Shop hours

From 10 or 11 to 6 or 8 (travel agencies 9 to 5). These hours are less strictly observed outside Lima. Not all shops close on one day a week; when they do it is usually Saturday.

Bank hours

Usually from 8.30 to 12 (11.30 in summer); closed on Saturdays and Sundays. Some branches of the Banco de la Nación are also open in the afternoon.

Office hours

From 9 to 5, without a lunch break; usually closed on Saturdays. Government departments often close at 11 for lunch and are open between 3 and 5 in the afternoon; they are also open on Saturday mornings.

Church opening hours

Churches open very early in the morning (sometimes at 6 a.m.), but close after the celebration of mass, opening again only if there is an afternoon service.

Museums and monuments: opening hours

Hours vary from place to place and ares ubject to change. The guide will expect a tip. Recently some churches (e.g. in Cuzco) have begun to make an admission charge for tourists.

Punctuality

Peruvian ideas of time are much more flexible than in Europe and the United States. It is common practice to have lunch in the later afternoon and to have dinner very late, as in Spain. If, however, an invitation contains the word *hora inglesa* or *hora exacta* you are expected to arrive at the exact time stated.

Emergencies

Police, fire, ambulance: dial 05.

Bargaining

This is a normal and accepted practice, except in shops with marked prices.

Etiquette

When in a friend's house take care not to admire anything too enthusiastically. Your host would then feel bound to offer it to you: an offer which would not be refused without causing grave offence.

Pickpockets

Peru has no monopoly of this trade, but they are active here as in all areas with crowds of tourists. Take care, therefore, to avoid tempting them.

Telephone

Local calls are free to subscribers up to a maximum of 150 per telephone per month. For foreign trunk calls dial 08 (reduced charges between 7 p.m. and 6 a.m., and on Sundays).

Telegrams

The porter in your hotel will despatch a telegram for you. The telegraph service is run by a nationalised body, *Entelperú*, Las Begonias 375, Lima (tel. 409 906). Only head post offices handle telegrams.

Postal services

The head post office (Correo Central) in Lima, where poste restante mail can be collected, is in the city centre, just north of the Plaza de Armas on the left-hand side of the Palacio de Gobierno.

Languages

The language of Peru is Spanish, with some differences of vocabulary and pronunciation from Castilian, but the differences are of relatively minor importance. English is understood in hotels, though those who speak it may be disrespectfully classed as gringos. French is spoken by a select few, particularly in Lima, but in country areas and provincial towns few people understand it. The Indians speak Quechua and Aymará (round Puno). Spanish and Quechua are both official languages.

Photography

Films are dear in Peru, and it is therefore better to bring your own. Remember that the light is very strong at high altitudes and that an ultraviolet filter must be used. Do not photograph people without their agreement (a small payment will sometimes be found to facilitate matters).

Health

Above 3000 m visitors tend to suffer from *soroche*, altitude sickness, which brings on blackouts and headaches. Serious consequences are rare, but people with heart conditions and pregnant women should be wary. It is advisable to have with you such preparations as Nautamine, Micoren and Coramine glucose (which can be obtained in chemists' shops in Peru). An infusion of coca leaves or a green lemon can also produce beneficial effects; and chewing cloves is a useful remedy for toothache (which is fairly common at high altitudes). Visitors who can afford the time will do well to go to Cuzco (alt. 3400 m) via Arequipa (2350 m) and spend a few days there before continuing to Puno (3900 m) and Cuzco by train. This will avoid the worst effects of *soroche*, felt by those who arrive by air from Lima after a 90 minute flight. During the first few days of their stay visitors visitors should avoid exertion, walk slowly, eat moderately and take no alcohol.

Visitors travelling by road may suffer from diarrhoea. They should avoid raw vegetables and salads and eat moderately of highly spiced dishes. They should not drink water outside the towns, taking beer or mineral waters instead. In Amazonia the water is particularly dangerous on account of amoebas and parasites. Visitors to Amazonia should also remember to take preparations containing quinine with them.

Since the air is very dry at high altitudes in July and August, rub your skin with moisturising cream.

There are excellent doctors in Peruvian towns, sometimes speaking English, French or German, and pharmacies with a convenient all-night service.

The following are the principal nursing homes in Lima:
International, Washington 1475 (tel. 288 060).
Anglo-American, Alfredo Salazar 300, San Isidro (tel. 403 570).
Javier Prado, Av. Javier Prado Este 499, San Isidro.
San Felipe, Av. Escobedo, Jesús María (tel. 613 041).

Public holidays

1 January, Mid-Lent, Good Friday, 1 May, 29 June, 28–29 July, 30 August (St Rose of Lima), 9 October (Day of National Dignity), All Saints, 8 December and 25 December.

Street numbering

In towns (usually laid out on a regular geometric plan) a block is known as a *cuadra*, and the corner of a block (often used in giving directions) is an *esquina*. Streets are numbered odd on one side, even on the other. No. 657 in a given street (*jirón, calle* or *avenida*) is in the 6th block on the odd-numbered side.

Many streets have changed their names in recent years, but in popular usage (including taxi drivers) they are still known by their old names (e.g., in Lima, Avenida Wilson rather than Garcilaso de la Vega).

Newspapers

The "Lima Times" is a weekly publication in English which gives full information about the events of the week in Lima. Its office is at Carabaya 928 (tel. 284 069).

The ABC bookshops (with branches in the Hotel Bolívar, at the airport and in the town) sell newspapers and books in foreign languages, particularly English, American, French, German, Italian and Spanish publications.

Useful addresses in Lima

British Council, Edificio Pacífico–Washington, Av. Arequipa (tel. 279 697).
Peruvian–British Cultural Association, Camaná 787 (tel. 277 927).
British Commonwealth Society, Av. Miló Quesada 309.

American Society of Peru, Calle Retiro, Miraflores (tel. 20 659).

Peruvian–North American Cultural Institute, Cuzco 446 (tel. 283 530).

American Chamber of Commerce, Juan de Arona, San Isidro.

Comercial Peruano–Canadiense, Av. Garcilaso de la Vega 1264 (tel. 243 546).

Alliance Française, Av. Garcilaso de la Vega 1550 (tel. 317 766).

Franco–Peruvian Chamber of Commerce, French Embassy, Plaza Francia (tel. 249 914).

German–Peruvian Cultural Association, Ica 426 (tel. 277 827).

Enturperú (Peruvian Tourist Office), Conde Superunda 298 (tel. 288 225).

Touring y Automóvil-Club, Av. César Vallejo 699, San Isidro (tel. 403 270).

YMCA, Carabaya 664 (tel. 277 827).

Peruvian Scouting Association, Av. República de Chile 284 (tel. 326 046).

National Association of Writers and Artists, Unión 1050 (tel. 236 139).

San Marcos University, Av. Venezuela, Ciudad Universitaria (tel. 322 665).

Lima University, Parque Universitario (tel. 401 820).

Pacific University, Av. Salaverry 2020 (tel. 235 936).

Federico Villareal National University, Av. N. de Piérola 262 (tel. 328 294).

SINAMOS (National System of Support for Social Mobilisation), Centro Cívico, Sheraton Hotel (tel. 289 775).

Peruvian Cultural Institute, Ica 426 (tel. 280 534).

Travel agencies in Lima

Chábez, Colmena 733 (tel. 277 777).

Coltur, Camaná 868 (tel. 289 935).

Sudex, Plaza San Martn (tel. 286 054).

Receptour, R. Torrico 889 (tel. 312 022).

Lima Tours, Ocoña 160 (tel. 276 624).

Puno–Cuzco Tours, Av. N. de Piérola 742 (tel. 318 575).

Wagons–Lits Cook, Ocoña 170 (tel. 279 907).

Universal, R. Torrico 965 (tel. 289 815).

Panorama, Garcilaso de la Vega 955 (tel. 288 380).

X. SHOPPING

Peru is rich in handicraft products of all kinds, and tourists will frequently be tempted. It should be remembered, however, that there is a strict ban on the export of pre-Columbian antiquities and on works of early colonial art (statuettes, carved and gilded woodwork, mirrors, etc.).

For a general survey of Peruvian arts and crafts, see p. 80. It is worth bearing in mind that although a wide range of craft goods from all over Peru can be found in Lima prices are higher in the capital than in the areas where they are produced. The best plan, therefore, is to avoid making too many purchases immediately after your arrival in Lima, but to have a final round of shopping there just before your departure, after you have seen what the rest of the country has to offer. Very fine pieces of silver, wood-carving, leather goods, woollen articles (in either sheep's wool or alpaca wool), jewellery, textiles (ponchos), pottery, etc., can be found in a whole series of shops and handicraft centres in Lima. Most of the handicraft shops are round Av. Colmena and Jirón de la Unión. The following is a brief and very far from exhaustive list:

Artesanía del Perú, Av. Orrantia 610, San Isidro (tel. 409 135); El Chasqui, Colmena 876 (tel. 234 303); Sylvania Print and Peru Print (printed textiles), Colmena; Platería Carlos Mario Camusso (silver), Av. Mariscal Benavides 679 and R. Rivera 788, San Isidro; Vasco (modern jewellery based on ancient models), San Isidro; EPPA (Empresa Peruana de Promoción Artisanal), Tambo de Oro, Belén 1066. See also the Art Center at Miraflores; and above all do not miss the Feria Artisanal in the Avenida de la Marina in Pueblo Libre (bus No. 48), where there is an open air display of their work by small craftsmen, where prices are lower than in the city and haggling is in order.

In the smaller towns good bargains can be found in the local markets (often held on Sunday). The following is a brief list of the products in which particular areas specialise:

Arequipa. Embroidered cushions in ancient designs or in contemporary folk style; woollens; carved and painted wooden articles; leather goods; statuettes in *sillar* (the local stone: see p. 185); necklaces made of *fideos* (spaghetti).

Ayacucho. Woollens; tinplate articles (*hojalata*); objects in Huamanga stone (human figurines); silver filigree work; gourds decorated in pokerwork and painted (*mates burilados*); carpets; Quinua pottery (miniature churches); "reredoses" (*cajones de San Marcos*) with small-scale figures, painted in bright colours.

Cajamarca. Mirrors framed in painted and gilded wood; brightly coloured ponchos; straw hats; rag dolls; leather goods; pottery, particularly copies of prehistoric ware.

Callejón de Huaylas. Woollen articles (ponchos, bags); leather goods; wrought iron.

Chiclayo. Ponchos and bags; straw hats.

Cuzco and surrounding area (*Pisac, Paucartambo*). Ponchos and other articles in alpaca; carved and painted wood; pottery of various kinds; *tupus* (brooches for fastening shawls) and silver filigree articles; felt hats. A visit to the craftsmen's quarter in Cuzco, San Blas, is recommended.

Huancavelica. Leather goods; alpaca articles; multi-coloured cuffs.

Huancayo. Gourds decorated in pokerwork; straw hats; silver; embroidered blouses; alpaca articles. See the famous Sunday fair.

Iquitos (*and Pucallpa*). Articles produced by the Indians of the Selva: native weapons (bows, blowpipes); textiles in geometric patterns; feather necklaces; small stuffed animals; brilliantly coloured Amazonian butterflies; Indian pottery (Pucallpa).

Juliaca, Puno. Ponchos, *chullos* (caps) and shawls of alpaca wool; llama skins; basketwork from Lake Titicaca; carnival masks; pottery bulls from Pucará.

Piura and Tumbes. Gold and silver filigree work (Catacaos); cotton cloths; straw articles.

XI. FOOD AND DRINK

Peruvian cooking offers visitors a richness and variety which they will do well to explore (though of course the restaurants have also a wide range of European dishes). It is notable for the strength of the condiments it uses, in particular pimentoes (*ají*, the small elongated yellow pepper, and *rocoto*, red pepper), purple onions, green lemons and various spices, colouring substances and herbs (coriander, *huacatay*, *hierba buena*, etc.). The result is to produce some very highly spiced dishes, usually served with steamed potatoes, sweet potatoes (*camotes*) or corn on the cob (*choclos*), which help to temper the fiery taste of the pimentoes and onions. Sometimes, however, the dishes are less highly seasoned and the pimentoes are served separately.

Soup is the mainstay of Peruvian cooking, particularly for the poorer classes. There are so many varieties that several different terms are used—*sopa, chupa, chilcano, pepián. Sopa* usually means a clear soup derived from European cuisine, with eggs, vegetables, vermicelli, etc. *Chupe de camarones*, eaten both on the Coast and in the Sierra, has crayfish as its main ingredient, together with a great variety of vegetables. *Chilcano* is a fish soup (often made with fishes' heads only). *Cazuelas* and *pucheros* are really hotpots containing vegetables in great variety.

By way of **entrees** there are a variety of dishes: stuffed avocados (*paltas rellenas*) and *piqueo criollo*, which is a meal in itself, consisting of a number of separate dishes like *anticuchos* (pieces of meat, particularly beef hearts, broiled on skewers), *chicharrones* (crackling of pork, salted and grilled), *empanadas* (a kind of pasty filled with meat, onions, hard-boiled eggs and black olives), *tamales* or *humitas* (found throughout Latin America— corn flour pasties filled with meat and wrapped in a maize husk or banana leaf and boiled), *choclos* (tender maize cobs, sometimes served with cheese), *papas a la huancaina* (boiled potatoes in a sauce made of goat's milk cheese and *ají*), *ocopa arequipeña* (a sauce served with steamed potatoes, containing peanut oil, various herbs and *ají*) and *causa a la limeña* (a kind of potato puree with a sauce containing *ají*, onions and lemon juice). Another popular dish is *ají de gallina* (chicken in a kind of béchamel sauce containing eggs, cheese and a strong seasoning of pimentos); and finally mention must be made of the various kinds of *escabeche* and *salpicón*—salads incorporating pieces of meat, chicken, fish and boiled vegetables.

Fish forms the basis of a number of typical dishes, particularly on the Coast. The most popular is *cebiche*, in which the fish (together with shellfish in the case of a "mixed *cebiche*") is marinaded, and practically cooked, for several hours in the juice of green lemons mixed with onions and *ají*. The fish most commonly eaten are *corvina, lenguado, pejerrey* and *cojinoa*. They are served boiled or fried, with a variety of sauces—*a la criolla* (with onion rings and *ají*), *a lo macho* (with shrimps and shellfish), *a la chorrillana* (with tomatoes and *ají*). Shrimps and crayfish (*camarones*) are used in various highly seasoned *chupes* (soups) and *piquantes* (sauces). Shellfish are seldom eaten raw; they are sometimes heated in the oven to make *sudados* (i.e. so hot that they sweat). In the Sierra there are trout (*truchas*) and *suches* (a kind of catfish).

In considering **meat dishes** it should be remembered that *lomo* is fillet steak, while *churrasco* is the rib. *Montado* is either *lomo* or *churrasco* with a fried egg, fried potatoes and rice (and sometimes also banana fritters). *Saltado* consists of small pieces of meat sauté'd with onions, tomatoes and potatoes. *Estofado* and *seco* are sauces served with meat, the former seasoned with coriander, the latter rather drier. *Lechones* (sucking pigs) and *cuyes* (guinea-pigs) are eaten grilled. In the Sierra they are rubbed with green lemon juice and exposed to the sun for several hours before being cooked. They are accompanied by *tamales* (see above) and *rocotos rellenos* (stuffed red peppers). In the Sierra they are sometimes served with potatoes cooked in the ground (*huatia*) or in heated stones (*pachamanka*) in accordance with a Polynesian tradition. Tripe is used in the preparation of sauces (*mondongo*, *cau-cau*). The peasants, who in general have a diet containing little meat, eat dried salt meat in the form of *charqui* (jerked beef), *sesina* (mutton), or *chalona*.

The commonest **vegetables** are potatoes in all their forms, maize (boiled cobs or *choclos*; boiled maize grains or *motes*, served with cheese, in a pancake, etc.) and *yuca* (sweet manioc). *Chuño* and *moraya*, forms of potato starch produced by exposure to frost and to the sun, are used mainly in Indian dishes, but are also used in certain soups in the Sierra. Kidney beans (*fréjoles*) and Lima beans (*pallares*) are also popular. Noodles (*tallarines*) are eaten with various sauces (including one made of mushrooms and seaweed).

Sweet dishes include *mazamorra* (a jelly made with corn flour), *alfajores* (pancakes filled with a mixture of honey, walnuts and crushed orange peel), fruit, either fresh or in syrup (*almibar*), *gelatinas* (jellies—a borrowing from the United States), *buñuelos* (doughnuts), various preserves (*dulces*) and *manjarblanco* (a blancmange made of very sweet boiled condensed milk).

The most popular **drinks** are the traditional *chicha de jora* (a light beer made from maize), *chicha morada* (non-alcoholic) and *cerveza* (beer brewed from barley). There are excellent wines in the Ica and Tacna valleys. The local wine brandy is known as *pisco*; *aguardiente* is a kind of brandy made from the juice of the sugar-cane. *Emolientes* (herb teas) and *ponches* ("punch" made of milk and eggs flavoured with ground almonds, cinnamon and sometimes brandy) are sold in the streets and at fiestas. Large quantities of "*Inca-Cola*" are also drunk.

Regional specialties. *Secos* (of goat meat and mutton) are typical of northern Peru. The various *piquantes* and dishes using crayfish and shellfish are specialities of Arequipa. Cuzco is noted for *rocotos rellenos*, *chicharrones* and *cuyes*. Specialties of the *Selva* are *paiche* (an Amazonian fish), particularly in the form of *picadillo* (dried, with a sauce containing garlic, tomatoes and eggs), manioc doughnuts, maize *humitas* and "*Juanes a la brasa*" (pasties made of corn flour containing chicken, eggs, rice and various condiments).

Most towns have restaurants specialising in grilled chickens and fried potatoes (*pollos a la brasa*) and *chifas* which serve excellent Chinese meals.

GASTRONOMIC GLOSSARY

Aji de gallina: chicken in a sauce made of cheese, walnuts and peppers.

Anticuchos: pieces of beef heart marinaded in vinegar and broiled on a skewer, accompanied by corn on the cob, sweet potatoes and a highly seasoned sauce.

Carapulcra: pork with dried potatoes, onions and peanuts.

Cau-cau: a thick sauce containing tripe, potatoes, onions and peppers.

Causa: a cold dish containing potatoes, onions, lemons, olives, hard-boiled eggs, shrimps, etc.

Cebiche: a sea fish, marinaded in the juice of green lemons and served with peppers, onions and boiled maize. *Cebiche* is also made with shrimps or other species of seafood.

Charqui: dried llama meat or beef.

Chicharrones: crackling of pork.

Chilcano: a fish soup containing onions, tomatoes, peppers and lemon juice.

Chupe: a soup made of fish or crayfish, with fresh cheese, eggs, condensed milk, garlic, onions and potatoes.

Escabeche: fish (sometimes chicken) cooked with onions and vinegar and served cold with vegetables.

Empanadas: pasties filled with meat or cheese.

Lomo a la chorrillana: grilled beef served with onions and tomatoes.

Parihuela: soup made with seafood.

Patita con mani: pig's trotters with potatoes, onions and peanuts.

Seco: kid or lamb stew.

Sopa a la criolla: a meat bouillon containing tomatoes, onion, garlic, small pieces of meat, peppers, etc.

Sancochado: brisket of beef with various vegetables.

Tamales: corn flour pasties filled with meat.

Restaurants in Lima and other towns: see p. 298.

HOTELS

In spite of the considerable progress made in recent years Peru's hotel resources are still inadequate, and are likely to remain so for some time. It is essential to book in advance, particularly in Lima and in the larger towns and tourist centres. This is even more necessary during the main season (July to September), when there are large numbers of foreign tourists.

The State organisation *Enturperú* runs a chain of "Turistas" hotels which can be particularly recommended. They are mostly new buildings with a high standard of comfort, and sometimes of luxury (parks, swimming pools, patios, etc.). Rooms in these hotels are in great demand, and it is sometimes difficult to obtain bookings. Apply to Enturperú, Conde de Superunda 298, Lima (tel. 287 815, 281 608, 288 225): open 8 a.m. to 6 p.m.

There are no luxury hotels except in Lima. These hotels, like those in the 1st category, offer every comfort and amenity, but tend to be dear. In the following list luxury hotels are indicated by the letter L, 1st category hotels by ***. The medium-grade hotels (2nd category, indicated by **) are often excellent, although not all rooms have private bathrooms. The more modest hotels (indicated by *) will appeal to those with shorter purses, but do not of course offer the same amenities as the hotels in the higher categories. There are also, particularly in Lima, guest-houses or pensions providing accommodation at lower rates than the hotels, and some of these are often pleasant and comfortable. Some of them provide only bed and breakfast; others serve meals as well. Finally there are the *alojamientos*, modest inns offering minimum standards of comfort at low rates, in which the unit of accommodation is the bed rather than the room.

Service and various taxes are added to the bill, making an addition of perhaps 22 to 25%. It is worth remembering that the more modest hotels do not usually supply towels or toilet paper.

Students can apply to the following addresses in Lima: Residencia Universitaria, Av. Graú 1190; Ciudad Universitaria, Camino de Callao, Av. Venezuela; Bienestar Estudiantil, Edificio Kennedy, Av. República de Chile 291; YMCA, Jirón Augusto N. Wiese 664 (with a new hostel in Pueblo Libre, Av. Bolívar).

Camping is not easy in Peru. There are no organised sites, and *camping sauvage* is not recommended.

Tel.

Abancay
** Turistas, D. Bárcenas 500 (22 rooms)   017

Arequipa
** Turistas, north of town centre, Selva Alegre
    (103 rooms)   22 140
** Presidente, Piérola 207   22 584
** Chrismar, Moral 107   27 339
 * Sucre, Sucre 201   25 045
 * Pensión Fernández, Quesada 106, Yanahuara   24 051

Other hotels: Country, Calle San Martín; International, 3 blocks
from the Plaza de Armas; Metro; Lira; Excelsior; Santa
Catalina.

Ayacucho
** Turistas, 9 de Diciembre 102 (59 rooms)   127
 * Colmena, Cuzco 114 (an old colonial house)   366

Other hotels: Huamanga, Asamblea 112 (near Plaza de Armas);
Sucre, Portal Constitución; Trocadero, Lima 115. Accommodation can also be obtained in the University.

Cajamarca
** Turistas, Plaza de Armas (60 rooms)   2470
 * Sucre, Amalia Puga 811   –

Other hotels: Becerra, Arequipa 195; San Francisco, Belén 570;
Plaza, Plaza de Armas.

Camaná
** Turistas, Lima 138 (18 rooms)   115

Chachapoyas
 * Amazonas (35 rooms)   –

Chala
 * Turistas (17 rooms)   –

Chiclayo
** Turistas, Av. Arteaga (90 rooms)   3711
 * Europa, Elías Aguirre 486   2015
 * Astoria, Balta 647   –
 * Americano, Balta 1169   –

Other hotels: Royal, San José 787; Mediterráneo, Balta (near Plaza de Armas).

Chimbote

* Chimú, Gálvez 109	2061
* San Felipe, Pardo 515	–

Chincha

** Canaveral (40 rooms)	2189

Cuzco

*** Espinar, Portal Espinar 142	5128
*** Savoy, Av. Sol 953	2480
** Turistas, Heladeros 135	2400
** Garcilaso, Garcilaso 233	3654
** San Agustín, San Agustín 332	2881
** El Virrey, Portal Comercio 165	3912
** Los Marqueses, Garcilaso 256 (house of colonial period)	4180
** Conquistador, Belén 588	3142
** El Sol, San Andrés 338 A	3816
** El Dorado, Av. Sol 341	3373
** Cusi, Av. Huáscar 115	2289
* Ollanta, Av. Sol 346	3043
* Santa Catalina, Santa Catalina Ancha 366	2841
* Continental, Estación del Sur	3589
* Ambassador, Tullumayo 440	2358
* John Kennedy, Av. Sol 819 A	4053
* Niza, San Francisco	2898

Other hotels (cheap): Machu Picchu, Calle Nueva 438; Trinitarias, Trinitarias 261; Imperio, Chaparro 128; Plateros, Plateros 340; Colonial, Matara 288; Panamericano, San Agustín 339; Bolívar (one block from Plaza de Armas).

Huancavelica

* Turistas, Plaza de Armas (20 rooms)	–

Huancayo

** Turistas, Plaza Huananmarca (70 rooms)	2701
* Huaychulo, Odriozola 176	–
* Confort, Ancash 297	–

Tel.

* Iman, Av. Ferrocarril 1298   3951
* Prince, Calixto 578   3901

Other hotels: Colmena, Jauja 618; Central, Loreto 452; Colón, Plaza de Armas; Palermo; Internacional; Príncipe; Olímpico; Iquitos.

Huánuco
** Turistas, D. Beraún 775 (30 rooms)   2410
** Cuzco, Huánuco 612   2041
* Confort, Huánuco 603   –

Other hotels: Astoria; Inca; Nacional; Oriental; Internacional.

Huaraz
** Monterrey (7 km north)   Monterrey 1

Huarmey
** Turistas, A. Reyes 201 (8 beds)   31

Ica
** Turistas, Av. Maestros   2116
** Mosone (5 km south-west)   Huacachina 9
* Colón   –

Other hotels: Confort; Salvatierra; Imperial; Bolívar.

Iquitos
** Turistas (70 rooms)   2523
* Imperial Amazonas (no restaurant)   –
* Isabel   –
* Lima   –

Other hotels: Excelsior; Olímpico; Perú; Internacional; Europe. In the Selva, reached by boat (1 hour), is the Amazon Lodge (bookings Putumayo 112, Iquitos, tel. 4494).

Jauja
** Turistas (at Paca, 4 km away)   2111

Juli
** Turistas (7 rooms)   –

Juliaca
** Turistas, M. Prado 335 (30 rooms)   435

Tel.

Lima

L	Sheraton, Paseo República 170 (325 rooms)	329 050, 315 265
L	Bolívar, Plaza San Martín (175 rooms)	276 400
L	Crillon, N. de Piérola 589 (320 rooms)	283 290
L	Country Club, Av. Golf, San Isidro (75 rooms)	404 060
***	Riviera, Garcilaso de la Vega 981 (150 rooms)	289 460
***	Savoy, Cailloma 224 (224 rooms)	283 520
***	Alcázar, Camana 564 (80 rooms)	276 290
***	Claridge, Cailloma 477 (75 rooms)	283 680
***	Continental, Puno 196 (75 rooms)	275 890
***	Maury, Ucayali 201 (72 rooms)	276 210
***	Columbus, Arequipa 1421 (80 rooms)	710 129
**	Oriental, Cuzco 696	288 051
**	Wilson, Chancay 633	288 670
**	Hostal del Sol, Ica 388	–
**	Playa Hermosa, Garcilaso de la Vega 1592	–
**	Richmond, Unión 706	–
**	Colmena, N. de Piérola 286	–
**	Leuro, Benavides 699, Miraflores	–
**	Domasco, Ucayali 199	–
*	Roma, Unión	–
*	San Martín, Arequipa 1851	229 210
*	Premier, Paruro	–
*	Belén, Unión 1049	280 959
*	Casa Vasca, Carabaya 1033	280 459
*	Miramar, Malecón Cisneros 1244	–
*	Pensión See, Herna Velarde 38 46	–

Other hotels (cheap): Pensión Americana, Carabaya 664 (tel. 278 995); Pensión Alemana, Arequipa 4704; Universo, near the Parque Universitario; Sardia, Sardia; Corona, Abancay (near the Parque Universitario); Europa and Pacífico (near the station); Amat, Cuzco 777; Alojamiento Hamburg, N. de Piérola 459.

Machu Picchu

** Turistas (15 rooms)
   (Book well in advance)

Mollendo

*	Salerno, Arequipa 209 (30 rooms)	202

Tel.

Moquegua
  ** Turistas, Av. de la Villa (30 rooms)   554
Also: Los Limoneros, Lima 441 (tel. 422).

Nazca
  ** Turistas (34 rooms)   60
Also: Montecarlo.

Oroya, La
  ** Junín (with permission of Cerro de Pasco
       Corporation, Lima)

Paracas
*** Paracas (90 bungalows)   2220

Pisco
Small hotels: Pisco, Humberto, Graú.

Piura
  ** Turistas, Libertad 875 (40 rooms)   2681
   * Terrazza (2 blocks from Plaza Graú)   –
Other hotels: Christina; Hispano; Residencial Piura.

Pucallpa
  ** Amazonas, Coronel Portillo 733   180
  ** Berlín   –
  ** Turistas, San Martín   481
  ** Mercedes, Raimondi 610   481
  ** Cabañas (bungalows on Lake Yarinacocha)   477
  ** Sisley, Coronel Portillo 654   191
  ** Choy Sánchez   –
Other hotels (cheap): Roma; Perú; Don José; Europa.

Puerto Maldonado
  ** Turistas (16 rooms)   –

Puno
  ** Turistas, A. Ugarte 255 (43 rooms)   24
  ** Ferrocarril, La Torre 185 (41 rooms)   409
  ** Motel Tambo Titikaka (near the lake)   –
   * Monterrey, Graú 154   343

Tel.

* Venezia, Av. Tacna —
* Tito, Los Incas 208 453

Other hotels (*cheap*): Colón, Tacna 290; Palace, Tacna 786; Roma; Torino; Cielo.

San Ramón
** Turistas (at airport) 2051

Santa Rosa de Quives
** Turistas —

Sicuani
Manzanares 161

Small hotels: Mollendo; Ferrocarril.

Tacna
** Turistas, Bolognesi 300 (70 rooms) —
* Gran Hotel Central, San Martín 561 3064
* Emperador, San Martín 558 3410

Other hotels: Lima, San Martín 442; Chiclayo.

Talara
* Talara 815

Also: Royal.

Tarapoto
** Turistas —

Other hotels: Juan Alfonso; Gran Hotel.

Tarma
** Turistas 2411

Other hotels: Plaza; Ritz; Vargas.

Tingo María
** Turistas (34 rooms) 2047
* Gran Hotel —

Other hotels: Viena; Coloso.

Trujillo
** Golf —

Tel.

** Turistas, Plaza de Armas (70 rooms)   2201
** San Antonio, Gamarra 774   5490
** San José (5th block, Graú)   –
** Opt Gar's (5th block, Graú)   2591
 * Americana, Pizarro 758   –

Other hotels: San Martín; Premier; Internacional; Lima; Giralda; Latino.

Tumbes
** Turistas, San Martín 76   2056
 * Rodrigo   –

Yura
** Turistas   –

Zorritos
** Turistas   –

RESTAURANTS

In this section no account is taken of restaurants in the hotels listed above.

Arequipa. The local cuisine ranks as one of the best in Peru, with such specialties as crayfish, stuffed peppers (*rocotos rellenos*), roast guinea-pig (*cuy chactado*), pork stew (*adobo*), potatoes with pimento sauce (*papas con ocopa*), etc. There are numerous *picanterías* (small, reasonably priced, restaurants). Among the more fashionable establishments are *Chez Nino*, San Francisco 125 (seafood); *La Estancia*, General Morán 106 (grills: music in the evening); *Astoria*, Calle San Domingo; and *Los Candiles*, Zela 320 (an old colonial house).

Ayacucho. Poorly provided with restaurants. There are a few reasonably priced establishments, including the *Fortaleza*, 9 de Diciembre (near the Turistas hotel) and the *Trocadero*, Lima 115 (modest).

Cajamarca. Excellent beef dishes, good cheeses; specialty of *manjarblanco* (blancmange). Two small restaurants which can be recommended are the *Salas* and the *Florida*.

Chiclayo. Good fish (*cebiche*); duck with rice (*arroz con pato*), kid stew (*seco de carbito*); *King Kong* (a meringue-covered cake made of *manjarblanco*, walnuts, groundnuts, pineapple, etc.). There is one good restaurant, *La Caleta de San José*, and several Chinese restaurants (*chifas*) where an excellent meal may be had.

Cuzco. Many excellent dishes, including roast guinea-pig, pork (fried and soufflé), maize with goat's cheese, *chuño cola* (a thick soup containing meat, rice and dried potatoes) and *receta del tiempo* (a stew of various kinds of meat, vegetables and fruit). There are numerous restaurants, usually of excellent quality, most of them round the Plaza de Armas: *Roma, El Cabildo, Cuzo, Café Astro, La Ñusta, Café Canoe*. Also the *Koricancha*, east of the Plaza de Armas at the junction of Calle Maruri and Calle Pampa del Castillo.

Huancayo. A local specialty is *papas a la huancayna* (potatoes in a highly spiced sauce made with white goat's cheese). There are a number of reasonably priced restaurants, like the *Olímpico* (the best), the *Mandarín* (Chinese), the *Inca* and *El Porteño*. To the north of the town is a drive-in restaurant, the *Puppos*.

Ica. Noted for its wines and its brandy (*pisco*), and for its *tejas* (preserved fruit served with *manjarblanco*). The *Estancia* restaurant is to be recommended.

Iquitos. Amazonian specialties—*chonta* (a salad of hearts of palm), turtle soup, *humitas*; *cazuela* (a thick soup containing various kinds of meat, vegetables, milk and wine); *paiche* (a large river fish which is eaten dried). Recommended restaurants: *Chez Victor* (town centre), *Chifa Central* (Chinese: town centre), *Río Nanay* (north of town centre).

Lima. There are large numbers of small restaurants in all price ranges all over the city, but particularly round the Plaza San Martín. Cafeterias, drive-in restaurants, etc., on the North American model are becoming increasingly common. Visitors can find restaurants serving regional specialties from all over Peru, as well as excellent Chinese, French, Italian, Argentinian, etc., restaurants. The restaurants of the large hotels of course provide an international cuisine, but their menus also include typical Peruvian dishes.

International cuisine

Tambo de Oro, Belén 1066 (tel. 310 046), in an old colonial mansion furnished in period style (fairly expensive).

Trece Monedas, Ancash 536 (tel. 276 547), in an old colonial mansion (fairly expensive).

Roof Garden 91, Garcilaso de la Vega 911 (fairly expensive).

Unicorn, Paseo República 3030, San Isidro (tel. 404 065) (expensive).

Raimondi, Av. Miró Quesada 110 (tel. 277 933), near the Merced, in an old colonial house (prices in middle range).

Aquarium, José Granda (Country Club) (tel. 404 060) (middle range).

Willy's, Jirón de la Unión (middle range).

Ebony 56, Las Begonias 730, San Isidro (tel. 226 691) (middle range).

Peruvian cuisine (*Comida criolla* or *peruana*)

Most of these restaurants (some of them open only for lunch or for dinner) have folk dancing and singing.

Raimondi, Tambo de Oro, Trece Monedas: see above.

Rosita Rios, El Altillo 100, Rímac, with a shady garden (lunch only) (tel. 815 105): moderate prices.

Tradición, Av. Dupetit-Thouars 1900 (dinner only): fairly dear.

El Chalán, Av. Limatambo 3091, San Isidro (dinner only) (tel. 408 611).

El Huerto de mi Amada, Canturias 160, Miraflores.

El Parral, Rímac (near the Arena de Acho).

Rinconcito Cajamarquino, Rímac (Cajamarca specialties).

Todo Fresco, Miguel Dasso 116, Miraflores (fish and seafood).

La Barca, Av. del Ejército 2195, Miraflores (fish and seafood).

La Luna, Muelle de Pescadores, Callao (fish and seafood).

La Granja Azul, between km 13 and 15 on the Carretera Central (the road to La Oroya, east of Lima) (tel. 350 777): specialises in chicken.

José Antonio, B. Monteagudo 200, San Isidro (tel. 619 923).

Hacienda Villa, Antigua Carretera, km 18 (tel. 670 086).

El Mesón de Marqués, Azángaro 532.

Chinese restaurants (*chifas*)

There are many *chifas* in the Chinese quarter, the Barrio Chino (Calle Capón), but there are also newer and more sophisticated Chinese restaurants in other parts of the town:

Kuo-Wha, Plaza de Armas, Pasaje Santa Rosa. There is a more luxurious establishment of the same name at Paseo República 5046, Miraflores (tel. 458 539).

El Dorado, Arequipa 2450, top floor (tel. 221 080).

Lung-Fung, Av. Limatombo 3165, San Isidro (tel. 226 382).

El Pacífico, Av. Diagonal 156, Miraflores (tel. 450 639).

Argentinian cuisine

Rincón Gaucho, Parque Salazar, Miraflores.

El Cortijo, Plaza San Martín 998 (tel. 247 140): specialises in chicken.

La Querencia, Libertad 425, Madgalena.

La Estancia, Arenales 1100.

Periplo, Malecón, Miraflores.

European cuisine

French: *Café de Paris*, N. de Piérola; *Café de France*, Huancavelica 158 (tel. 286 437); *Saint Tropez*, F. Tudela y Varela 100.

German: *Rincón Toni*, Piérola 478; *Bavaria*, Av. Diagonal 220, Miraflores; *Taberna Alemana*, N. de Piérola.

Italian: *Giannino*. R. Torrico 899; *Firenze*, Av. José Pardo 225, Miraflores; *Pizzeria*, Av. Diagonal, Miraflores.

Scandinavian: *El Vikingo*, Av. José Pardo 254, Miraflores.

Swiss: *Chalet Suisse*, Piérola 560 (tel. 312 985).

Puno. Trout (*trucha*) from Lake Titicaca; *suche* (another local fish); *chairo* (mutton stew with *chuño* and beans. Restaurants: *El Arriero*, *El Lago*, *Asi es mi Perú*.

Trujillo. Specialties: fish from the Pacific, "King Kong" (see under Chiclayo), *tumbos* (a tropical fruit). A wide range of excellent restaurants: *Los Mariscos*, Gamarra 780; *Las 200 Millas*, Huáscar 226; *Gallo Rojo*, Graú 579; *Kuo-Wha* (Chinese), Gamarra 810; *Demarco* and *Romano* (7th block, Pizarro).

Tumbes. Specialties: rock lobsters and the shellfish called *conchas negras*. Restaurant: *El Parral*. *Motel Puerto Pizarro*, 14 km north.

SPANISH VOCABULARY

Phrases in everyday use
Expresiones de uso corriente

Good morning	Buenos días
Good afternoon, good evening	Buenas tardes
Good night	Buenas noches
Goodbye (for some time)	Adios
Goodbye (for a short period)	Hasta luego
How are you?	¿Cómo está Usted?
Very well, thank you	Muy bien, gracias
All right	Tal cual
I am not well	Estoy indispuesto
I am sorry	Lo siento
What can I offer you?	¿Qué puedo ofrecerle a Usted?
What do you want?	¿Qué quiere Usted?
Please sit down	Sientese, por favor
Can I ask you to do something for me?	¿Puedo pedirle un favor?
Of course, by all means	Yo se lo ruego
Do you understand?	¿Comprende Usted?
I do not understand	No estiendo
Speak slowly, please	Hable despacio, por favor
Tell me	Dígame Usted
Do you speak English, French?	¿Habla inglés, francés?
I should like to have . . .	Querría tener . . .
Where is it?	¿Donde está?
What is it called?	¿Cómo se llama?
Please	Por favor
Thank you	Gracias
Yes, no	Sí, no

Time
El tiempo

Day	Día
Week	Semana
Month	Mes
Year	Año
Century	Siglo
January	Enero
February	Febrero
March	Marzo
April	Abril

May	Mayo
June	Junio
July	Julio
August	Agosto
September	Septiembre
October	Octubre
November	Noviembre
December	Diciembre
Sunday	Domingo
Monday	Lunes
Tuesday	Martes
Wednesday	Miércoles
Thursday	Jueves
Friday	Viernes
Saturday	Sabado
Today	Hoy
Yesterday	Ayer
Tomorrow	Mañana
The day after tomorrow	Pasado mañana
Morning	La mañana
Midday	El medio día, la doce
Afternoon	La tarde
Evening, night	La noche
Midnight	La media noche
An hour	Una hora
A half-hour	Media hora
A quarter of an hour	Un cuarto de hora
A minute	Un minuto
Two o'clock	Las dos
Feast day, holiday	Día de fiesta
Working day, weekday	Día de trabajo
New Year's Day	Año nuevo
Palm Sunday	Domingo de Ramos
Holy Week	Semana Santa
Easter	Pascua de Resurrección
Corpus Christi Day	Corpus Christi
All Saints Day	Todos los Santos
Christmas	Navidad
New Year's Eve	Fin de año

Numbers	**Números**
Nothing, zero	Cero
1 – 1st	Uno, una – primero (declined for number and gender)

2 – 2nd	Dos – segundo	do.
3 – 3rd	Tres – tercero	do.
4 – 4th	Cuatro – cuarto	do.
5 – 5th	Cinco – quinto	do.
6 – 6th	Seis – sexto	do.
7 – 7th	Siete – séptimo	do.
8 – 8th	Ocho – octavo	do.
9 – 9th	Nueve – noveno	do.
10 – 10th	Diez – décimo	do.
11	Once	
12	Doce	
13	Trece	
14	Catorce	
15	Quince	
16	Diez y seis	
17	Diez y siete	
18	Diez y ocho	
19	Diez y nueve	
20	Veinte	
21	Veinte y uno, una	
22	Veinte y dos	
30	Treinta	
40	Cuaranta	
50	Cincuenta	
60	Sesenta	
70	Setenta	
80	Ochenta	
90	Noventa	
100	Ciento	
200	Doscientos	
500	Quinientos	
1000	Mil	
Million	Un millón	

In a restaurant

En el restorán

I should like to have a meal	Deseo comer
Menu	La lista, el menú
Place setting (knife and fork, etc.)	El cubierto
Bread	Pan
Butter	Mantequilla
Salt, pepper	Sal, pimienta
Oil, vinegar	Aceite, vinagre
Meat	Carne

Roast, grilled	Asado
Boiled	Cocido
Steak	Filete
Chop	Chuleta
Game	Caza
Lamb	Cordero
Beef	Res
Veal	Ternera
Pork	Chancho
Ham	Jamón
Gravy, bouillon	Caldo
Fried eggs	Huevos fritos, al plato
Omelette	Tortilla
Salad	Ensalada
Vegetables	Legumbres, verduras
Fish	Pescado
Chicken	Pollo
Hen	Gallina
Cheese	Quesco
Soup	Sopa
Fruit	Frutas
Cakes, pastry	Dulces, pasteles
Dessert	Postre
Tart	Tarta
Ice	Helado
The bill	La cuenta

Drinks / **Bebidas**

Bring me a glass of water	Tráigame un vaso de agua
A cup of black coffee	Una taza de café solo
Beer	Cerveza
Red, white wine	Vino tinto, blanco
Ordinary table wine	Vino corriente
Tea	Té
Orangeade	Naranjada
Lemonade	Limonada
A bottle	Una botella
A half bottle	Una media botella
A glass	Una copa

In town / **En la ciudad**

Bank	Banco
Where can I change money ?	¿ Donde puedo cambiar moneda ?

20

Have you an English newspaper?	¿ Tiene Usted un periódico inglés?
Interpreter	Intérprete
Guide	Guía
Doctor	Médico
Dentist	Dentista
Chemist's shop	Farmacia
Bookshop	Librería
Tobacconist's shop	Estanco
Newspaper kiosk	Puesto de periódicos
Optician	Optico
Dairy, grocer's shop	Mantequería
Butcher's shop	Carnicería
Fruiterer's shop	Frutería
Baker's shop	Panadería
Hairdresser	Peluquero
Shoe-shop	Zapatería
Tailor	Sastre
Haberdasher's shop	Camisería
Watchmaker's shop	Relojería

In the hotel

Hotel

A double room	Una habitación con dos camas
Room with bath	Habitación con baño
Outside room (on street)	Habitación con ventana a la calle
Inside room	Habitación con vista al patio
How much, including service?	¿ Cuanto vale, servicio incluido?
How much is it for full board?	¿ Cuanto la pensión completa?
I should like an extra blanket (pillow)	Quisiera una manta (almohada) más
I shall be leaving tomorrow afternoon	Me marcho mañana por la tarde
Please call me at six o'clock	Haga el favor de llamarme a las seis
Let me have the bill	Prepáreme la cuenta
The waiter	El camarero
The chambermaid	La doncella
Floor (storey)	Piso
Bring my breakfast at 7	Entreme el desayuno a las siete

Where is the bathroom, lavatory?	¿ Dónde está el cuarto de baño, el lavabo?
Hot water	Agua caliente
Breakfast	El desayuno
Lunch	El almuerzo
Dinner	La cena
Meal	La comida
I have some laundry	Tengo ropa para lavar
Will you post these letters for me?	¿ Quiere echarme estas cartas al correo?
Are there any letters for me?	¿ Hay alguna carta para mi?
Have you writing paper?	¿ Tiene papel de cartas?

The post office

Correos

Where is the head post office, the nearest post office?	¿ Dónde está el correo central, la estafeta más próxima?
Give me a . . . stamp	Déme un sello de . . .
What stamp do I need?	¿ Cuanto cuesta el franqueo?
A postcard	Una tarjeta postal
Poste restante	Lista de correos
Postal (telegraphic) giro service	Giro postal, telegráfico
I should like to send a telegram	Quisiera enviar un telegrama
What does it cost per word?	¿ Cuanto cuesta cada palabra?
Reply paid	Respuesta pagada
Urgent	Urgente
Post-box	Buzón

Travelling by train

Ferrocarril

Station	Estación
Timetable	Guía de ferrocarriles
A first-class ticket to . . .	Un boleto de primera clase para . . .
Return	Ida y vuelta
What is the fare?	¿ Cuanto vale el boleto?
When does the train go?	¿ Cuanto tiempo para el tren?
Is the train late?	¿ Viene el tren con retraso?
Is this the train for . . .?	¿ Es éste el tren de . . .?
Where do I check in my luggage?	¿ Dónde se facturan los equipajes?
Where can I buy a packed lunch?	¿ Dónde podría comprar una bolsa de merienda?

Restaurant car	El coche-restorán
Sleeping car	El coche-cama
Left luggage room	La consigna
Exit	Salida
Station official	El mozo de estación
Seat reservation	Reserva de asiento
Is this seat free?	¿Está libre este asiento?

At the customs

Aduana

Nothing to declare	Nada que declarer
I have only personal belongings	Sólo llevo efectos personales
No tobacco	Tabaco, no
No spirits	Licores, no
Suitcases, pieces of luggage	Maletas, baules
Here are the keys	Aquí están las llaves
Passport	El pasaporte

Motoring

En la carretera

Where does this road go to?	¿A donde lleva esta carretera?
What is the road like?	¿En qué estado está la carretera?
What is the quickest way to...?	¿Cual es el camino más corto para llegar a...?
What is the name of the next village?	¿Cómo se llama el primer pueblo?
To the left, right	A la izquierda, a la derecha
How long does it take to reach...?	¿Cuanto tiempo se necesita para ir a...?
Where can we find a room for the night?	¿En qué sitio podremos encontrar alogamiento?
Garage	Garaje
Service station	Estación de servicio
40 litres of petrol, please	Quiero cuarenta litros de gasolina
Change the oil	Cambie el aceite del carter
Fill the radiator, please	Haga el favor de llenar el radiador
Grease the car	Por favor engrase mi coche
Regulate the brakes	Por favor ajuste los frenos
Wash the car	Por favor lave mi coche
Check the tyre pressures	Por favor vea la presión de los neumáticos

Check the battery	Por favor reliene mi batería
I have a puncture	He tenido un pinchazo
I have broken down	Tengo una avería
The car won't start	Mi coche no arranca
When will the car be ready?	¿Cúanto tardará?
It will be ready this evening	Estaría listo esta noche
In three hours	Dentro de tres horas
Bridge	El puente
River	El río
Mountain	La montaña
Climb (uphill gradient)	La subida
Descent	La bajada
Speed	Velocidad
To park	Aparcar
Parking permitted	Sitios de estacionamiento
No parking	Prohibido estacionar
No entry	Prohibido el paso
Closed	Cerrado
Open	Abierto
Danger	Peligro
Slow	Despacio
Look out!	Atención! Precaución!
Road works	Obras
One-way street	Dirección unica
Curve, bend	Curva, vuelta

The car	**El automóvil**
Engine	El motor
Plugs	Las bujías
Valve	La válvula
Cylinder head	La culata
Water pump	La bomba de agua
Distributor	El distribuidor
Contact point	El ruptor
Ignition	El encendido
Switch on	Conectar
Dynamo	La dínamo
Carburettor	El carburador
Choke	El estangulador de aire
Accelerator	El acelerador
Clutch	El embrague
Gear-box	La caja de cambios
Brake	El freno

Fan-belt	La correa
Steering	La dirección
Steering wheel	El volante
Rear, front wheel	Rueda trasera, delantera
Headlights	Las luces
Windscreen-wiper	El limpiaparabrisas
Horn	El claxon
Petrol tank	El tanque
Coachwork	La carrocería
Number (plate)	La matrícula
Spare parts	Piezas de recambio

INDEX

This book has been set, printed and bound
by Nagel Publishers, Geneva (Switzerland)

Legal deposit No. 713

Printed in Switzerland

PERU - PEROU

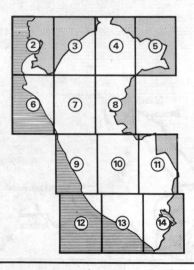

◉ { Capital de départements / Chef-lieu de département / Provincial capital / Provinzhaupstadt

+++ { Ferrocarriles / Chemins de fer / Railways / Eisenbahnen

━━━ { Principales carreteras / Routes principales / Main roads / Haupstrassen

══ { Carreteras / Routes / Roads / Strassen

+ + + { Limite internacional / Frontière d'Etat / International boundary / Grenze

0   50   100   150   200 km

Pl. 2

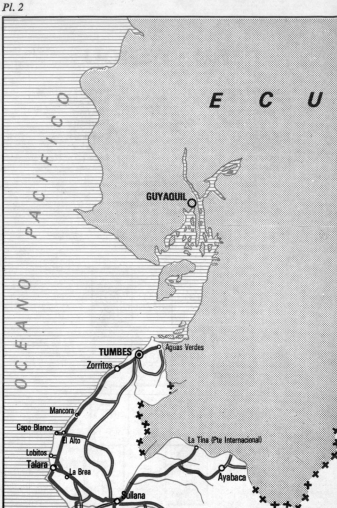

Pl. 3

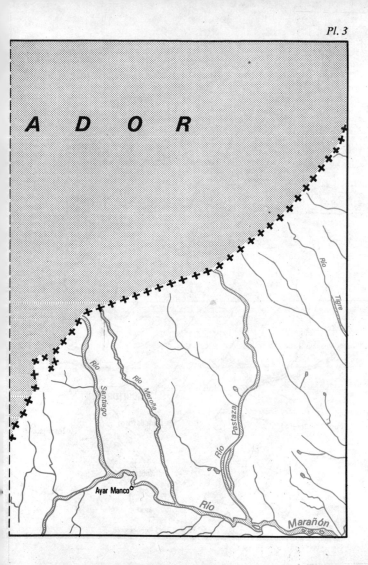

A D O R

Río Tigre

Río Santiago

Río Morona

Río Pastaza

Ayar Manco

Río

Marañón

Pl. 4

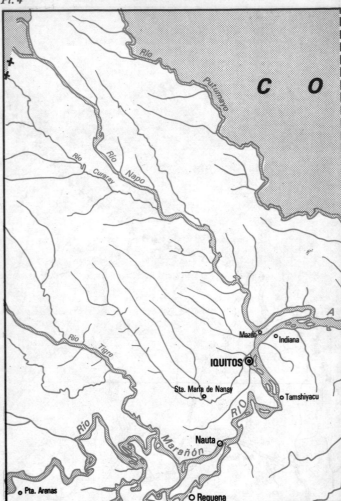

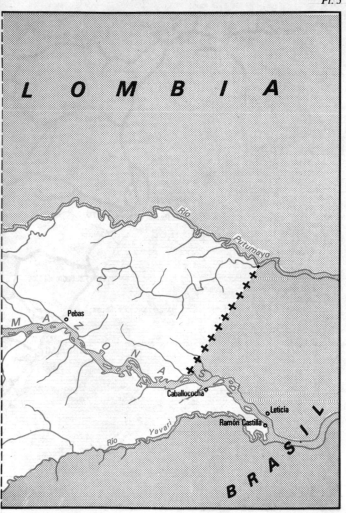

Pl. 5

Pl. 6

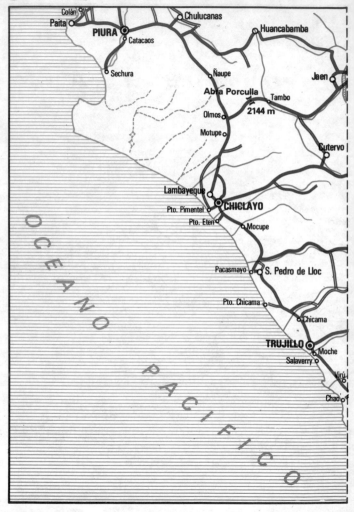

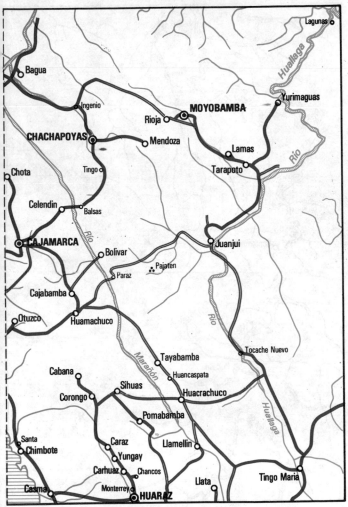

Pl. 7

Pl. 8

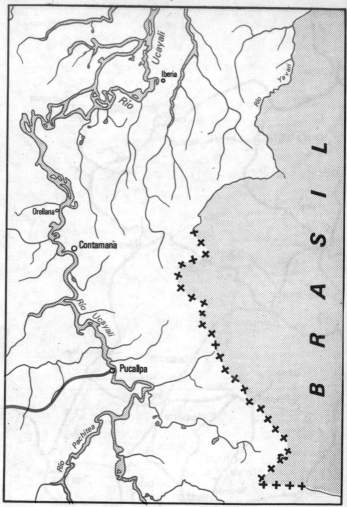

Pl. 9

Pl. 10

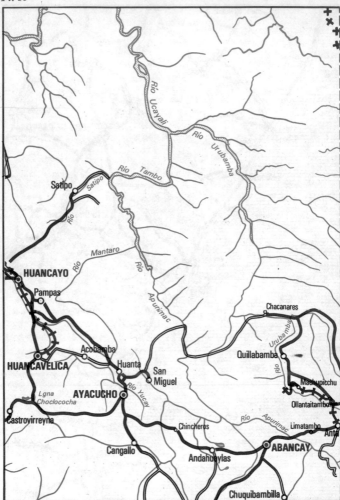

Pl. 11

Pl. 12

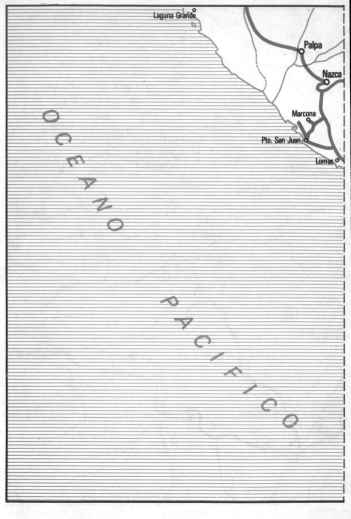

Pl. 13

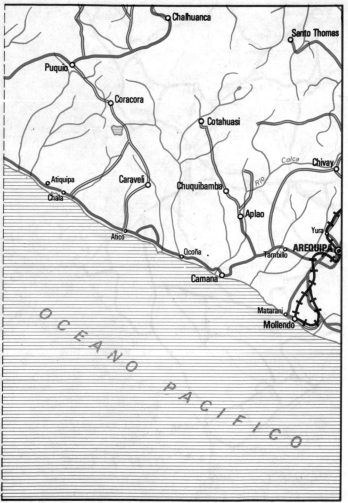

Pl. 14

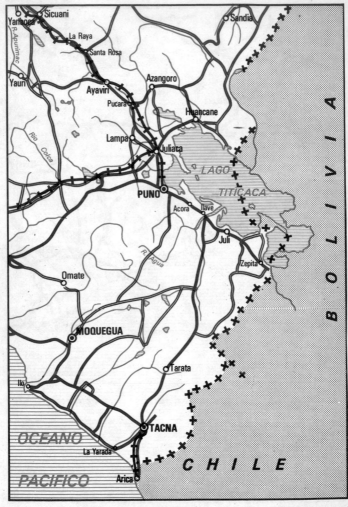